MW01039818
Montgomery, AL
Pensacola, FL
Tallahassee, FL
Jacksonville
Palatka, FL
Orlando,

The 10

The 10

A Memoir of Family and the Open Road

E. A. Hanks

G

GALLERY BOOKS

New York Amsterdam/Antwerp London
Toronto Sydney/Melbourne New Delhi

Gallery Books
An Imprint of Simon & Schuster, LLC
1230 Avenue of the Americas
New York, NY 10020

For more than 100 years, Simon & Schuster has championed authors and the stories they create. By respecting the copyright of an author's intellectual property, you enable Simon & Schuster and the author to continue publishing exceptional books for years to come. We thank you for supporting the author's copyright by purchasing an authorized edition of this book.

No amount of this book may be reproduced or stored in any format, nor may it be uploaded to any website, database, language-learning model, or other repository, retrieval, or artificial intelligence system without express permission. All rights reserved. Inquiries may be directed to Simon & Schuster, 1230 Avenue of the Americas, New York, NY 10020 or permissions@simonandschuster.com.

Copyright © 2025 by E. A. Hanks

Some dialogue has been re-created, and some names and identifying characteristics have been changed.

All rights reserved, including the right to reproduce this book or portions thereof in any form whatsoever. For information, address Gallery Books Subsidiary Rights Department, 1230 Avenue of the Americas, New York, NY 10020.

First Gallery Books hardcover edition April 2025

GALLERY BOOKS and colophon are registered trademarks of Simon & Schuster, LLC

Simon & Schuster strongly believes in freedom of expression and stands against censorship in all its forms. For more information, visit BooksBelong.com.

For information about special discounts for bulk purchases, please contact Simon & Schuster Special Sales at 1-866-506-1949 or business@simonandschuster.com.

The Simon & Schuster Speakers Bureau can bring authors to your live event. For more information or to book an event, contact the Simon & Schuster Speakers Bureau at 1-866-248-3049 or visit our website at www.simonspeakers.com.

Interior design by Jaime Putorti

Art by Madeleine Eve Ignon

Manufactured in the United States of America

10 9 8 7 6 5 4 3 2 1

Library of Congress Cataloging-in-Publication Data is available.

ISBN 978-1-9821-3129-6
ISBN 978-1-9821-3131-9 (ebook)

For Charlotte, Michaiah, and Olivia
and in memory of Scott John Hutchison

My family had come to Sacramento in the 19th century. . . . Don't you think that sometimes people are formed by the landscapes they grew up in? It formed everything I ever think or ever do, or am.

—JOAN DIDION

Where I was born and where and how I have lived is unimportant. It is what I have done with where I have been that should be of interest.

—GEORGIA O'KEEFFE

Introduction

Who the Hell Is Moomat Ahiko?

> Miraculously [Los Angeles's] extremes include excessive tolerance.
>
> —REYNER BANHAM

Santa Monica isn't easy to find. It's on a lot of maps. You can drive there, if the traffic isn't too bad, but it's always too bad. You can walk around Santa Monica for hours, among the unhoused and the tourists and the rented scooters that pile up on street corners, and still wonder if you're there yet. Santa Monica taught me that it's possible to know exactly where you are and still be lost. It's the kind of place whose main characteristic is the sneaking suspicion that there is no there there.

Los Angeles specializes in this sort of sleight of hand. Getting to know a city takes time, the sort of time that eludes most tourists—and being as spread out as LA is, I don't know how someone can take in the whole scope of it. So, people go to places like Santa Monica and confuse it for Los Angeles. The German poet and playwright Bertolt Brecht lived here and called Los Angeles "Tahiti in the form of a big city." He didn't like it very much, but then, he lived in Santa Monica. (At 1063

Twenty-Sixth Street, where he paid $60 a month and which would now sell for over $2 million.)[1]

Some cities you walk out the door and, *bang*, you're in it. The city is open to you and you know what you're in for, places like New Orleans, Berlin, and Glasgow. Los Angeles, on the other hand, is like Paris: the meat of life here happens behind closed doors. While the landscape is open and spread out, social hierarchies exist in closed groups, closed rooms, closed restaurants. If you think you're getting the real City of Light by just looking at the Eiffel Tower, if you think you understand LA because you people-watched in Beverly Hills for a few strange hours, you don't understand the lives of cities. We are a city of actual magic castles (I can think of at least two, off the top of my head) and specialize in such trickery: it may look easy because the sun is shining, but the living can be hard. We are clinging to the side of the continent and our days are numbered, so lord help you if you get in the way of someone trying to make their time count.

The American city Los Angeles gets paired with most often is New York. Occasionally someone will confuse Los Angeles and San Francisco as sister cities, though never someone from California. There's been an unfortunate spate of tech companies draining out of Silicon Valley and moving into LA's Westside (anything between the ocean and Beverly Hills), chasing good weather and buying up whole swaths of Santa Monica and Venice. As of yet, this influx hasn't brought any significant change to the culture of the city other than further inflating the real estate bubble and the previously mentioned piles of scooters. Most gold-seeking whites arrived directly in San Francisco from America's East Coast via ships that rounded Cape Horn around 1849, hence the term *forty-niner*. Whereas in Los Angeles, the majority of white settlers came via trains out of the dust bowl, nearly fifty years after the gold rush. San Francisco and Los Angeles are only sister cities if you think of them as the sort of siblings who don't speak to each other.

In fact, the city with which LA has the most in common is Washington, DC. They are single-market towns—with one major industry at the center around which all the other businesses circulate. There might be other hustles in DC, but politics is the point; likewise, show business is at the heart of Los Angeles. They both run on one source of power. The only difference is that in DC power is centralized; everyone can measure their standing by how close they are to one oval office. In Los Angeles, power is decentralized among various studios, agencies, individual actors, producers, and writers. This free-for-all means that everyone is rising and falling, with only the highest echelons maintaining a steady level over the years. Given all this fluidity, there's a lot of attention paid to who is up and who is down, and so Los Angeles is a fraught city. There is more than one type of fault line.

One must not conflate Hollywood and Los Angeles because, while this is an industry town, there is a difference imperceptible to most outsiders but obvious to the millions of people who live here and have nothing to do with either film or television. Hollywood and Los Angeles are a bit like Santa Christmas and Jesus Christmas, in that the difference really only matters to believers. Outsiders and nonbelievers can't be bothered to see the nuance. Why should they?

The truth is that this tension made by the diffusion of power didn't begin with Hollywood. Perhaps it, and the good weather, just meant that Los Angeles happened to be the best place to make movies. This decentralized existence comes from the fact that the city has, since the days when the Californio ranchers divided this basin, been defined by what separates us. First it was the empty miles between pueblos, but now it is time itself. What should take twenty minutes between point A and point B now takes an hour and a half, so everyone tries their hardest to stay where they are, separated across what Reyner Banham called the Plains of Id, "where the crudest urban lusts and most fundamental aspirations are created."[2]

Unlike most every other major American metropolis, Los Angeles did not grow outward from one epicenter, rippling out across the land. Instead, pueblos and villages became ranches and cities that grew alongside each other until these organisms eventually absorbed each other, resulting in the pulsing megatropolis we have now.

There are two parties happening in Los Angeles. The first, which is the one everyone knows about (even people who don't live here), is invite-only. It happens behind closed doors, behind velvet ropes guarded by girls with clipboards. These are the glittering fêtes on sprawling grounds somewhere up in the hills, or beyond the imposing gates, where the valet guys have to sign nondisclosure agreements, promising not to discuss Santa Christmas. It is also the small dinner parties, intimate gatherings that function as postmortems, poring over the data from lives lived in an air so rarified, even the most grounded of them seem like hothouse orchids to the rest of the city's people. That is the party a lot of people want to attend—and they spend years trying to figure out how to get an invite. They've forgotten, or just never cared about, the other party, which only people who live in LA know about.

This party requires no invitation, but you do have to know where to go. It happens at taco trucks in parking lots, on picnics by reservoirs humbled by drought, jammed into Koreatown studio apartments, and at used bookstores downtown. It is the daily life of Los Angeles, somehow both bohemian and bourgeois at the same time. The most expensive offering at this party is the pot, which is phenomenal.

There is also an existence between these two parties: the noir. Noir flourishes in Los Angeles, because it requires the urban but it also needs space. Alone in our cars, we surpass the anonymity of other cities and achieve true loneliness. With no centralized power, chaos reigns and corruption flourishes. Between the two parties is a life spent with headlights shining in your eyes, angry, furtive, looking for what you were promised. My friend Suzanne, who was once the director of development for an Oscar-winning director, likened show business to a simple door. Some people get here and just walk right on through. Some people spend months, years, outside the door, listening to the party on the other side, getting darker and angrier. Noir LA is not just for Raymond Chandler characters; it's for all the people who don't understand why "it" isn't happening for them. If they were smart, they'd move and become the funniest bartender in Boulder, and heaps happier, but they don't. Maybe they get a job in Santa Monica, trying to be close to something they just can't touch, reaching for an invitation to walk through.

I don't know if other people tell themselves stories like these about the places they live. I only know that for the past two years, all I can think about is the lands where I've grown up, about Moomat Ahiko, about the interstate, and about what happened in a small town in Florida. I started collecting my own stories, and now it's time to go through them, to sort out what's real and what isn't. I didn't know where to start, so I went to school.

One balmy November afternoon, I wandered the UCLA campus, a leafy and indiscriminate place spackled with young people all wearing athleisure, burning some time before I met with Dr. Dana Cuff, a professor of urban design, an architectural theorist, and the founder of cityLAB, a think tank that studies how cities function—or don't. We met in her basement office, where a dog bowl and bed were tucked under a desk, but there was unfortunately no dog that day. Dr. Cuff was wearing a great necklace with little dogs on it, though, and all black clothes. With her very chic, large green glasses, she looked like your favorite elementary school teacher if she only shopped at the

MoMA Design Store. "The dominance of individual landowners and developers was the shaping hand of the Los Angeles landscape. And that stays true. We've never had a strong civic culture or government," Dr. Cuff said, phlegmatic. "I think that has had its effects on the built landscape, and maybe that was why the federal highway program was so powerful here, because it was such a free-for-all between the highways."

Like myself, Los Angeles grew up with no one really watching, no one keeping an eye on her. With no one person in charge, I suspect information, rumor, and gossip have been our real currency since well before the first movie was shot in a barn on the corner of Gower and Sunset.

Of the 114 neighborhoods and 158 cities that make up the whole of Los Angeles, Santa Monica draws large crowds of tourists with its shopping opportunities. I hope these people are also going to the Watts Towers, to the Grand Central Market downtown, to the Getty Villa in Malibu, but that's up for grabs. For my money, the way to be a tourist in Los Angeles is to rent a kitted-out Sprinter van and drive your hotel room wherever you want to go.

Santa Monica lures visitors with the Third Street Promenade and the redone Santa Monica Place mall, both of which offer out-of-towners all the stores they could shop from back home, with one or two spikes of LA exoticism. There's also a weekly farmers market, and the Santa Monica Pier with a roller coaster and carousel. The original pier was built in 1909 to carry sewage out past the breakers. It was also a stylish esplanade where early Angelenos marveled at the ability to walk over the water and held swimming competitions. Guess they forgot about the sewage. Shortly after the municipal pier opened, the land just to the south was bought and developed into a pleasure pier, iterations of which have stood until this day, with names like the Horseshoe Pier & Pavilion, the Crystal Pier, and the Million Dollar Pier, all offering casinos, dining, theaters, and saloons.

The name Santa Monica, like so much else in this land, is from our Spanish forebears. The Portolá expedition of 1769 brought the Spanish to California. In what would eventually be known as Brentwood, where the O. J. Simpson car chase ended but also where I took the SATs, sixty-three soldiers, a hundred mules, and a couple of priests made camp by a small Tongva village and the Kuruvungna Springs. If the Tongva had any idea what was good for them, they would have killed the Spaniards that first night without blinking.

The Spanish did not think much of the name for the springs, which translated means "a place where we are in the sun." Several names for the area show up in the writings of the secretary of the expedition, Father Juan Crespi, including San Vicente (now the name of a wide boulevard with tree-dappled islands) and El Berendo, but the first use of *Santa Monica* is in a grazing grant from 1828. Originally a wild outpost connected to the pueblo by the rail line, and then a frivolous holiday spot, Santa Monica's fate was sealed when the "Great Free Harbor Fight" of the 1890s resulted in San Pedro, thirty miles to the south, receiving federal funds to create a deepwater port. Serious money and big business had bypassed Santa Monica, and it's been a shopping and tourist destination ever since. There is very little in Santa Monica that you can't get anywhere else, except for the view, which is monumental. And Moomat Ahiko.

Most people who live here could not guess who or what Moomat Ahiko is, though most people I've asked assume it's the name of a Japanese

American interned during World War II. That is, if they've heard of it at all. Only Westsiders might recognize the name of a small access street that takes cars from the Santa Monica bluffs down to the beach level by the pier and the Pacific Coast Highway. The truth is, Moomat Ahiko isn't a person. Or a thing. Just like Santa Monica, Moomat Ahiko is a bit hard to define.

California is the America of America—people still move here in their own personal manifest destinies, leaving behind the East with its winters, the old families with old obligations. They think they're moving to a place with no history, no ties to the past. They think we are the clowns of the frontier. We inspire envy and not a little wonder: Who could live with all those fires and earthquakes?

We have as much history as the East, but instead of Puritans and Dutch settlers, we have Spanish monks and Mexican ranchers as our forebears. But before statehood in 1850, before the Californios, before Mexico and before Spain, there were the Tongva.

When I lived in upstate New York, the names on the signposts were as exotic to me as the woods: dense to the point you couldn't see between trees, so unlike the solitary sequoias I grew up with. In the Hudson valley, the Dutch left the fingerprints of early white settlers in names like Peekskill and Spackenkill and Fishkill—*kill* being Dutch for creek or river. But there were also names like Wiccopee, Minnewaska, and Napanoch, words my mouth never seemed able to form correctly. In Los Angeles, if something is old, it's in Spanish. Except. Except for Moomat Ahiko.

The Tongva tribe has lived in the Los Angeles basin for centuries; archaeological sites date back from eight thousand to fifteen thousand years. Exploring the frigid Pacific in their *Ti'at*, ocean canoes, the Tongva settled up and down the Southern California coast and valleys. The Spanish missions and later the Mexican and Californio ranches were built on the slave labor of the Tongva, who were not recognized under California state law until 1994. Their language is Shoson.

Moomat Ahiko, it turns out, isn't a Japanese American, not a Polynesian place, but something else altogether. It's Shoson for "breath of the ocean." Formerly Route 187, Moomat Ahiko was the winning suggestion from an online poll to rename an access road. I'd forgotten about the street, and my fascination with it, while I was on my East Coast adventure. But soon enough I was back in Los Angeles, a city I'd sworn off forever, unable to write and aimlessly working at a series of bookstores. I felt like I'd gone backward, that I was stagnant, and it seemed to me that the only way I was going to get out of the mess I was in was to start thinking about beginnings and endings. Moomat Ahiko marks where the Pacific Coast Highway becomes Interstate 10. Or maybe vice versa. Neither necessarily ends, but both definitely begin. I started to think about how you don't understand a place simply because you're in it. You don't understand a place because you're from there. You don't even understand a place just because you're new to it. I started thinking about how place informs person. I began to wonder whether if you don't understand where you are, you don't understand yourself. So Moomat Ahiko became way more important to me than most people would judge as normal.

I write about Los Angeles with an outsider's eye because I am not from here, and I can dish on Los Angeles because I'm a wallflower at the invite-only party. I am a very good example of a certain species of person wholly *of* Los Angeles but not *from* Los Angeles: I am a kid from the First (non-famous) Marriage. My father is the actor Tom Hanks; my mother was his first wife, Susan Dillingham. They married when my older brother, Colin, was already two years old and divorced when I was five. My only memories of my parents being in the same place at the same time are Colin's high school graduation, then my high school graduation. I have one picture of me standing between my parents. In it, my mother's best wig is slightly askew.

When someone asks me where I am from, I usually say that I'm Californian. This is because I am torn between Northern and Southern California, which is a bit like not knowing if you're a cat or a dog. How do you *not know*? I was born in Burbank, one of the many smaller cities that make up LA, but after my parents split up, my mother took my older brother and me to live in Sacramento. I have few memories of the early years in Los Angeles. Eventually a divorce agreement was settled, and I would visit my dad and stepmother (and soon enough my younger half brothers) on the weekends and during summers, but from ages five to fourteen, years filled with confusion, violence, deprivation, and love, I was a Sacramento girl.

Sacramento is a city of gold and trees. The punishing valley heat of the summertime leaches color out of the tall grass, and leaves the fields and yards Andrew Wyeth yellow. Soggy winters aren't quite Seattle damp, but they turn the rice paddies emerald nonetheless. I lived in a white house with columns, a backyard with a pool, and a bedroom with pictures of horses plastered on every wall. As the years went on, the backyard became so full of dog shit that you couldn't walk around it, and the house stank of smoke. The fridge was bare or full of expired food more often than not, and my mother spent more and more time in her big four-poster bed, poring over her Bible. One night, her emotional violence became physical violence, and in the aftermath I moved to Los Angeles, right smack in the middle of the seventh grade, when teen herd dynamics are at their most brutal. My custody arrangement basically switched—now I lived in LA and visited Sacramento on the weekends and in the summer. When I was fourteen, my mother and I drove across America along Interstate 10 to Florida, in a Winnebago that lumbered along the asphalt with a rolling gait that felt nautical, as if we were crossing oceans instead of the vast expanses of the South.

My senior year of high school, she called to say she was dying.

Back to Santa Monica. It rests on bluffs above the beach, and in between, in the very slim margin between the ocean and the palisade, is the Pacific Coast Highway, California's Route 1. If you follow it north, it will wind up through Malibu, where Joan Didion kept a dubious eye on the fire-prone hills, and unfurl, hugging the corners up the coastline, through the grandiosity of Big Sur, and well past San Francisco.

In Santa Monica, however, the PCH veers inland, away from the ocean, under Moomat Ahiko and Tongva Park, which used to be a parking lot but now has plants that are indigenous to Southern California, which means it looks like the canyons of Mars by way of Dr. Seuss. From there, the highway heads into the McClure Tunnel. Originally built for the train from downtown and rebuilt for motorcars in 1935, it was named for Robert E. McClure, the editor of the *Santa Monica Outlook* newspaper, which began reporting local news in 1875 and ran its last issue in 1998. The McClure is a gateway from the inner guts of Los Angeles to its beaches. The tunnel, I found out, is cleaned every sixteen months, when the city borrows a truck rig from San Francisco, plugs up all the drains, and scrubs down the entire interior. What happens then? "We pack up our equipment and move on," according to a foreman of the California Department of Transportation cleaning crew. Fair enough.

The McClure looks like any municipal tunnel, but I suspect something else happens in there. Maps will tell you that the 10 starts somewhere around Fourth Street, a couple miles east of the McClure, but the maps are wrong. The 10 manifests itself into existence somewhere in the McClure, somewhere beneath Tongva Park. When the PCH bends and heads east, morphing into the 10, it becomes a path toward not a place, but a time. To go eastward is to head into the past, a reversal of manifest destiny, a search not for a glorious end, but for a missing point of origin or perhaps original sin. This is the road I find myself on. This is the road the red journal and Moomat Ahiko have brought me to, a path back to the small town in Florida where I think it all started.

I do not know where my mother was born. Sometimes she said she was born in Florida and grew up around Cuban refugees. Sometimes she said she grew up in deep Georgia, picking ticks out of her skin and sipping sweet tea. Other times she said she was from the Bay Area and grew up going to Ramones shows, exploring just how much patchouli one white girl could douse herself in.

I do know where her mother grew up: Palatka, Florida, population 10,452, plopped between Jacksonville and the Ocala National Forest. Harriet Collins was a teacher, and she and John Raymond Dillingham had four children, three boys and one girl. I know that John was a soldier, was awarded the Purple Heart when he was injured in combat, and is buried in Arlington National Cemetery. When I told my mom that I'd veered off from my eighth grade trip to the cemetery to see his grave, she did not speak to me for several days. I never saw a photograph of him, and neither my mother nor my grandmother ever spoke of him. He was a ghost I never noticed was haunting me, until I found the journal.

Not knowing where my mother was from was not so unusual. Her relationship with reality was fluid. There would usually be a grain of truth that was fed through the meat grinder of mental illness and came out the other side sordid and upsetting. There was a time she'd bought me a CD from a popular born-again Christian rock band. I looked at it, gave a typically teenage "Yeah, thanks," and put it down on the counter. Days later, in a restaurant and sobbing to one of her few friends, she described me throwing the CD at her face and screaming at her. She wasn't being manipulative; that was truly how she remembered it. Because she couldn't keep the past in line, I knew very little about her life—I don't know the cards she was dealt, and in turn dealt to me.

I once asked my father if I was a "save the marriage" baby. "No," he assured me, "but you were a 'someone died and I feel the urge to create life' baby." Turns out, after her father's death, my mother wanted another child. Without the death of John Raymond Dillingham, I never enter the picture.

Just before Christmas in 2000, my mother called to tell me that she was dying. Smoking multiple packs a day had finally caught up with her: her entire lung was filled with tumors and the cancer had spread to her bones. She died in the spring. Exhausted and baffled by what we'd just gone through, my brother and I put most of her belongings into storage. Life happened, and before we knew it, ten years had passed before we went back to sort through it all.

Opening the boxes years after her death was like opening a time capsule to my childhood, left behind in Sacramento, a city that while I wasn't looking had transformed from my hometown into something else. I was embarrassed to have to look up directions to the storage facility. There were boxes of my show ribbons from horseback riding, a slew of romance novels. My mother had countless boxes of mass-market editions of Shakespeare. I never knew what she was buying them for, or why she needed fourteen copies of *The Tempest*, but she hoarded them like they'd be the currency in the world after the apocalypse. Speaking of apocalypses, there were also boxes of canned food she'd moved out of the Y2K panic room she'd built in our basement. Unlike all my friends whose first apartments were stocked with family castoffs and hand-me-downs, I'd never had anything of my mother's, and I leapt to collect the relics of my Sacramento life. Small things and homely things I kept: a potato masher because it made me think of all the pale Scots-Irish bog women who peeled and pounded potatoes before us. I took the once pink, now nearly bone-white quilt, threadbare and ink-stained, that had been on my bed all those years ago, and in the RV across the 10. I took her dictionary. Amid everything I found a white binder of poetry and a dozen reporter's notebooks filled with paranoid notations about her phones being tapped and people following her. I grabbed all of these papers, with a vague plan to go through them one day.

"One day" turned into another three years down the line, as I floundered through the end of my twenties. When I finally sorted through all the papers, reading her poetry and legal documents and grocery lists, I found a red journal, the sort flogged on the first floor of a Barnes & Noble. In it I read her thankfulness for the Dead Sea Scrolls being found, that God had evicted all of the drug dealers out of Sacramento. Then I read that Jesus had saved her from going insane when her "mind remembered [her] father butchering, torturing, murdering, raping, dismembering 6-year-old girl Natalie."

This was the first time I'd ever heard my mother mention her father. It is hard to remember what I thought about my mom before I found the red journal. It is hard to remember if I ever thought of her as a victim of anything beyond mental illness. She was never diagnosed; as an adult she refused therapy, and I assume that, when she was a child, her family decided it was best just to look the other way. What else were they looking away from? Where was the grain of truth in this horror? What if it was more than a mere grain?

My mother was raised by a southern woman. I was raised by my mother. I call myself a Californian, but how much of me was not made in the rice paddies outside of Sacramento, or the freezing waters of the Pacific, under the fragrant eucalyptus of the Santa Monica Mountains?

How much of me was molded by a landscape that is as strange to me as I am to it? I've tried for thirty-five years to figure out what part of California I'm from, but what if the meat of my life, the bones of my personality, aren't western at all, but southern?

Like all Sacramento girls, the first traveling stories I heard were of the Donner party: a family of pioneers who had veered off the trusted path to the West Coast in search of a shortcut and found themselves stranded in the Sierra Nevada in an early winter. Of the eighty-seven members who set out, only forty-seven survived to reach California, where lurid tales of cannibalism followed them the rest of their forlorn lives.

For a period of my childhood, my summers were spent traveling wherever my father was working, to places like Evansville, Indiana, or Beaufort, South Carolina, where I ran barefoot and feral, learned how to crab, and kissed a boy. Now when I travel, it's as a woman alone. Without children or a partner, I find myself camping on the lunar mesas of Nevada, or driving from Idaho to Seattle through a snowstorm, because I can. For me, travel has become the greatest reward of a solitary life. Travel takes time, and I am rich with hours to myself.

I am setting out on the 10, through the American South, because there are no shortcuts. There is no way to understand what the red journal means, if anything, without going back. The narrative I have of the South, as an outsider, is that the past there means something else. That it is both ever present, and never spoken of. That it is indefinable and yet inescapable, an atmosphere that both hovers and is breathed in at the same time. I have my own stories about the places along the 10, the truck stops and tourist traps I visited with my mother on the way to Palatka. I want to see those places again, to find the Moomat Ahiko truth of those spots. I want to know what happened to my mother,

Susan Jane Dillingham, who could read a five-hundred-page novel in a single afternoon, who did enough cocaine she collapsed her sinus cavity, who got sober through the power of her Lord and Savior, Jesus Christ. I want to know who John Raymond Dillingham was. I want to know what he did.

I am setting out on the road because I never knew what Moomat Ahiko meant until I thought to ask. I am starting this journey because I am yet another girl trying to make sense of her dead, crazy mother. I want to understand the land that made her, to see if it made me too. Because somewhere my mother stops and I begin, just like how somewhere in the McClure Tunnel the 1 stops and the 10 begins. Something magic happens in that tunnel. Something that I think is wholly American. I am going into that tunnel. I am heading east, and I don't know who I'll be on the other side.

Forget Moomat Ahiko. Who the hell am I?

Part I

The Desert

Chapter One

Minnie

I wasn't supposed to be in this van.

Originally I was driving a Fiat, a teeny tiny convertible that was great for parking in Los Angeles but would not have worked for a six-month road trip. Luckily, I was in a car accident. A man driving a Porsche SUV didn't check his side mirror and barreled into me on the Sepulveda Pass. While the Fiat was only slightly dented, the insurance company declared the car totaled since the whole thing is basically made of three wraparound pieces of plastic, and I was in the market for a new ride.

All the research about "best road trip" vehicles said Subaru, and I eventually settled on a Subaru Outback, which felt like driving a living room sofa around. I started spending a lot of time looking at Subaru blogs, at all the ways people have kitted out their Outbacks for camping. Everything fell apart when I actually took the car camping.

I was parked in the woods of Kern County, home to Bakersfield, California, and not long after I got home, my engine service light started flashing at me—not great for a brand-new car. When I took it in to get serviced, they broke the news to me: some rodent of an unusual size had chewed completely through the engine suspension cords, and the engine was in danger of "falling out the bottom." Of course, the fix was thousands of dollars. While the Outback was in the shop, I called my dad to ask if I could borrow the Shit Box.

While my dad does have a "nice" car, he doesn't like it very much, so he usually drove the small minivan he affectionately called "the Shit Box." It looks like a box with wheels on it. Driving it across Los Angeles from my parents' home to my apartment, I realized, *Oh, this is just a little higher up off the road; I can really see a lot more. Especially with this big windshield and side windows. Gosh this seat is comfortable. You know, if I took the seats out of the back, I could have a bed and still be able to sit up way more comfortably than in the Outback. . . .*

By the time I got to the Eastside, I had already texted my dad and asked if I could take the van, technically a Ford Transit, on the trip.

Take it! Go go go! Drive safe!

So that's how I ended up with the Shit Box.

Except she was not a shit box! I cannot sing the praises of this vehicle enough. I put over five thousand miles on this car, and all I ever had to do was put gas in it. I did give it an oil change once I got to Florida, but that was it. To be able to take this minivan completely for granted was a blessing. She never got stuck in sand or water. She never got a flat, and her air-conditioning always worked. She just needed a couple of adjustments before I hit the road.

First up, I could not go around calling her "Shit Box" in my head. I've always named my cars—there was Edna (my high school ride) and Bertha (the Outback). I've come to love the minivan so much that when I eventually get home, I will cry hysterically when I return her.

First I took her to the friend of a friend to disconnect all the back seats. Then I took her to a woman who works as a carpenter for a theater to build a sleeping platform, and in the process of chitchatting, I realized I had been calling the minivan, appropriately enough, Minnie. So, Minnie she was. I like this because I have a soft spot for Minnie Mouse, and also because it seems like a nice echo of the vehicle in which my mom and I drove across the 10 in 1996, a Winnebago that we called Winnie. Then, Winnie; now, Minnie.

The only mistake I made with Minnie was that by trying to conserve headroom in the back, I left myself no under-the-bed storage. Since I wanted to be able to get into the driver's seat from the bed without getting out of the van, all of my things got crammed into the passenger side's footwell and chair at night. That would not have been safe had I parked and slept overnight in residential neighborhoods, but I was either in the middle of nowhere or in a Walmart parking lot, which usually had security. It was a pain to have everything either on top of my bed or on the passenger seat—occasionally it could feel claustrophobic.

But that is my one and only complaint about Minnie the Wonder Van. I was blessed with Minnie.

PACKING LIST

Books (for full list, check bibliography)

Hiking boots

Camp dining utensils

MSR PocketRocket backpacking stove and isobutane/propane canister

Patagonia sun-protection shirt

Single-person tent and lightweight sleeping bag

1 Ikea twin mattress and 1 set Ikea bedding

1 set Parachute queen-sized linen sheets

1 set Parachute towels

Cabela's folding rocking camp chair

Curtains

Emergency bag with snakebite kit, first aid kit, and electrolyte powders

6 gallons water

PG Tips tea bags

2 sets packing cubes

1 set professional-grade clear makeup artist travel bags

1 pair espadrilles

2 pairs butt pants

1 pair wide-leg cropped pink jeans

1 USS *Kidd* baseball cap

1 cowboy hat

2019 At-a-Glance Standard Daily Reminder diary

Index cards

Legal pads

Smith Corona typewriter

Chapter Two

The Desert Begins

And yet in this fantastic wonderland there are no endings, only beginnings.

—*THE LIVING DESERT*

In 1996, when I was fourteen, my mother and I made the drive to Florida as quickly as possible. We never stopped at tourist attractions or stayed a couple of nights in different places to get to know the vibe of a city. We only stopped to eat and sleep, usually at Kampgrounds of America. This was in part because my mom wanted to get to Florida and my grandmother as soon as possible, but also, we were on a schedule: from Florida we were driving on to Georgia and the 1996 Summer Olympics.

What I remember is long, interminable stretches of driving; a lumbering, smoke-filled Winnebago; my mother listening to turgid Christian rock and lectures while I listened on my Discman to one-half of the Beatles' *White Album* on repeat in my bunk bed, a fan on my face to keep the fumes of her constant cigarette smoking away. We didn't speak to each other often, except for when she asked me to make coffee. She would drive all day, late into the night, and then pass out on the back bed while I set up the water and sewage lines at whatever random campground we pulled into.

My plan is to take my time on my trip east. The landscapes of the 10 mark the pillars of the legend of America: California, the Southwest, the Deep South. These places are the crux of some of our strongest myths: manifest destiny, the virtue of independence and bootstrap gusto, the gothic and gallant South. To the best of my knowledge, no little kid ever played that classic game Vermont Maple Syrup Farmers. No, they played Cowboys and Indians. Even whatever is going on in Florida is part of contemporary America's self-concept—its weirdest, most chaotic self, but part of our identity nonetheless.

But the first stretch of the 10, from the Pacific coast through the belly of the city and out through the sprawling inland empire to Palm Springs, is marred by a nearly unending stream of strip malls. Any Angeleno can tell you that a random strip mall can be home to real deal cuisine, but they're not beautiful. Even with the San Bernardino Mountains looming lovely in the distance, this is a drive I usually do at night. My favorite view en route from Los Angeles and on to Phoenix is the field of wind turbines northwest of Palm Springs in the San Gorgonio Pass. Hundreds of them standing like sentinels over the land, and I like seeing how long they linger in my rearview mirror as I head for the California-Arizona border.

Every time I travel, there inevitably comes a moment when I start listening to a lot of Joni Mitchell. This is in part because I have a theory that every culture has either a statement or a question at its core. As a Californian, I think our culture is built on a question of innate optimism: "What do you want to be?" So you're a Canadian painter who wants to start singing? Why not? Make up your own chords, while you're at it. Maybe the Golden State better refers to a golden state-of-being: the identity you take on when you're in charge of yourself. This innate question—"What do you want to be?"—made the summer I spent working in Connecticut a serious culture shock (the only popped collars I had ever seen were on the villains in John Hughes movies of the eighties), to say nothing of the year I lived in Scotland (there is no collar more popped than on an *inherited* rugby jersey). Since I live in a place that values the new and flashy, I also feel a deep yearning for the old and prestigious, but if I stay too long in a place where the money is so old that it's "ye olde money," or the emotions are repressed, Joni goes on repeat. I start scribbling lyrics on spare pieces of paper: "But I wouldn't want to stay here / it's too old and cold and settled in its ways here / Oh, but California, California!" The South will certainly not feel cold—I remember the thunderous heat of Florida in 1996—but old and settled in its ways? That seems likely. As deep as my ambivalence about old places runs, I sure do like to read about them a lot. Old places, old people, old events.

I didn't know I was a history nerd until other people told me just how much of a history nerd I am. If my mother gave me Shakespeare, Yeats, and Tennyson, my father gave me E. H. Gombrich's *A Little History of the World*, William Manchester's *A World Lit Only by Fire*, and Anna Funder's *Stasiland*. I read. A lot. Constantly, even, often about fascism, and cults, but there is forever space for my always question: "What happened here?"

It's not hard to imagine why I'm so fascinated by history, beyond what I picked up from my father. I don't have any sense of my own history. Am I from Los Angeles, where I was born and went to high school, or Sacramento, where I truly grew up? I don't even know where my mom went to high school. I only have a vague idea of what my mother's father looked like, and no idea where he came from or who his people were. Who my people are. This trip is not only my attempt to discover where my mother ends and I begin, but an effort to place myself in some sort of historical lineage. If the stories we tell about the places we're from become part of the stories we tell about who we are, I owe much to place. We all do. But which place?

I want to understand, as best I can, the places I visit on the 10 as I re-create the path my mother and I took in 1996. Naturally I start with reading the history of a place. Then there's local news coverage (distressingly hard to find in some spots). From there, I dip into the pop culture most associated with it, its best-known fiction, its fine art, its movies and music. I think someone can learn just as much about Sacramento by listening to Cake and watching *Lady Bird* as they can by reading Joan Didion and visiting Sutter's Fort.

Once my brain is stuffed with research, it's time to throw all that out and get going. Walk around, see and taste things. Do what I do best: talk. This is the part I'm most excited for on this trip, talking to people. As I've been reading, I've been reaching out to writers, friends of friends, asking if people are available for a cup of coffee and a chat. I want to ask strangers about the places they're from, the places they live, how they think about identity. You can't meet a place unless you meet some of its people.

I want to shake hands with all these places the same way I'm trying to shake hands with my mother: *Hello, it's nice to meet you. I've heard a lot, but I'd like to get to know the real you.*

These plans are all well and good, but all seem stupid as I'm trundling along the highway, looking at the landscape of cacti and rocks out my window and thinking, not without some guilt, *No thank you!*

I think there are desert people and then there is everyone else. It takes something specific to flourish in the desert, to find its beauty obvious, to take root and weather the dry heat, the epic and swift flash floods. Only certain people figure out how to blossom in a landscape where everything wears its bones on the outside, where scorpions wander in the front door and tarantulas have migrating seasons. I also think there are many people who live in the desert who never actually engage with it, floating between air-conditioned bubbles and perversely green and verdant oases, golf courses, and luxuriantly watered lawns.

When I was a little girl, we lived momentarily with my grandmother Harriet, who at the time was also living in Sacramento. I can't remember if this was before or after we spent some nighttime hours on a quilt in the driveway while my mother sobbed and begged the police to come because she was adamant that men were inside the house, waiting to do horrible things to us. We stayed with Haha for a while, though, and in her house, Sunday evenings were for *The Magical World of Disney*. I vividly remember watching *The Living Desert*, which won the Academy Award for best documentary feature in 1953; the animated opening of winds, cherubic faces blowing Spanish ships across the seas:

> Here in the shadow of [Mount Whitney] the wasteland begins. This is Death Valley, bitterest of all deserts and the lowest point on the American continent. . . . But this desolate basin is only the beginning of the great American desert. From the vicinity of Death Valley it reaches to the plains of Texas, and from a corner of Oregon, deep into old Mexico. For the granite blockade has created one of the largest deserts in the world.

The truth is, I am not headed into a great American desert. I am headed into an American, Mexican, and, soon enough, Canadian desert. The landscape that most defines the Southwest is actually three massive deserts, each of which is growing: the Sonoran Desert, at 100,387 square miles; the Chihuahuan Desert, at 139,769 square miles (both of these begin in Mexico); and the Mojave Desert, at 4,580 square miles. North of these deserts, reaching up into Canada, are the Central and Northern Basins, creating an arid kingdom "incredibly ugly yet fantastically beautiful," as *The Living Desert* put it, whose reach is only expanding in a time of fires, droughts, and climate change.

Sitting on my grandmother's living room floor watching *The Living Desert*, I thought: *That is not a place for me.* I was terrified by the dancing scorpions, the fighting tarantulas, the screaming javelina pigs. Life on Mars looked like it would be rough for a bog person like me.

My skin is made for misty green places and sweaters. Any place where other people would complain of the cold and the damp? That's where I'm happy. Family trips to sunny, bright places usually result with me inside, reading, trying not to get aloe vera all over the pages of my book. That said, I made a general peace pact with heat. Living in Brooklyn with no air-conditioning for six years had forced me into a détente with humidity, which I learned to wear with little complaint. Rather than figure out how to install and remove a window AC unit, like thousands of New Yorkers do every spring and fall, I found it easier to create an intricate schedule. Before I left for work at *Vanity Fair*, I would put my dry sheets in the freezer. At night, I would down a ZzzQuil, take as cold a shower as possible, make my bed with the frozen sheets, point a fan directly at it, and hope I fell asleep before everything thawed. This seemed less intimidating than calling a handyman to install a standard window-unit air conditioner, and I did this for six years. Anyway, I got used to being hot.

Heading east on the other side of the mountains, dipping in between great basins and climbing the great Arizona/New Mexico Plateau (74,467 square miles), it is easy to forget about the Pacific Ocean behind you. These deserts are so big, it looks as though you are on a planet of deserts. It takes me reading a book called *Horizontal Yellow* by Dan Flores to realize that a lot of what I find so discombobulating about the desert is the lack of trees. But just because there aren't any trees does not mean that this landscape is "barren."

"What I want to say is that those of us who are repeat devourers of the Chihuahuan Desert recognize it as the living refutation of *deserted.* Hot and beautiful, it is spare only to forest-trained eyes," Flores writes. "Looking out from the highway, across the endless creosote bush flats is to misapprehend. Ignore economics and this desert is a paradise, the most ecologically rich and diverse desert in the United States."[1]

It's some brutal economics to attempt to ignore, but in the months I am here I will try my hardest to become a desert person; I will eventually learn to see the signs that distinguish the Sonoran from the Chihuahuan; I will learn what Georgia saw that kept her in the clouds, painting her black door. But first I have to make it out of Phoenix alive.

Chapter Three

Phoenix

> Dead shopping malls rise like mountains beyond mountains
> And there's no end in sight / I need the darkness, someone please cut the lights
>
> —ARCADE FIRE

All anyone in Phoenix wants to talk to me about is Los Angeles. Half of the people I speak with assure me that Phoenix is just like LA, nearly an extension, another suburb. There's just as much money to be made, just as much culture, a quality of life that even supersedes LA, with more room, slightly better traffic, and better golfing. The other half tell me Los Angeles is a nefarious cloud on the horizon, infecting Phoenix with bad actors (the politics kind, not the show business kind) and increasingly bad traffic. They bemoan people who live here but commute to LA, making the congestion worse.

"It's a magnet for people escaping California," writer Francisco Cantú explains to me, "weirdly just bringing all the problems of California with them." Problems like traffic, and adding to the Phoenix sprawl, which has this Angeleno floored at its expanse and flatness. Out of this desert plain rises the Camelback, a red mountain that lords over the city, a reminder of all the land underneath this extravaganza of strip malls.

When I try to explain to people what it is I'm doing, my example is that we all know that Arizona must be different from Louisiana. But how is Arizona different from New Mexico? Perhaps there's an obvious answer to the people who live here, but not to everyone else. How, if at all, is Phoenix different from Tucson?

The first thing I notice about Phoenix is that many of the streets are six-lane-wide thoroughfares, with entrances to strip malls directly off the main road. A lack of side-street entrances means I enrage the people behind me by slowing down to pull into parking lots. These streets as big as highways, I will learn, are known as "stroads," part road, part street, all bad news for urban planning, local economies, and quality of life.

While here, I'm staying with the parents of some friends, happy to point me in the direction of some of Phoenix's attractions. They teach me to never leave any door open for too long, because of wandering scorpions. Their library features many biographies of both Bush administrations, and their home is decorated with fine art. In their neighborhood, many driveways feature white Teslas and Land Rovers.

One morning, before the sun rises, I join my host and his friends for their daily walk. I am not fully out of the back seat of one of those white Teslas before a small older man, legs bowed with age but wearing expensive workout gear, marches toward me, putting his own book into my hands. Gary Driggs wrote *Camelback*, a guide to the hikes up the mountain as well as its art and stories, in 1998. We have not been introduced before he begins, "You must understand that I have a veneer of knowledge about many things. A veneer is a thin layer—"

He decides that I can't hear him well enough in the single file that the hike requires, so we "hike" back and forth on the concrete path between the car and the trailhead, over and over.

"The story of America is a story of progress," he tells me. "And it's better than it's ever been. All this 'Henny Penny, the sky is falling!' It's just not true. It never has been. That's all politics."

At some point Driggs pulls me over to inspect a flower and asks what I see.

"It's lovely."

"How many petals does it have?"

"There are five."

"And what color are they?"

"Yellow."

"No. There are four yellow petals and one white one. You see, there's a hidden story behind everything, if you only think to look." I notice that his sunglasses are Gucci and are women's sunglasses.

Eventually we meet with the rest of the hikers, who take turns telling me stories of their time in Phoenix, extolling its virtues as a great place to raise children, run a corporation.

I meet up with a friend of a friend at Changing Hands, a bookstore with a full bar and a café that also hosts various book clubs and lectures. I ask what makes Arizona, Arizona.

"Arizona has a very independent, 'we do it ourselves' kind of mentality. Underlying, there's still the idea that Arizona people are very self-sufficient. Bootstrapping," she says to me, smiling and rolling her eyes at the same time.

In this, Arizona is very American, but maybe especially western. Why else would the metaphor include boots?

Speaking of boots, Dana Armstrong has a fantastic pair. She has even better hair. She has a Stevie Nicks/Dolly Parton coif, a seventies do that is part shag, part bouffant that no mortal woman should be able to pull off. Yet when she meanders into our first meeting at a familiar-feeling Mexican food joint filled with neon lights and generous portions of guacamole for our lunch, she pulls it off so easily, it's intimidating. My first impression is of a woman who knows precisely what she likes, and what Dana likes is Phoenix, country music, and a good bar.

"I'm totally okay with Phoenix being an uncool place," she tells me. "You can't count on a place to make you happy." That may be, but I'm certain that you can count on a place to make you unhappy.

Dana's father, Frank, was the co-owner of a local joint called the Dirty Drummer, which opened in 1975. Eventually there were fourteen bars around the Phoenix area under his banner. Although he stepped down from the business in the nineties, and died in 2012, Dana's ties to the bar remained strong. When she learned that the Drummer franchise was due to close, she and her friends stepped in. When we meet, a new lone Dirty Drummer bar is slated to open in the coming months and she is stressed about the new woodwork for the bar top.

Dana leads me far from the country clubs and green lawns. We go out for tacos and margaritas, and then to her favorite place to drink: the Arizona American Italian Club. Imagine all the perfectly cast extras from *The Sopranos*—that's who's drinking at the bar of the Arizona American Italian Club. A local soul duo with an electric keyboard entertains the slim crowd, and some hock glasses of house red keep our table of young Phoenix folks merry. When I ask any of them about their city, nearly everyone makes some mention of how much they like that Phoenix is not cool. Fuck cool. Fuck hipsters. It's easy to have a good life in a cool city—but somewhere else?

"I feel most inspired here," Dana tells me. "It feels original here."

* * *

As I'm driving around Phoenix, I keep thinking about the Disneyland parking lot. Every time I'm at Disneyland, just after I've parked and I'm headed toward the trams that take visitors to the park entrances, I wonder what the walk back will feel like. Will it have been a good trip? Will I have noticed something new? How many corn dogs will I have consumed? In my early explorations of the desert, I'm aware of how new it all is—all my gear is shiny and clean, all my clothes are tidily folded away in their packing cubes. I don't feel comfortable in Minnie yet, and I'm nervous that I don't have everything I'm going to need, or that I have a lot of things I don't. (Did I really need to bring the collected works of Keats?) I haven't camped yet—will I be ready for that? Should I start on a residential street, or out on the land? I'm terrified of the knock on the door in the middle of the night. The last time I was regularly interviewing people was in my midtwenties when I was at *Vanity Fair*, and my skills are rusty. I ask leading questions, I interject, and I bail out my subjects when I can tell they've talked themselves into corners. On top of this, my journalistic curiosity has been piqued by too many local stories that would keep me here, happily distracted from my journey east. I talk with a woman about her work advising the Navajo Nation on green technology contracts, and the closing of a coal plant that employed a huge number of Native Americans in the area. I associate coal with West Virginia, not Arizona, and that's enough to have me spinning out into a wholly different project. What I find out about Gary Driggs of *Cambelback* fame nearly seduces me with a particularly juicy Google. All this research, all these books, all these interviews, they're part of the writer, the sometime journalist in me.

Part of me wishes I could simply montage my way through these weeks of firsts: first interviews, first camps, first nights. Unfortunately, that's not an option.

To keep myself focused, I am working my way through the binder of my mother's poetry, some of which touches on the 1996 trip, and none of which I've read before; she never shared her writing with me when she was alive. I remember my mother seated at her large desktop computer, typing for hours, and the house was always littered with lines she scribbled down as they occurred to her. This isn't so far from my own life, filled with writerly knickknacks like an unending supply of notebooks and Post-it notes, index cards with research in my loopy cursive, which looks uncannily like my mother's handwriting. The difference is that my mother's writing reflects the violent, uneven nature of her personality. The poems veer uneasily from gentle pieces about nature to screeds of religiosity:

Satan is law rules
[. . .] Satan is the liar, not God
Satan is the bringer of death upon the world
Satan is the bringer of AIDS

Pages and pages of this sort of thing. Looking through this binder, I feel a queasy sense of embarrassment. Often they're not even poems per se, more akin to diary entries with line breaks. Maybe as a kid I found it easy to see my mother as a great artist who never got her chance, but as a professional writer with twenty-plus years of experience, it's impossible to set aside my taste to preserve the image I once had of her. Some of my discomfort comes from the gap between my mom's ambition and her ability, a disparity that haunts every artist. And my mother had ambition:

i have struggled with my desires and jealous envy
inflamed by the taunts of others.
why [am I] not more rich, nor famous, nor acclaimed?
no one ever became rich by being a mother and a poet.

why then am I not a famous feminist theologian?
by then Christ, not I was sent to preach the gospel.
why am I not a famous actress?
but two helpless children need more than any audience.
why are my works as a mom not for God?
but Christ alone is the suffering servant,
who does the words of and for God,
and Christ is who enables me to Mother,
and grace needs no assistance.

She would have been a famous poet, but that doesn't pay. She would have been a famous actress, if not for having kids. She would have been a "famous feminist theologian" (because there are so many of them around), but all glory belongs to Christ. She sounds like the barflies who hover around Los Angeles who *would* have a hit show on television, but they were unwilling to lower their standards to appease the morons who hand out show business careers.

Then I wonder what it must have been like for her to watch from the sidelines as my dad became one of the most famous people on the planet through a heady mix of once-in-a-generation talent and the windfall VHS/DVD market that overlapped perfectly with the height of his fame. Now I'm not so keen to scoff.

Not to mention that sometimes, when she doesn't try so hard, her writing conveys images with startling poignancy, like this moment from a poem about Sacramento that immediately sent me home:

peregrine falcon
tawny hills
oaks
the three rivers join

That is exactly the way to describe the gentle slopes of northern California: tawny hills. It might also now be my drag name.

I'm surprised to see several poems that feature me, one from our time on the Northern California coast, a place special to both of us.

Painted within my memory
is Elizabeth smiling.
Lounging on the greyed, bleached and weather worn deck,
rimmed by pointed firs . . .
[. . .] Her hair glinting gold
[. . .] Ocean surging as white waves race
each other to the shore behind her;
[. . .] She will always
be a part of this landscape
of the heart.

The first thing I notice is that I also spell it "grey," thanks to spending my junior year abroad in Scotland, where all my teachers took a sadistic joy in penalizing an American student for using foreign spelling. British spelling quirks, a twenty-four-hour clock, saying "trousers" rather than "pants," these stuck with me because they were the things I caught the most grief for. No true Scotsman, indeed. My mother, on the other hand, has no reason to spell the word "grey" other than a raging case of Anglophilia. The only known cure for this affliction is to spend a year as a visiting student at the University of St. Andrews.

But in this poem is the whole reason why I went to Scotland in the first place: it is the landscape of the heart. My heart, and my mom's too. The only place I saw my mom really happy was when we would go to the coast of Northern California, as dramatic a place as you can imagine, where redwoods ascend out of the earth until high grass meadows momentarily splay with reckless abandon before sudden cliffs plunge into the frigid waters of the Pacific. The only landscape I've seen that can match its drama is the coast of Scotland.

Maybe my reticence to dig into my quest, this trip, doesn't have anything to do with Phoenix, but more to do with my struggle to connect with a woman who has been dead for nearly twenty years, and who, even when she was alive, was incomprehensible.

It wasn't too long after she died that I started talking to her all the time. Not the way I usually talked to her when she was alive, on eggshells, but the way I could talk to her on a rare good day, when she could listen, root me on, make jokes. It is, admittedly, a one-sided conversation. Reading and editing her poems feels like the first conversation we've had in two decades in which she responds, with as much baffling and heartbreaking bluster as when she was alive.

Still, when I look up from this binder and remember the enormity of this task I have set for myself, trying to understand this woman, my mother, and maybe this place, America, it feels like Phoenix, with its sprawl and its malls and its chain stores, hasn't done me any favors.

Chapter Four

Tucson

> Betcha on land they understand / Bet they don't reprimand their daughters
>
> —*THE LITTLE MERMAID*

I don't know squat about Tucson. All I know is that Tucson is the city where Congresswoman Gabrielle Giffords was gunned down while hosting a town hall at a grocery store and survived. Thirteen people were shot and injured that day, and six people died. The first bit of recent news, however, that everyone wants to share with me is that Diane Keaton recently bought a place in a trendy neighborhood that is the focus of a lot of conversations about gentrification. (She will put it back on the market a few years later.)

I have settled into something like a routine: I wake up and meditate. I drink a cup of tea and write out everything that happened the day before. I make oatmeal, which is cheap and easy to make whether I'm camping (which I haven't done yet) or in an Airbnb. I usually spend the early afternoon at a museum or a tourist attraction, and lunch is either an opportunity to try a local favorite while reading at the same time, or to share lunch with an interviewee.

I'm a Sacramento girl who went on to live in New York and work at a Condé Nast magazine, so it is safe to say that I have always respected Joan Didion, whose early career followed the same trajectory. Didion's famous collection of essays, *The White Album*, begins with the line: "We tell ourselves stories in order to live." Every interview I've done so far, I've noticed how eagerly people have responded to the question "Tell me a story about where you're from." I keep thinking about the connection between identity and location, about origin myths and whether we've adopted new, modern myths to explain why, where, and how we live. The oldies station in Sacramento used to play songs from the fifties and sixties (now they play songs from the nineties, gulp), and I remember driving under sunny skies listening to the Beach Boys singing, "I wish they all could be California girls." "The West Coast has the sunshine," crooned Mike Love, "and the girls all get so tanned." Not this California girl. The closest I get to tan is charbroiled. Nevertheless, I heard that song and thought, *That's a song about me*. I am a California Girl. But what does that mean, other than being "the cutest girls in the land"? How much do the places we're from inform who we are?

I've been listening to people's stories, remembering how often my mom would tell me about growing up eating Cuban food in Florida, and trying to square that with other stories she told, of being a young woman at the infamous Altamont Rolling Stones concert where Hells Angels worked as security and consequently several people died. My mom would have been seventeen. The stories my mom told me often veered between a childhood of crinolines and proper Sunday social calls, and the scary abandon of the counterculture of Northern California, and her personality seemed to swing on the same fulcrum. Growing up, I was taught where the dessert spoon went versus the coffee spoon, but my mother was also extremely frank about sex and masturbation and was happy to draw female anatomy on any napkin. She was both Deep South and NorCal hippie.

I am sitting outside my Tucson rental, a tiny guesthouse behind a classic adobe house that was designed flawlessly by my host, whose family has been here for years. My bedroom, with worn leather accents and teal woven blankets, looks like a Ralph Lauren store in miniature. As I sit outside, watching the Tucson sunset, it seems to me that the stories we tell about the places we're from ultimately become part of the stories we tell about who we are. That place is personhood.

That reminds me: Why did I only have half of the Beatles' *White Album* to listen to constantly on that earlier trip? Had I lost the second CD? Did I purposefully throw it out? I remember sitting outside the Winnebago and surreptitiously cutting up the liner notes to my Green Day *Kerplunk* CD because I was convinced my mother would flip it open to find the lyrics "'Cause I love feelin' dirty / And I love feeling cheap / And I love it when you hurt me / So drive those staples deep!"). In the past, my mother had found a beloved copy of the original *Little Mermaid* on my bookshelves. She was deeply disturbed by the imagery of the transformed mermaid feeling the stabbing of swords every time she took a step with her magical human feet. I came home from school to find my book torn to shreds in my trash can, and the only explanation I was given was that the fairy tale was "rooted in the law, not in God's grace."

If that was how she felt about a traditional retelling of *The Little Mermaid*, who knew how she'd have reacted to a song titled "Dominated Love Slave." Although . . . for every time my memory serves up an image of my mother as a straitlaced Puritan, I can easily recall her buying me a copy of Janis Joplin or sitting me down to show me her favorite Monty Python bit, a knight being hacked to bloody bits while arguing "'Tis but a scratch!"

* * *

The first thing I notice in Tucson is that, unlike in Phoenix, I hear Spanish everywhere I go. Katherine, my third-generation Tucsonan host, tells me part of this is life in southern Arizona—more liberal and closer to the border. Native faces and Latin faces and "Anglo" (as white people are called around here) faces greet me all over the city—though not many Black faces. The second thing I notice is that, unlike in Phoenix, you never forget about the desert in Tucson (named after a Native rancheria/village Chuk Sohn)—the city makes no effort to hold it at bay. I have finally arrived in the southwestern aesthetic.

"We are living in an age of a desert aesthetic and even a desert chic," wrote Dan Flores in his 1999 book. "Many of us grow up now with romantic notions about cactus-studded landscapes lit by neon sunsets, notions some scholars think may be the emerging landscape stereotype of the American West in the eyes of the world."[1] Flores must have had his finger on the pulse—because if 1999 marked the emergence of a desert aesthetic, we are still in the full flush of a major desert romanticism.

Pinterest boards and homes across America are dedicated to a spartan look of succulent plants, Edison bulbs, and simple plywood tables—this also describes nearly every coffee shop I've been in, not just in America but in Europe as well. Instagram has homogenized style to the point where a café in Tucson can look remarkably similar to one in Vienna. And while I'd previously thought that this sparse look was derived from Scandinavia, when I eventually stand in Georgia O'Keeffe's kitchen a couple of days hence, I'll realize that in large part we have her to thank for this moment where midcentury modern meets the Mojave.

Walking toward the museum at the University of Arizona, I think about how Tucson embraces the desert, its beauty and austerity, in a way that Phoenix does not. Here I don't see discordantly green lawns or modern glass buildings. Some in Phoenix seemed to consider, with pride, their own city as a mere extension of Los Angeles; but as the 10 dips south, Tucson feels distinct, with the touches that feel officially southwestern. Everywhere I go now it's small adobe homes with spiny cacti out front, iron decals of desert foxes and coyotes, *ristras* (strings of red chilies) hanging from front doors.

On my first day, over tea on the small patio outside the Airbnb, I read from local writer Francisco Cantú's *The Line Becomes a River: Dispatches from the Border*. Cantú grew up here in Arizona and, after studying international relations, realized he wanted to come back to the landscape and political situation that his classmates spoke about in the hypothetical but that he knew personally. Then he joined the Border Patrol.

Cantú and his book have come under fire from immigration activists and undocumented persons who feel that, of all the stories to be told about the border, do we really need the one from the guy who can pass as white and who worked for the Border Patrol? And for the most part, Cantú agrees with them—there should be more undocumented voices highlighted, their stories deserve to be told; nor does he absolve himself of any of his actions while working for the Border Patrol. When I eventually meet up with Francisco, or Paco, as he is sometimes known, we talk about why he wrote the book he did.

"The writing was to come to terms with what I had been a part of, and what I was participating in, and understanding that on a deeply personal level," he says to me.

As I move east, I've been thinking about the experiences we have that depend on being in a specific place. Border life can only happen on the border, and when I ask Francisco about this place, for his thoughts about Phoenix versus Tucson, he has an immediate response.

"Tucson is a place with a long lineage of desert rats," he tells me over barbacoa and birria tacos at Taqueria Pico de Gallo. "Phoenix is very much more like a boomtown; its older roots are more obscured than in Tucson, where I think it's kind of a source of pride for a lot of Tucsonans. The Mexican history of Tucson is also a source of pride. We have our problems and our issues of gentrification and obscuring people's narratives and stories."

In Southern California, it's par for the course that Mexico is part of the conversation about America; but here in Arizona, the fact that all this land once belonged to our neighbors south of the border seems all the more prevalent. Unavoidable, even.

"People talk about the American Southwest and the borderlands, sometimes as distinct things, sometimes interchangeably. And they all touch each other and rub up against each other and transition in and out of one another," Cantú points out. *Transition in and out of one another* perks my ears up—it reminds me of the Pacific Coast Highway blending into the 10, the way we "become our parents." When I headed south from Phoenix, I slipped into the borderlands, and I won't leave them until I arrive in Houston.

Francisco is an affable, soft-spoken man with an impressive mustache who can swear a blue streak. We trade thoughts on our favorite horchata recipes and we talk about our mothers.

"My mom was an interpretive ranger; she's always telling stories," he tells me. "I grew up very attuned to those stories and narratives, and as they connect specifically to the landscape. . . . One thing that played a big part in my decision [to join the Border Patrol] was—I talked to recruiters, and I remember a lot of them were like, 'Oh yeah, you love being outdoors, you like hiking outdoors. You're gonna be doing that all the time.' Which is fucking true. . . . I mean, if you're lazy and you don't want to get out of your car, you could be that kind of agent."

There are desert people, and Francisco is a desert person.

"Part of the idea of this place, the borderland deserts as being a wasteland, is tied into the erasure of these cultures that knew how to flourish here," he points out.

While we're talking, I can't take my eyes off a family nearby: a grandmother, mother, and two little girls. The mother has a large, badly infected wound exposed in the crook of her arm. Her little girls have the sort of shoes that light up, and they fight over who gets to watch something on an iPhone. The crushed ice in their Styrofoam cups squelches noisily.

"The idea of the desert as an inhospitable place is just so prevalent," Francisco says. "But it's a beautifully functioning ecosystem for the plants and animals that have evolved to live here. And for the people that lived here."

And there were a lot of people who lived here. Of all the myths of the west, of the great experiment of manifest destiny, perhaps the most pervasive is that the West is and always was defined by emptiness—the vast expanse of land untainted by human presence. All that empty land—it's ugly. Filled with spiny, needly plants and creatures that scuttle. This myth of emptiness is necessary to perpetuate the idea that this land was just waiting for some capable, brave folks walking by the strength of their own bootstraps to turn it into something worthy. And just why were these deserts so empty anyway? Because an estimated 60 to 90 percent of the Indigenous population was eradicated in a single generation—*60 to 90 percent.*[2] The Southwest wasn't an open land of opportunity to the Spanish, or to the Anglos who came west later—it was a crime scene.

Francisco and I speak for over an hour, politely ignoring just how messy taco eating can be and comparing notes on editors we've had and magazine people to avoid. When we talk about his time in the Border Patrol, I notice how often he ends up speaking about his mother.

Whenever I think of my mom, I think of Sacramento, because I don't have many memories of her away from our home. Other than driving the 10 to Palatka, there's a trip, again to Florida and Walt Disney World, that I barely remember, and the odd excursion to Sea Ranch on the Northern California coast. My mom and Sacramento are almost the same for me. When I go back, I see her in the mist that rises over the American River in the winter. I can't remember if the scent I associate with her is how she actually smelled, or maybe is just the smell of water on concrete baking on a summer's afternoon. I miss her like I miss the wide, tree-lined streets of East Sacramento. Francisco's mother comes up not only when we discuss his old job but also when the conversation returns, as it does again, to the desert. They are intertwined for him, I think.

"I was being put in the situation of fear and/or aggression, and that kind of plays into the way that you understand the landscape," Francisco says, keeping his mustache tidy. "Because to me the desert has always been this place of fascination. This place of beauty. I got that from my mother. One of my first memories [in the Border Patrol] is showing up at the station after finishing the academy. It was our second day in the field, and we found foot signs of people right on the border road. We followed it up a couple miles and we never found the people, but they left their backpacks and their dope, and then with the tacit permission of our supervising agents, people are just taking everything out of the backpacks and stringing it on plants. Throwing clothes on top of saguaro cactus, lighting shit on fire, pissing on things."

"So that the people can't go back for it," I say. It was one of the details from his book that I found most upsetting.

"All this destruction. And then leaving it. Leaving it in the fucking desert. I'm the son of a park ranger. What, am I going to complain? What am I going to do? I'm like a fucking baby. Somebody'll spit in my face. Or make me do push-ups or something crazy. So, this is what happens out here." He throws his hands in the air. The woman with the hole in her arm plays with her little girl's hair.

"So, this is how people think about this landscape. This is how people treat it and indoctrinate others to regard it. . . . We're told to fear these places. Or they're places of inspiration or vision. Why can't it just be a place? It could just . . . be a place."

Why *can't* a place just be a place? I'm not sure, but I think it has something to do with stories. *We tell ourselves stories in order to live*—and all stories, even the dumb ones, need a setting. We can't help but make everywhere we go into a stage. But does the stage dictate the type of story you're in? And what happens when you want, very badly, for the story to end?

I drove into Tombstone
Thinking myself immune
To cowboy and indian dreams [. . .]
Wild west fictions
And found myself yielding
To the truths of history
Which are far more interesting
Than the pale imitations of fiction
Of Walt Disney's America.
[. . .]
Our mythologies, our story tellers
Are too simple
[. . .]
No inconvenient realities, no follies, no ironies
No existential cowboy moments.
[. . .]
Our heroes, our myths, our legends, our realities
Collide in unexpected places,
In ways that are both humorous and intriguing.
Existential humorous cowboy moments happen.

—Susan Jane Dillingham

Chapter Five

Tombstone

"Why, Johnny Ringo. You look like somebody just walked over your grave."

—*TOMBSTONE*

I'm baffled by my mother's fixation with Tombstone. I didn't care for it the first time I was here, and I really don't care for it now. What I did enjoy was Val Kilmer.

I don't know if it started before our trip, or if it was the 10 that spawned it, but her obsession with Tombstone never ran out of steam. Over and over she would go back to the 1993 film with Kurt Russell as Texas lawman Wyatt Earp, Bill Paxton as the hotshot younger brother, and Sam Elliott as the stoic eldest brother. She had many books about Tombstone. Most of these books were self-published, and like all my mother's other books, she owned doubles and triplicates of them. I thought the movie was cheesy—kids these days would say "cringe"—except for Val's consumptive Doc Holliday; "Doc" came from his day job, which was dentistry. Everyone remembers "I'm your huckleberry," but teenage me was overcome by Doc's dandy style, his insouciant pout, the strange combination of being a killer while slowly dying. Those pale cheekbones topped by that cynical glare . . . swoon! Maybe I only fell for Keats when I was in college because he reminded me a bit of Doc Holliday.

Many of my strongest memories of our 1996 trip on the 10 are of our time in Tombstone. For one, it was where I met cousins and uncles for the first time. The only member of my mother's family that she spoke of was my grandmother. My mother's brothers were mysterious figures who were occasionally mentioned, but only in passing. I never heard stories about them, about Thanksgiving dinners or Christmas mornings. I never saw pictures of any of these people, or even knew the names of my cousins. My mother's family was simply off-limits. Any direct question about them was evaded, and any question about my grandfather would have brought heaps of trouble down on me.

So it was strange when my mother announced as we drove along the 10 that we would be meeting up with two of her three brothers, as they lived along the interstate. Suddenly there we were, wandering around the ruins of a cowboy town with people who looked like us. My cousins seemed nice, and I wondered what they had heard about us. About my mother.

Seeing her with her older brother, seeing her as a sister, was strange. Our lives had already begun to shrink; I rarely saw my mother interact with anyone outside her limited circle of friends, most of whom were never around for long. Seeing her with people other than my brother and me was novel, though I'm sure most teenagers don't imagine their parents having a life beyond them.

Growing up, I would get flashes of normal family life that only made how strange life with my mother was all the more clear. When I was young, my mother's mother, Harriet, with her *The Magical World of Disney* evenings, still lived in Sacramento, as did Haha's brother, Uncle David. There would be periods when my brother and I would stay with her, when Mom's drug use was still rampant. Grandma Haha would play

Prokofiev's *Peter and the Wolf* on her record player for Colin and me to act out around her living room. Harriet left Sacramento when I was still a young girl, mourning her brother and I think exhausted by my mother, years before it ever occurred to me that here was someone who might have been willing to answer all the questions that would come.

My father's sister also lived in Sacramento, in a large and stately Victorian home that was *so* large and stately, it had a golden plaque on the porch that read NOT A BED-AND-BREAKFAST. Inside it was a bohemian hodgepodge that excited me: paintings, books, epic ceilings. I only saw her on the rare occasions that my Hanks family would be in town. Those didn't feel so much like formal family gatherings, but more like hangouts that were goofy and loud. In elementary school there were several Grandparents Days when Grandma Haha; my father's mother, Janet, who lived north of Sacramento in Red Bluff; and his stepmother, Frances, accompanied me. I was the only girl with three grandmothers. Walking around with Frances, who still spoke with a thick Mandarin accent thanks to a childhood in the bubble of San Francisco's Chinatown, confused a lot of people.

But the family I spent the most time with by far was my Greek stepfamily, on weekends in Los Angeles and every summer. I was usually with my two cousins, as blond and tan and thin as I was not. I watched them, mystified by the idea of having a sister, and got used to being around people who didn't look at all like me.

The idea that I had cousins who had my freckled skin, my auburn hair, was novel. Who were these people who argued about classical music (I assume we all got the bug from Harriet) and traded Monty Python barbs? But I could also see the strain of keeping it together placed on my mother, of trying not to talk to herself quite as much, and I saw the polite blankness that would fall over my cousins' faces when she started to talk about Jesus.

* * *

When I pull into Tombstone in the heat of midafternoon, I have to pause for a stagecoach, driven by a man wearing chaps and a headset microphone. All of Tombstone is a couple of blocks down one main street plus a couple of little side streets. Nearly every storefront is a different attraction requiring a different ticket. From the moment I exit my van to the moment I get back in the driver's seat, exhausted and near tears, it is at most twenty-five minutes.

I know I'm in trouble when I cannot tell the difference between paid reenactors and people who love Tombstone enough to spend their Saturdays cosplaying as cowboys and prostitutes, like a Yeehaw Western Renaissance Faire that never ends. Soon enough, aggressive carnival barkers attempt to entice the growing number of passersby into buying tickets to a re-creation of the shootout at the O.K. Corral, now walled up so only ticketed tourists can see anything. I'm implored to buy tickets to ghost tours, tickets to stables, tickets to an abandoned mine. I start keeping to the shadows to avoid people coming up to me. After the fourth person in a cowboy hat calls me "little lady" and tries to get me to buy something, I turn off the main drag, passing a bar that has bucked the western kitsch theme and is blasting AC/DC. I try to remember if my mother made us buy tickets to the Bird Cage Theatre, still mottled with bullet holes (over 140, it's rumored), where the longest poker game in the world took place. Back in the van, I save myself the twenty bucks and watch the shootout scene in the O.K. Corral from the movie.

The gunfight at the O.K. Corral, supposedly only thirty seconds long, is the world's most famous shootout and did not happen at the O.K. Corral. On October 26, 1881, in a narrow lot beside a photography studio, town marshal Virgil Earp, his brothers Wyatt and Morgan, and Doc Holliday took on five cowboys and won. Virgil was maimed for life after a retaliatory attack in December, and in March, Morgan was murdered. Wyatt, then US deputy marshal of Cochise County, swore vengeance, but it's possible Tombstone's sympathy was with the dead cowboys. Photos of nineteen-year-old Billy Clanton, twenty-eight-year-old Tom McLaury, and his brother, thirty-three-year-old Frank, in their glass-faced coffins, cheeks gaudily rouged, were incredibly popular, and the funeral procession to the cemetery on Boot Hill brought out the whole town. Boot Hill has markers that read 3 FINGERED JACK DUNLAP and the elegiac: TWO COWBOYS.

I get Minnie running and immediately set out. I feel a momentary blip of guilt for not trying to wrangle an interview out of one of the reenactors, or maybe the glum teen who sold me some postcards. Everything in my body is telling me to get out of Dodge. Maybe it could have been fun with a friend, but alone and unaware of the black clouds of emotion rolling in behind me, Tombstone just feels like a sad tourist trap that has no secrets to give up.

The whiff of desperation that lies over the town makes sense—with no one to buy tickets to the shootout, to the silver mine, to the theater, there is no economy—but the constant carnival barking has my teeth grinding, and my skin overly sensitive, like a migraine building. My mother may have had cowboy dreams, but on that day, I did not.

What was it about Tombstone that so appealed to my mother? She scoffs at "the pale imitations of fiction / Of Walt Disney's America," but if there is any grain or grit of truth to be found here, I've completely missed it, not to mention beauty. I think she liked to think of herself as a Shakespearean actress lost in the wild—another trope she got from the movie. In it, a ravishing city girl comes to the dusty backwater of Tombstone to perform as the devil tempting Faust at the Bird Cage.

Wyatt, married to an opium-addled bit of baggage, falls for the actress the way only a tall drink of water can, the lady swoons, and eventually they ride off into the sunset for a lifetime of room service.

I think that when she never became a famous theater actress, or any type of actress, my mother considered herself a thoroughbred of the highest order put out to pasture in Sacramento way before her time. To her, Tombstone was a place where all the burnouts, all the people who never made it, could congregate and make something new of themselves. To me, then and now, it is a tourist trap that makes my skin crawl. Something isn't right with me, but I'm not sure what. I blame it on Tombstone and try to leave it all behind me.

Chapter Six

Gila Bend

> We all begin as a bundle of bones lost somewhere in a desert, a dismantled skeleton that lies under the sand. It is our work to recover the parts. It is a painstaking process best done when the shadows are just right, for it takes much looking.
>
> —CLARISSA PINKOLA ESTÉS

About an hour outside of Tombstone, I make my way to a campsite at the Cochise Stronghold in the Coronado National Forest. The lone country road, with the Anglophilic name Middlemarch Road, passes an abandoned mine of the same name, then takes a turn up into the Dragoon Mountains. From there it turns into a gravel road, passing over a couple of dry riverbeds. It's remote enough that I wonder if I'm going to see another human being for the next twenty-four hours, so it's confusing that when I finally arrive at the camping area, it's crowded enough that I can't find anywhere to set up that isn't less than twenty-five feet from anyone else. I settle for the spot farthest from a family with blaring speakers. Even with the crowd, I can see the beauty of this place, shady thanks to the evergreen oaks. We're hemmed in by great stacks of granite boulders, home to fairy sword ferns that splay out in the wet season and curl up in the dry. Everything here has to adapt.

This place was named for a chief of the Chiricahua band of the Apache, Cochise. When America took over the Arizona and New Mexico territories in 1850, Cochise was mostly friendly with the new Anglos in charge. Then a young kid went missing from a nearby ranch.

When the Chiricahua chief and several family members came to speak with local military officials to deny that they had kidnapped the child, Lieutenant George Bascom decided to take the group hostage. Cochise escaped, and in retaliation, Bascom had the rest of the Natives hanged. The missing child, it turns out, had been taken by a different group of Apache.

After the murder of his family members, Cochise took up active rebellion and joined in the large fight to fend off US efforts to wrench Natives off their land and "relocate" them on reservations hundreds of miles away. This stronghold was where the Chiricahua hid out and based their military operations. The man who united the Apache said, "No one wants peace more than I do. Why shut me up on a reservation? We will make peace; we will keep it faithfully. But let us go around free as Americans do. Let us go wherever we please."[1]

Eventually Cochise successfully negotiated with the US government; while the Chiricahui were confined to a reservation, it was on their own ancestral land. The leader died June 8, 1874, and is buried somewhere in this mountainous area, covered in dense brush and lovely trees. When I go for a hike, nervous after reading too many stories about solo hikers taken down by mountain lions, I notice a marker.

CHIEF COCHISE

GREATEST OF APACHE WARRIORS

DIED JUNE 8, 1874

IN THIS HIS FAVORITE STRONGHOLD
INTERRED SECRETLY BY HIS FOLLOWERS
THE EXACT PLACE OF HIS BURIAL WAS KNOWN TO ONLY
ONE WHITE MAN—HIS BLOOD BROTHER
THOMAS J. JEFFORDS

Thank goodness Jeffords got his moment in the sun. This is the first of many iffy monuments I will see on my trip.

On our original trip across the 10, I got my period for the first time in Gila Bend, Arizona. It was on the way home—I remember that because we had a dog with us. While stopping in El Paso to spend some time with the eldest of my mom's brothers, for some reason we ended up taking his absolutely insane, fat Jack Russell terrier, Fern. Fern liked to bolt out the front door given any chance, leaving my mother to chase her down the street, almost always in some state of undress, screaming her name, until giving up and getting in the car and driving back and forth with the door open because then and only then would Fern come running. Like nearly every pet we had, Fern was vanished, simply gone one day when I got home.

So it must have been on the way home, because I remember my stomach hurting while Mom and I wrangled Fern into a red suitcase (not a hard case, though I'm not sure that makes it any better). We sneaked the dog into the motel, and at some point I took my cramping stomach to the bathroom. Mom hugged me and told me I was a woman. That was twenty-three years ago. I still don't really know what she meant by that, because no piece of advice my mother gave me about being a woman wasn't actually about men. Being a woman meant to be constantly watched, lusted after, always at risk. Getting my period meant that now I had to constantly position myself in relation to men. Female friendship, community: if these mattered to my mother at some point, by the time I was a teenager they were no longer really part of her life. There were a number of infinitely patient women who had known my mother, but over the years they would be alternatively banned from and re-invited into our lives. It is safe to say that I did not have committed, honest friendship modeled to me, so the fact that I am still close with my core group of high school girlfriends is a blessing, but also a testament to how closely I watched my older brother, Colin. I saw the way his friends protected him, took him in whenever he needed another place to crash, and felt true envy. I wanted that. I wanted everything my mother lacked: friendship, partnership, consistency, cleanliness.

Returning to these places where I've been before with my mother brings no wellspring of emotion, no surge of nostalgia. Maybe it's just been too long. I remember, a couple of months after she died, bursting into tears at the sight of a can of Arizona iced tea, because we drank so many of them on the road in 1996. But nearly twenty years after her death, everything is muffled: my memories of her voice, the cadence of her touch. Mostly my mother, and the life I lived with her, seems like a strange dream now. Did I really spend years worshiping her and fearing her? Did we really drive across the country together, in relative silence? Basic facets of life seem bizarre to me: What was family dinner like? It's hard for me to recall sitting at the family table with Colin and my mother, yet I know it happened countless times. Being here, in Arizona, brings back little flashes: I remember the dog squiggling around inside the red suitcase; I remember the sound of the disposable camera as she took pictures of everything, truly everything, in Tombstone. But I don't remember what it felt like to be my mother's daughter.

I don't remember, I mean, what it was like to relate to her, to talk to her, to share space and time with her. I only remember her telling me that being a woman meant you were always in danger, yet she was by far the most dangerous thing in my life. I think I'm only really figuring that out here, on the road, while I stare at places I know I've visited in the past, and feel no closer to her than I did before. Did I wait too long to do this? Why didn't I go through all those boxes of her papers sooner? Maybe she's just been dead for too long. Maybe there's no part of me that can reach any part of her.

This campground is basically a parking lot in the middle of the mountains. Minnie is berthed beside my own picnic table and a fire pit, and the area is shady with trees, but most of the other campsites have been set up like outdoor living rooms. The family next to me has three huge inflatable sofas, with a loud generator keeping an impressive array of electronics running: an electric grill, a mini fridge, and a bunch of plug-in lanterns. My setup is pretty feeble by comparison. I don't have any firewood for the pit, so I use my tiny propane canister to boil some water, add it to a bag of camping enchiladas, and crack a seltzer water. My other direct neighbor is a woman with the taut body of a marathon runner, whose tent setup is as beefy as she is slight. She comes over to let me know that, with my sliding door open, Minnie's lights are on. I slather on some mosquito repellent, turn on my lantern, and read more from my mom's white binder of poetry. It was in the red journal that I read about her father, and the crime she believed he'd committed. The writing in that little book is mostly one-off sentences, prayers that are a paragraph long. This binder is heavy, with hundreds of pages, some with poems, some with train-of-thought ramblings. I can only read a little at a time; it's too exhausting trying to process everything she's throwing at me.

> *I was low on gas on a highway in the desert of Arizona so I was relieved that I was able to turn around on a grass strip and head*

back to the nearest gas station, near the Gila river. The local station had a dangling sign, unkempt with peeling paint and tumble weeds blowing past the gas pumps. Relieved to find a man there to pump the gas, I pulled in. Seemingly friendly, as he pumped gas, he talked to me, telling me a story. About how a woman and her child had been locked in their car in the desert just yesterday, and he answered a rescue call to save them. Had driven up and down the highway for hours looking for them without a trace and had finally given up.

As he talked, I noticed his faded blue denim shirt was buttoned all crooked, and food still stuck in his teeth where he hadn't brushed them. I became very aware of the fact that I was a woman alone with him in the middle of the Arizona desert, with my daughter in the car. I worried that I had to pay the bill inside where the cash register was. Worried, I followed him inside.

"Let me show you my cancer scars." He showed me the scars on his neck from cancer surgery. There were two huge scars where he pointed to and said there had been two large tumors removed.

"I used to look just like the elephant man."

Then he told me of the mysterious doctor just over the border in Mexico he had gone to, hinting that he might tell me of a secret cancer cure, which he obtained during his trips into Mexico.

The doctor cured him by giving him herb teas. The old lady in the nearby towns believes the tea to have tasted similar to the roots of the saguaro cactus. How the doctors here have been amazed at the miracle of his recovery, and he knew it was of God. Then he told me he had not read much of the Bible but he wanted to preach me the gospel, if I would only listen, then he would give me the name of the mysterious herbalist in Mexico. But what he preached was law. The law of diet. No meat, vegetarian food. No mention of Christ came to fulfill the laws and nail them to the cross along with our sins. How we died with him so that the life of the Holy Spirit might flow into us bringing new life. So that we might begin again brand new. He preached one more of the hundreds of versions of law being passed off as the gospel. Here in the desert as God has said, those who ignore his Christ will fulfill and cancel his own law, so he might bring us into freedom. In their hubris they seem to fulfill the law on their own and live in God's wrath as a result. Ironically we are not far from Alamogordo, reminding me of Sodom and Gomorrah where God's judgment on our attempts to keep the law was demonstrated. Where the result of law and wrath are evident. My daughter called to me screaming. I hurried back to the car which had become filled with hundreds of flies, which appeared in a swarm. I left him there as I pulled out. Standing next to a garbage can filled with swarming black flies, covered in flies, still talking in my window about how I could be saved by God if only I would follow the law. I pulled back out onto the highway, too scared to cry.

I remember the black flies in the Winnebago very clearly, but that happened in Barstow, California, not near the Gila River, the oldest wilderness preserve in America. Barstow is on the 40, not the 10. There was no way my mother was going to drive through Los Angeles, home to all my father's success and, I think in her mind, all her failures. We cut southwest after Bakersfield, and probably took Route 93 south to Phoenix and *then* got on the 10. No Moomat Ahiko for my mother and me.

We were parked at a gas station while refueling, and my mother was sure that our tires were going to melt on asphalt on the verge of boiling. I remember her going in to pay and her taking a very long time, and then coming back to find me dealing with the swarm of flies that had invaded the moment I'd opened the door to invite a breeze. She had that spooked, jumpy look about her that meant she felt threatened by someone or something. Chances are, this guy was a chitchatty oddball who tried to make small talk. After my mom died, I asked the people who had known her best when they knew something about her was off. Some people would dodge this question, reading insult in it, and chide me for criticizing a woman who was "doing her best."

My dad knew exactly what I meant and told me a story of one time she returned to their Hell's Kitchen apartment in New York with that look in her eyes, like when a horse's eyes roll and show white. He asked her what was wrong, and she told him that a Black man in a bodega had assaulted her and threatened to rape her; she ran from the store screaming. Horrified, my dad marched down with her to the corner store to confront the man. When my mother pointed out someone, it was just a middle-aged guy going about his business, browsing the crowded shelves. Something about the man's stance, his indifference, the quiet of the store around them, the normality of it all, tipped my dad off. He eyed the cashier: nothing beyond a casual head nod. It was clear that nothing had happened.

When I think about this story now, I remember a moment during the legal proceedings around when I switched custody and moved to Los Angeles. I read something she had submitted to the judge: it was a description of how I had screamed at her to drop everything she was doing because I needed new, expensive blue bedsheets. I had badgered and bullied her into buying these sheets that she could not afford. In reality, I had no idea what she was talking about. At some point I had arrived for one of my court-appointed visits and found that she had bought new *pink* sheets, and simply left them unopened on the bed. What's funny about it now is that eventually I gave up on having sheets on my bed at all. I was a teenager and not inclined to do laundry, and my mother gave up on cleaning altogether at some point, so I just dug up an old sleeping bag and put that on my bed instead. My mother's versions of events often included ominous men, violence, and drama.

Inside Minnie at night, I cuddle up between a loose pair of hiking boots and a stack of books on the desert I've been reading at truck stops and diners. In 1996, my mother and I mostly ate fast food. She would park the RV and I would go in and order for us, and then we'd eat seated at the little table that could fold into another bed. There was the occasional Cracker Barrel, which at fourteen I thought was the most delicious thing in the world. It was, compared to the Taco Bell we ate for many, many meals back home. This time around, I have been much more thoughtful about where I eat in the cities, trying out independent cafés and asking people for restaurant recommendations; but along the stretch from Tucson to Las Cruces, New Mexico, I'm mostly eating at hole-in-the-wall taquerias and truck stops. I would say that I like the anonymity of these places, but the truth is that I stick out like a sore thumb, being alone, being a woman. I do remember stopping with my mom once or twice at one Love's truck stop or another. I would watch with fascination as truckers bought shower time—Love's is famous for its clean showers, which I will not be experiencing since I signed up for a twenty-four-hour gym chain for this express purpose. I think all the men at the truck stops made my mom nervous, so we stopped doing anything besides fueling up. I don't mind stopping for a cup of coffee when there's a diner (and maybe for the occasional chicken-fried steak, something I would never order back home), but that's usually in the morning. Even today, I made sure to get to the Cochise camping area well before sundown—I try not to be on the road, or at gas stations, after dark.

When the campground finally quiets, the dark is so dark, and the quiet is so quiet. Camping in an organized campground has saved me from being nervous about an angry knock on the window in the middle of the night. Before I left for the trip, I was bingeing videos on van life, and the dreaded night knock seems to be a rite of passage. Curled up in my surprisingly comfortable bed, I wonder if I'll make it through the whole trip without some sort of nighttime drama. Before I slip into sleep, I cross my fingers for good luck. For some reason I dream not of the desert, but of water. Water everywhere, gray waves carrying me inside my van, like a little black boat, away.

Chapter Seven

Albuquerque

> To Don Quixotes from everywhere, this has always been a durable and baffling land.
>
> —DAVID LAVENDER

The 10 as it crosses from Arizona into New Mexico looks exactly like the epitome of the American Road Trip road, the physical manifestation of a Bruce Springsteen song, two lanes headed out into a landscape you wouldn't want to get lost in, on foot or otherwise. It looks like this road never ends.

The last time I was driving through the desert, I sent a picture of it to my friend Scott, far away in Scotland. "Yep," he responded. "That's THE American highway right there. Don't make them like that anywhere else." Scott was a musician who toured America extensively; he knew his American roadways, so different from the kamikaze country lanes of Scotland. There, the smaller and narrower the single-lane road, the faster people drive. It's unhinged. It doesn't matter if you're traversing the Highlands or crossing a loch-speckled isle, country roads are minuscule and murderous. Just like I have so many times since I left LA, I instinctually go to text him, maybe send a picture of where I am, but Scott died a year ago. Since our friendship was mostly a long-distance one, I have to remind myself that he's not just on the other side of the globe. His absence is a wound I keep picking at. I don't want to get used to it.

As I drive through this postcard desertiness, the other thing I keep thinking about is, as usual, Disneyland. When you grow up with the beloved, fake version of something, seeing the real deal can be a bit of a shock. Specifically, I think about the Cars Land ride in Disneyland's California Adventure, where at night the fake rocks that look like Cadillac fins are lit perfectly, the ideal vista for a quiet dinner of passable fried chicken. The ersatz vista can't compete with the real thing, though. Am I starting to see with desert eyes? In the real world, when I pull over for gas, I take deep breaths—away from the highway, the air is cleaner than back home in Los Angeles, and I don't take it for granted. Sometimes I think I can smell rain coming from far away, but I won't see rain for a long time to come.

Albuquerque is not on the 10. In fact, it's quite north. I'm here because I want to see my father, who happens to be shooting a movie here, before I continue north to visit Georgia O'Keeffe's house near Santa Fe.

While filming, my dad has a rental house on a hillside that offers a view of the whole city. ABQ is nearly invisible during the day. The brown of all the adobe and the heat-friendly taupe color scheme blend with the desert scrub. You can only really see the city at night, a blanket of lights spreading out through the dark, finally showing you the size of this place. Nearby is the Sandia Peak Tramway, which ascends to an elevation of 10,378 feet and a restaurant. My dad is looking trim, more in shape than he's ever been in his life, thankfully taking his type 2 diabetes seriously. He's careful about his daily walks and yoga, and his beard is full, but not *Cast Away* long. He loves anywhere hot and dry, and he's in his man sandals constantly. With a hat on, he looks like any other tan New Mexico retiree. Over paleo pancakes and diabetes-friendly syrup, my dad tells me that I've been up the tramway before—when my mother was pregnant with me.

I treat any snippet of information about my biological family as if I have stumbled onto a scrap of paper from a presumed-lost sacred text. My dad never volunteers stories about his marriage to my mom, though he always answers my questions honestly and openly. Between his reticence to dig up the past, and my mother's version of events always being unreliable, I didn't know the beginning, or even the middle, of my own story thus far. Because of this, little throw-away memories like "You've actually been here before, with your mom and me" feel seismic. Any story of my family actually being together is mythic—from a time and place that seems so unlikely as to be totally made up. Sometimes it just feels weird, anachronistic even, to think of us all in the same place at the same time. *What if the Flintstones hung out with the Jetsons?*

My parents were in ABQ because my dad, having cut his teeth as a professional repertory actor at the Great Lakes Shakespeare Festival in Cleveland, Ohio, snagged a role on a little show that only lasted two seasons, *Bosom Buddies*. As part of the Paramount "family," he was invited to take part in the *Happy Days* celebrity charity softball game, which that year was happening in Albuquerque. The brief trip included a visit up the tramway, where my dad and my mom, pregnant with me, had dinner above this city, with all the other television stars of the early 1980s. I put this story in my pocket and, at night, lie in bed and wonder if my mom liked being pregnant.

* * *

When a friend asks me, "What was your mom like?" I sometimes wish for an easier answer. It's an uncomfortable truth that if she'd regularly hit me, I could say, "She was abusive," and everyone, as the lyrics of one of her favorite records put it, "would know exactly what I was talking about." The truth is, she had never really hit me before. She pushed me, shook me, pulled at my hair, and locked me in a closet once or twice, but never really had she hit me. Instead, she told me there were men hiding in her closet who were waiting for us to go to sleep to come out and do horrible things. She painted a picture of dozens of miscarried babies, my lost siblings, and insinuated that I'd join them in eternal limbo. She also was the only person who could instantly gauge my mood and backed me in every situation, except the one between us. She told me I was smarter than all the other kids, and that I could have been an Olympic equestrian if I had wanted to, and she drove me all over California to horse shows at ungodly hours. For every time she grabbed me by my hair and yelled in my face, she also cut up cookie dough for my friends sleeping over and let me dye my hair every color I wanted. For every friend I had who was not allowed to come to my house, I had another for whom my mom was "the cool mom."

But at nearly fourteen, I had started to understand that something was not right. That there should have been more food in the house on a regular basis, that I should have had help with homework, that I needed clean clothes, and that being woken up at three in the morning to hear an impromptu lecture on why yoga was the devil's work did not happen in other houses. Also, things were starting to fall apart. There had been a time when the house wasn't quite as messy, and my mom actually went outside. She went places, did things like seeing the Eagles in concert; she used to take classes in ancient Greek, with the goal of studying theology, perhaps going to seminary. All that was starting to fade; I only really saw her leave the house for necessary errands.

* * *

Anyone who has buried someone from a wasting disease knows something very specific about trauma. Most people imagine trauma to be something like a car crash: a sudden cataclysm in a specific moment in time with a definitive before and after. Oftentimes, though, trauma is more akin to a slow tide coming in. The change is so incremental, you don't realize you're drowning until it's too late. This incremental trauma is commonly dismissed because it is so quiet and happens in relative stillness. Trauma, it turns out, is often very boring.

Grief is such a trauma, which is why it's so deeply misunderstood by those who have yet to experience it. Americans, as a culture, do not do well with long-term emotional labor. We have short attention spans and even shorter emotional bandwidths. Grief from mourning is acceptable for a month, perhaps three, but then our bootstrap mentality kicks in: "Well, you've got to get on with things," and "It's not good to linger." Crying at the funeral is one thing, but bursting into tears months later because of something nominally unrelated? It's so *dramatic*. It is unseemly, un-*American*.

Emotional abuse, years of insults, threats, and diminishment, is another example of this tidal trauma. Those who would dismiss it as "not that bad" are so sure perhaps because the water is only at their ankles. It wasn't until my twenties that I realized how much of a fingerprint my childhood had left on me. There are the psychological issues, like how I associate absence with love, forging a remarkable ability to pine for the unavailable. Like many people who grew up afraid of someone's anger, I am always ready with a joke to lighten the mood, a question to pivot the conversation. There was never any context where it was safe for me to be the angry one. The only time I remember yelling at someone was when I was twelve or so, when a cousin stole and hid my copy of *How Green Was My Valley*, frustrated that I was spending too much time on a family vacation reading.

But there are other, more concrete legacies of how I grew up. Personal hygiene was difficult for me to grasp because only sporadically did I ever have an adult telling me to brush my teeth, for example, let alone how or why I should. I was deep in my thirties when I realized it had been more than a decade since I'd seen a dentist. While I love to cook for friends and family, when I'm not expecting company, I struggle to keep food in my house on a consistent basis. Dinners in my mother's house would either be four courses, or fast food for the third time in a week. The steady day in, day out schedule of cleaning, feeding, even clothing myself is still not muscle memory to me—it takes conscious, specific effort on my part, like a new, nervous driver saying out loud, "First, I check my mirrors."

Most pernicious of all might be my habit of picking at my skin, excoriation disorder.

As with many people who grew up in perpetually tense circumstances, during the quiet time before bed, or lounging in front of a television—the times that should be relaxing—I'm tearing at myself. It's as if I'm falling asleep on the subway and have to jerk myself awake: I pick to keep myself alert. As an adolescent I started picking at spots no one could easily see, to the point of bleeding. These areas are now dotted with tiny, nearly pearlescent scars after years of picking, and scabs too from fresh wounds. I still pick badly, though I work hard not to. When I know someone is going to see me with my clothes off, I have to make special efforts to stop myself a couple of days in advance to give my skin a chance to bounce back.

After I moved to Los Angeles, and my exposure to my mom was limited, it was like I was a little wound-up toy car—I'd already been set to zoom off in one direction, and no change in custody was going to alter that. I was headed straight into an adulthood as dysfunctional as my childhood. I had all the symptoms of a kid who had grown up with a mother like mine: I honed my ability to make everyone laugh to diffuse tension and was sensitive to any change in mood, but could also be oblivious and hurtful to others to a shocking degree. I lacked loads of basic life skills, but felt resentful and hurt by any attempt to teach them to me. I was desperate to be loved, and mired in shame for not having it in the first place. All the men I dated in my late twenties and early thirties were versions of the same dude: smart, unavailable, and deeply unhappy. On the whole, they weren't bad men; they were just bad for me. Which is why I picked them. We survive emotional trauma, only to keep inflicting pain on ourselves long after our abusers are gone—by choosing partners with the same unresolved issues as our parents, by perpetuating cycles of bounty and deprivation, by picking at scabs that become wounds, that become scars that we open back into wounds. I grew up on a frozen lake, never quite sure how thick the ice beneath my feet was, and in my twenties I realized that I was the one pushing myself out onto the frozen water. I started serious therapy and began the work to dismantle the coping mechanisms that had once helped, protected me like a shield, but had begun to hinder, calcifying my emotional growth and creating a carapace, a barrier between myself and the intimate relationships I so desperately wanted.

I also read quite a bit, because that's my reaction to everything, in particular Alice Miller's brief and powerful text *The Drama of the Gifted Child: The Search for the True Self.* For a long while I had a quotation taped to my refrigerator door:

> Several sorts of mechanisms can be recognized in the defense against early feelings of abandonment. . . . Intellectualization

> is very commonly met, since it is a defense mechanism of great reliability.[1]

Shots fired. Is that what this trip is, a defense mechanism? Have I turned my relationship with my mother into a research opportunity, an excuse to read a bunch of books, so I can *think* about her, rather than *feel* anything about her?

My mother grew up in a military family that moved constantly. Her parents, by all accounts, at best deeply resented each other. Her father drank, had a temper. Eventually she herself was an alcoholic with a temper. She also did enough cocaine to make the members of Fleetwood Mac look like rookies, and more than one person told me she did quite a lot of acid as well. When was the water at her ankles?

This is why I pore over the two texts my mother left behind, the red journal and the white binder, like a Talmudic scholar. Actually, reading the red journal is more akin to picking up the Tao Te Ching: it is filled with mysterious snippets that get vaguer the more I try to understand them, but fills me with a sense of wonder, as if it holds greater truths just beyond my ken. The white binder, on the other hand, is more akin to the many hours I spent reading the Bible, filled as it is with writing that is often interminable and infuriating, but occasionally skews poignant under close scrutiny. I have both the red journal and the white binder with me, as well as my mother's hefty Bible, but at night on the patio, watching the lights of Albuquerque, I'm taking refuge in reading Lesley Poling-Kempes's book about women who ran away to and flourished in the Southwest, *Ladies of the Canyons*. Sometimes I wonder what my mom's life would have been like if, well, if she hadn't been the way she was. If she could pay bills on time, and not talk to herself, and take out the trash, and didn't think that her daughter sometimes had demons in her. If none of that were the case, I could see my mom being one of those women who moves to New Mexico and never looks back. She could have been happy, if only everything was different.

If any part of the red journal is true, where I read about my grandfather raping and murdering, my mother never stood a chance. If any part of the red journal is true, the water was at her neck by the time she was thirteen, the same age I was when everything changed. I'm reading these sacred, insane texts, wondering if she ever stood a chance, and I hit the road to figure out if I still stand a chance.

Chapter Eight

Abiquiú

You have no associations with those hills—our waste land—I think our most beautiful country. You must not have seen it, so you want me always to paint flowers.

—GEORGIA O'KEEFFE

I don't understand why people don't want to hear about other people's dreams. If it's boring or vague, I blame the storyteller, not the dream. To my mind, when someone asks, "Do you want to hear about my dream?" what I hear is "Do you want to know what's *really* going on with me?" and I want to know what's *really* going on with everyone.

After my mother died, every dream I had felt so real. If I dreamed of oranges, I woke up with citrus on my tongue. Sometimes the dream would just be about the feeling of lying in my bed in Sacramento on a summer afternoon, when 4 p.m. seems to go on for hours, when everything has a tangerine hue, and I can hear the clinking of the metal flagpole right outside my bedroom. Often the dream was of me stumbling through postwar bombed-out Berlin, nothing but bricks and burned-out cars. I come to a city square. In the center, there is a spike and on it a severed baboon head, blood slopping out of its raggedly hewn neck.

As I approach the baboon head, it swivels around on the spike to face me. Its eyes become my mother's eyes, its mouth opens and black flies pour out and flood my vision.

On my little mattress in the back of Minnie, as I'm drifting off a series of Proustian sense-memories flickers past me: the sound of the front door opening, the smell in my closet, the particular taste of the water from the tap in my mother's bathroom sink. My bedroom was a sleigh bed, horse posters, horse books, strings of horse lights, horse show ribbons. There was floral wallpaper, which eventually got painted white, and my mother let me paint a huge mural on the wall. My inspiration was a pierced and blazing heart wrapped in roses I definitely stole from Baz Luhrmann's 1996 *Romeo + Juliet*. The horse posters lasted longer than the mural, because my mom thought it meant I was planning on converting to Catholicism. Back to white walls, then.

I've driven north from Albuquerque, about 110 miles give or take, keeping west of the atomic testing site of Los Alamos. The views from Minnie's windows are expansive, but the view is mostly houses surrounded by the wreckage of broken-down cars, broken swing sets, heaps of tires.

Other than *The Living Desert*, the biggest influence on my thinking about the desert is the work of Georgia O'Keeffe. My ideas of the Southwest come from a Disney documentary and a white woman—I don't think that these influences are completely wrong, per se, but they are limited. They are a reflection of the commodified aesthetics of the Southwest, not the place itself. Georgia certainly didn't invent the iconography of the high desert, only captured it so perfectly she herself became synonymous with it. That, and vagina flowers.

Speaking of, she didn't think they had anything to do with vaginas. She was fascinated by the process of abstraction by simply getting as close as possible to something, an attempt at seeing the heart of it and conveying exactly what she saw—a flower, not a symbol: "Well—I made you take time to look at what I saw and when you took time to really notice my flower you hung all your associations with flowers on my flowers and you write about my flower as if I think and see what you think and see of the flower—and I don't."[1]

I'm inclined to side with Georgia, because I think that if she wanted to paint vaginas, she would have. It's just that flowers really look like vaginas.

There is a certain sort of woman who is into Georgia O'Keeffe. In my experience, she is usually over forty, likes clunky jewelry (or the silver that is synonymous with the Southwest), gives incense as a gift, and if she doesn't actually look like Joni Mitchell, she *feels* like Joni Mitchell. She's a hippie, really, which is ironic because outside of eating organic, Georgia was not remotely a hippie. Interviews with her show a sharp, wry woman with a direct sense of humor who was disinclined to read any deep spiritual or even intellectual meaning into her work. Color, line, shape—this mattered to her, not the critics' interpretations. My mom was too much of an Anglophile to be much of a fan of O'Keeffe, who openly tried to make the Great American Painting after getting bored of hearing so many men talk about their Great American Novels, Great American Plays, etc.

Like many, I'm curious about O'Keeffe not only because of her work, but her personal look—a woman samurai in the American desert, lugging bones around and arranging them beside her jazz LPs. I wanted to see her space—so I'm standing in her kitchen. It is exactly the way she left it the day she was taken to the hospital and never came back. She has a lot of teapots.

The only way into the adobe house in Abiquiu is to book a tour in advance. O'Keeffe's original house in New Mexico, a place called Ghost Ranch, is not open to the public at the time I'm visiting.

To see the Abiquiu adobe, you park at the O'Keeffe Welcome Center and board a small shuttle bus to begin your tour with Frank, if you're lucky. There's a specific sinking feeling when you realize you've been saddled with a bad tour guide, someone who just talks *at* you, reciting a list of facts, numbers, and names. Frank, on the other hand, knows how to tell a story. A painter himself, Frank sticks out for his comfortably stylish look: a large hat tipped back on his silver hair, linen blazer, fitted jeans, and sandals. Chic glasses finish off the look, as well as a binder with laminated examples of O'Keeffe's work.

This property was originally built by the Catholic church in the 1700s, and blessed the grounds with water rights, which anyone who lives west of the Mississippi can tell you means everything. O'Keeffe had to haggle with the church for ten years to purchase this place.

Nowadays O'Keeffe's extensive organic garden, from which she ate almost exclusively, and from which she donated large portions to the township of Abiquiu, is still run by the grandchildren of her gardener and factotum, Esteban Suazo. In fact, his granddaughter Agapita Judy Lopez is the director of historic properties at the Georgia O'Keeffe Museum in Santa Fe. Food from the garden is still donated to the local community.

While we tourists begin to wilt under the sun, Frank explains how a stone-lined miniature aqueduct brings the water from a nearby reservoir into the garden aquifer, lined with permeable rock to allow the garden to flood and then slowly drain throughout the incredible heat of the day. This water system has an interesting lineage. African Moors brought aqueducts to Spain; the Spaniards in turn brought the technology with them across the Atlantic. Some speculate that isn't the only influence the Moors brought to the Southwest—a jeweler I was chatting with in Albuquerque told me that she grew up learning that the famous squash blossom necklaces—the silver and turquoise pieces made by many Native artisans but perhaps most often affiliated with the Navajo and Zuni—have antecedents in African design. The shopkeeper explained to me that the *naja,* a sort of Navajo symbol for protection against the evil eye, could be traced back to the decorations on the bridles of Spanish horses, which the Spaniards had adapted from the Moors.

O'Keeffe came to New Mexico when she was married to the influential photographer and gallery owner Alfred Stieglitz. In a 1977 PBS documentary about O'Keeffe, you can hear a female producer suggest, "It was nice of Stieglitz to let you go to New Mexico every summer," and the ensuing exchange seems to me to sum up something about O'Keeffe:

> "Well, listen, he didn't let me go, I just went."
> "Was it hard convincing him?"
> "He was never convinced, but I went. I had to go."

Standing in the room that was her painting studio, so still and quiet, I think about people who know what it means to wake up and realize, *I have to go.* Not everyone does.

I was on the verge of turning fourteen when I realized I had to leave Sacramento. Since my parents' split I had lived in Sacramento with my mother and brother, and took pride in being from Northern California, the lesser-known half of my home state. Something happened, though, that made it very clear to me that I could not stay in my mother's house any longer. In the tumult of that night, only one flash remains perfectly lucid: the moment I thought to myself, *I have to leave Sacramento.* It's not clear if I was running from something or toward something, just as I'm not sure which was the case with Georgia, but I knew I had to go.

Months ago, that quiet voice that grew increasingly insistent told me, *You have to go back.* But not just back to my mother's house. I had to go beyond Sacramento, merely one stop on the timeline of my mother and me. I had to go east, further back. People have asked me why I'm doing this, and my only answer is that I have questions. I don't know what to do other than to literally go looking, to get up and go.

After Frank tells us about O'Keeffe's two chow chow dogs (whenever one died, she'd just get another, and sometimes recycled their names, Bo and Chia) and shows us "the room without a roof" where she would eat breakfast in the cool mornings, it's time for us to get back on the bus, but I take a moment to look at the black door.

It's this black door, behind which O'Keeffe kept her finished canvases, that made her want to buy the decrepit adobe in the first place: "The wall with a door in it was something I had to have. It took me ten years to get it—three more years to fix up the house so I could live in it—and after that the wall with a door was painted many times."[2]

These paintings of the black door are some of my favorites of O'Keeffe's. No one tries to argue what they are *actually* a painting of, and they do not carry the weight that contemporary viewers hang on O'Keeffe's landscapes. Standing in front of the door, a fresh glossy black, I imagined what it would have been like to be one of Georgia's friends, invited to visit her, way out here. The airplane. The train. A dusty ride down a dusty road—and then there she is, in her linen pinafore and her neat gray hair. Her big dogs and her expansive garden. She'd cook for you, play a record while you reported on the gossip from back in the city. There were already many people here in New Mexico, but Georgia brought different kinds of people here. She brought me here, north and away from the 10. I decided to veer north because it seemed to me that if I wanted to understand New Mexico, I needed to shake hands with the woman who created an iconography of the Southwest that is so pervasive, she and the place became synonymous.

I look at the door and try to see it the way she saw it. The different planes of the wall and sky, then the ground perpendicular with the squares of quadrisected tiles spaced out in the ground. Being in that place, one sees that O'Keeffe was the curator of her own life—and far from seeming elusive or cold or imperious, the thoughtfulness of the home and the life she created brings her very close. It's easy to see her sly humor, her appetite, her ambition. The way she lived, her home, was a reflection of her values, her aesthetic. Everything in the way she decorated, cooked, dressed, was intentional.

My mother's house, on the other hand, was chaos. She was always adding things: a random column in the kitchen, bars to the windows, making the small patch of grass in the backyard into a small hill. Projects she farmed out to random people who always took too long and charged too much. When the house actually needed something, there was never enough money. What did people see when they walked into my childhood home on Forty-Fourth Street in Sacramento; what did it tell them about my mother? By the time she left that house, there was no orderly room of books, shelved and dusted—but an explosion of them everywhere, reeking of cigarette smoke. If visitors came during one of her down times, they would have seen the piles of unwashed laundry, dishes stacked up, ashtrays everywhere, the overflowing litter box. The gun casually resting next to the television remote. When I was a child there were times when the house was tidy, usually the work of a housekeeper, but she wasn't able to keep one in her employ for very long. One woman didn't last after she argued with my mother over her shirt with the Buddha on it. The housekeeper's point of view was that the shirt depicted someone praying (really, meditating), surely that was a good thing? My mother's perspective was, "We don't need your services anymore, but I'll pray for you."

My own house resembles my mother's in that I also have stacks of books just about everywhere, usually crowned with a precariously balanced half-full cup of tea. Although my fear of sliding into Grey Gardens decrepitude has kept me respectably tidy, and I am very good at editing all my nonliterary possessions to a minimum. Maybe the biggest difference is, I host. I host all the time, because I love to have people over: Christmas parties, Halloween Dinners for the Dead, movie marathons. My guest room is always available to out-of-towners, and whenever I am traveling, there is usually a friend staying in my home, keeping it company. Maybe my hope is that by having people come and go, my house will never collect the stagnant dust of the lonely.

Did the rare visitors see my mother's loneliness? Did they see her intelligence, her romanticism? Or are there people in the world who don't understand that if you're paying attention, a person's home, just like their dreams, will show you everything. I mean, *really* everything.

Chapter Nine

Santa Fe

It's not even America, this place.

—EVE BABITZ

All around the world the American highway looms large in its legend, conjuring the ghosts of railroad laborers and pioneer caravans. I do my best thinking on long trips like this one, thanks to the soft eyes.

"You know what you need at a crime scene?" asks homicide detective Bunk Moreland of HBO's *The Wire* (played by New Orleans's own Wendell Pierce). "Soft eyes. You got soft eyes you can see the whole thing. You got hard eyes, you're staring at the same tree, missing the forest." Learning how to keep my eyes soft is what allowed me to start writing again after a decade-long block. It's what led me to learn Transcendental Meditation, and it's given me a slightly uncanny knack for finding things, like a small gold earring my sister-in-law lost on the bottom of the ocean floor. The trick is, don't look for an earring—just notice Not Rock. Driving long distances helps me keep my eyes soft—I'm not chasing down thoughts, merely letting them rise to the surface.

Stretches of highway lie low over the open landscape, and with no buildings, no billboards, no trees to distract the eyes, mine go soft enough to let my mind wander. When I think back to the trip with my mom in 1996, I remember Texas as the place with the big emptiness, the vast expanse of west Texas, but New Mexico's openness is impressive. Arizona, with the spread of Phoenix and Tucson, felt denser—which it is. In 2023, Arizona's population was counted as 7,431,344, whereas the census counts the population of New Mexico at 2,114,371. Arizona also has more than three times the GDP of New Mexico ($508.3 million versus $130.2 million).[1] I know that all I have to do is actually get out of the van and walk into the desert to experience how *not* empty it is (I shudder to think just how many spiders are outside my window at any time), but from inside Minnie, my combination bedroom, studio, and office on wheels, the path out to the horizon seems to flatten. Distance both expands and contracts.

My thoughts wander from the way my mother would gently bounce me in the pool as a child, to trying to place where all my brothers are at the moment—we're scattered over the country this summer. Sometimes I tune back into the podcast I'm listening to, Dan Carlin's *Hardcore History*. His five-part series on World War 1, *Blueprint for Armageddon*, is around twenty-two hours long, and this is my fourth or fifth time listening to it. A lot of people ask me, "What's with your dad and World War II?" One day I hope someone asks him, "What's with your daughter and World War I?"

It's simple, really: World War I is the birth of the modern world. Before that war, the world was run by the grandchildren of Queen Victoria. Russia's economy was based on serfs; women's hair was long and their dresses even longer. The Ottoman Empire was a thing, an extremely important thing. By the time the war was over, Coco Chanel's cropped hair inspired women around the world to chop not only their hair but their hemlines, and their corsets too. Czar Nicholas II abdicated and was murdered with his family by the Bolsheviks, and the waltz was deposed as the most scandalous dance by the Charleston. Jazz was born with the hit record "Livery Stable Blues," and the world was given its first taste of a wholly American art form.

On the way to Santa Fe, I think about how one of the greatest challenges we face is understanding the times we live in. The early WWI French soldier's uniform with its bright-red trousers, while a proud reminder of the country's Napoleonic triumphs, literally cost thousands of lives. They didn't understand that the times had changed.

On the micro scale, I *think* I understand the time I am living through, this strange decade of my thirties. For my closest friends it has been largely about marriages and babies, but for me it has been all about learning to keep my eyes soft. It seems to me that the thirties are when you realize: not everyone is going to make it.

Not all your friends' marriages will be happy ones, and dreams of success will go unrealized. People with drinking problems probably won't get help, and friends who desperately want babies won't be able to have them. My fear in my twenties was that we were all headed for some sort of cataclysmic denouement, but in my thirties I've come to understand that no one should fear rock bottom. What scares me now is not everything crashing down, but rather a long, unending arc of low-grade unhappiness, a quiet and workable dysfunction. As I ponder all this, time on the road slips by, and I pull into Santa Fe with my head full of shapeless thoughts, my stomach full of gas station taquitos, delicious if you don't look at them took closely, marveling at how old Santa Fe feels if you ignore the slickness of the rich retiree enclaves.

A couple of days later, I'm sitting across from Dan Flores at a hip little café called Modern General, which also offers expensive soaps and gardening tools, and we're talking about time.

"In the Southwest," he says, "you have to come to terms with the fact that we're not new here. In fact, we're in a place that has been this ancient homeland for thousands of years. . . . I kind of think of it as the most American part of America. And it has to do with what I just described: the inescapable fact that you are in an ancient place."

When Angeleno It Girl and magazine writer Eve Babitz wrote, "It's not even America, this place," Santa Fe was already *nearly four hundred years old.* Like El Paso and New Orleans, it's a city whose roots are still so evident it's impossible to sweep its pre-American identity under the carpet. Are there northern cities that feel like they're not even in America? "Except for Jamestown and Quebec, [Santa Fe] is the oldest European town in North America," says Flores. "And Jamestown and Quebec are only two years older and one year older. It's the oldest city in the West."

I reference Flores's book *Horizontal Yellow* many times during our lunch but have to remind him of what's in it. It's been a while. Dan also had a bit of a crossover hit into popular nonfiction with his book *Coyote America.* Back home, coyotes are mostly known as pests. They eat cats who wander into the backyard for a little sunshine, and small dogs aren't much safer. In my neighborhood, they come down from the Hollywood sign and scamper across the busy boulevards to eat trash. It makes me sad to see them, thin and rough-looking, navigating human garbage. A wild thing should get to stay wild.

"Can you understand the desert if you don't understand coyotes?" I ask him.

"No, you've got to understand that animal."

"What is it at the core of a coyote that is necessary for the desert and vice versa?"

"The coyote is an indigenous North American animal," he explains. "He has been adapted to the desert, and singing that original coyote national anthem, you know, for at least a million years. And to me, it's the song of the desert. They've managed to figure out a way to survive virtually everything that's thrown at them. Sort of the ultimate coyote knowledge."

Flores, on a random day in a nice café in Santa Fe, effortlessly has what the poseurs in Tombstone attempted and fumbled so badly: he makes being weathered look pretty good. For a longtime professor at the University of Montana at Missoula, he's got the slouch of a ranch hand off the clock for chow, complete with a long silver ponytail. The only time I get a real chuckle out of him is when I tell him a story about a coyote fucking up a film shoot. The movie my father is shooting has moved from ABQ to Santa Fe, and then on to Shiprock, a monadnock rising 1,583 feet out of the desert and a sacred ancestral site for the Navajo and the Ancestral Puebloans before them. One of the requirements of the tax incentive program that has brought large numbers of both television and film productions to New Mexico is that those productions must hire local crews, many of whom are Native American. I hear the crew use "Native American" and "Indian" interchangeably.

Chances are you've seen Shiprock in movies, like 2012's *John Carter*. Well. Maybe not that movie. This landscape is often used as a stand-in for other planets, as if this uncanny beauty couldn't possibly be earthly. Shiprock, visible for miles as you approach from a lone two-lane road, is a cathedral of stone; it appears in many Navajo myths, including their origin story, which says that the "stone with wings" was once a giant bird that brought the ancestors to this place. The people lived on the mountain and would come down to search for water and to plant crops. When Shiprock was struck by lightning and the trail to the peak was destroyed, those on the ground were stranded, as were those atop the mountain, left with no food or water. For this reason, no one is supposed to go anywhere near the base of Shiprock, as they might disturb the souls of those who died. One of the bored-looking security guards hanging around told me that, myths aside, sometimes you'll find beer cans and graffiti out near the base.

"Bored kids," he said, adjusting his gloves. There'd been ice on the ground in the morning, and a hailstorm was incoming. While photography for the day was winding down, catering started barbecuing dinner, and coyotes nearby began howling. At first everyone thought the biggest problem was for the sound department, but suddenly in the middle of a take, the dog in the movie, arguably the lead, *bolted* through the desert. I mean, that animal heard the call of the wild and took the fuck off.

I have been on a lot of movie sets, and I have been present on bad days when things are not going well for one reason or another and the mood is extremely tense. I have never, ever seen a set so absolutely terrified as that one when a whole squadron of people went running after the dog. It didn't help that he was sandy brown and completely camouflaged to blend into the land as twilight turned the evening violet. I was pretty sure that the dog, who had a bigger posse of minders and assistants than my dad did, was an absolute goner. Instead, after fifteen or so nerve-racking minutes, Seamus the dog was brought back on a leash, looking as unbothered as ever, his eyes brightened by the exercise. I watched them finish the scheduled shots with Seamus now on an invisible leash, and I read my book seated next to a prop of my dad's dead body. Movie magic!

The whole trajectory of my trip is to go from a landscape where there is simply not enough water to a landscape where there is way too much. Here in the Southwest, it feels like everything I see is on borrowed time: the golf courses, the green lawns, the suburbs and tract homes. *How long can this go on?* I wonder. *How long can these resources hold out, how long will the Colorado River last?* In the not-too-distant future, the suburbs of Phoenix will simply run out of water; newspapers already run stories about new developments and subdivisions with permanently dry taps. I gulp at the glass in front of me and ask Dan Flores: "And what can coyotes teach us about this changing landscape?"

He says, "Coyote evolved this adaptation that biologists call fission-fusion. They can live as packs." (That's the fusion part.) "And they do that very well, and as social animals. But when the conditions get bad, they scatter as singles and pairs across the landscape." (That's the fission part.) "And humans are one of the nineteen mammal species around the world that have this adaptation. One of the things that I always think of, when I think of the future of the Southwest: we may need to call on our fission ability, like coyotes do."

Coyotes, in other words, were here first, and I wonder if they'll be the ones to have the last laugh.

While the dog was escaping and the movie was being made, I finished Clarissa Pinkola Estés's immensely popular 1992 book, *Women Who Run with the Wolves: Myths and Stories of the Wild Woman Archetype*, a copy of which seemed to live in all the women's houses I went into as a child, and which I read huddled on a blanket beneath Shiprock (next to the dead body prop). One section jumped out at me: "Life in the desert is small but brilliant and most of what occurs goes on underground. This is like the lives of many women. The desert is not lush like a forest or a jungle. It is very intense and mysterious in its life-forms. Many of us have lived desert lives: very small on the surface, and enormous underground."[2]

Earlier in the week I was eating breakfast at the Dolina Cafe & Bakery in Santa Fe, and I struck up a conversation with the man sitting next to me. He was an Englishman who'd moved to the city and couldn't imagine living anywhere else. I asked what brought him here and what kept him here. Marital obligations had brought him here, but what kept him here, particularly as a husband and a father of daughters, he said, was that "I consider this to be a feminine landscape, and that seems like an important place to be these days."

What made him think that? I wanted to know. He said, "Because it's very rich with life, but it's all under the surface."

The day after my lunch with Dan Flores, I stop by Cafe Pasqual's, which everyone tells me is a must-do while I'm in town. I snag a seat during a very busy lunch service at the communal table, hoping to strike up a conversation, but no one is keen to chat. Want to order like a local in Santa Fe? Order your enchiladas Christmas-style: half red chile sauce, half green.

From Pasqual's I walk through the old Plaza, taking time to peek into the myriad shops that all seem to offer variations on the same things: turquoise jewelry, silver paperweights, paintings of cowboys and desert sunsets. Around the Plaza itself, beneath four-hundred-year-old porticos, Native folks sell various wares—a lot of small pottery, jewelry, and hair clips. Again, I see a lot of the same things scattered around, but people are friendly.

I walk to the Georgia O'Keeffe Museum and find myself staring, ensorcelled by *Horse's Skull with White Rose*, painted in 1931. What I can't get over is how black the black is—a deep well of black that doesn't convey darkness or ominousness at all, but wholeness, placidity. The way the blackness holds the cream of the horse bones, the white of the rose, makes me think of Georgia's black door back in Abiquiu. I feel like I understand why so many older women in my life have a sort of hero worship for her, because of a life that (at least from the observer's point of view) seems entirely purposeful. She meant to move to New Mexico; she meant for her house to feel a certain way, for her clothes to project a certain image. She knew what she wanted to eat, whom she wanted to visit, the art she intended to make. She was a woman in control, and perhaps that's something you desire more as you get older: to be in control of your own life.

I'm leaving Santa Fe soon, and after nearly two months in the Southwest, I'm finally starting to see with desert eyes. I don't see desolation anymore—but a different sort of fecundity, the kind you can't recognize as you drive past it. I have traded trees for the sky, but I am still nervous about the story I am trying to tell. About whether I have any right to tell it.

"When I found the beautiful white bones in the desert, I picked them up and took them home too," Georgia wrote. "I have used these things to say what is to me the wideness and wonder of the world as I live in it."[3] Maybe O'Keeffe was right, in her way. She painted the world as she saw it and didn't think that anyone would assume that her vision should stand as the singular truth of the place. She knew what her flowers meant to her, regardless of other people's ideas about them, and perhaps I can only tell the story of the trip, of my mother, as I live in it. There are bones only I know to look for. That only I can pick up.

Chapter Ten

Truth or Consequences

The loves we share with a city are often secret loves.

—ALBERT CAMUS

Before I left on my trip, I noticed a set pattern in the reaction I got when I told people what I was doing—namely, spending about six months, give or take, driving around the American South, camping for much of it. I told people I had questions about America, and questions about myself, and that they were oddly similar: What do we know about how we started? What happened to us? How do we move on? How does our relationship with the past, both personal and political, determine the future? The pattern was in the gendered responses I got. Nearly all the men responded with jealousy: "You're so lucky; I'd kill to get away like that." In their minds, I was escaping toward adventure. Women, on the other hand, mostly reacted with fear: "Aren't you afraid?" There was also the cheerier "Maybe you'll meet someone!"

When I asked women what exactly they were afraid of, it was being alone in nature, to be even more vulnerable, to be in a tent and not know what's outside. It's not that I'm immune to that fear. Last night I was waking up at the slightest noise. Minnie is so perfectly cozy, a little bower that protects me from the still frosty desert nights, but the moment the sun sets, the complete darkness of the desert is engulfing, and I can't see anything outside my windows. Every sound makes me sit up, worried someone is about to pound on my window. I finally fell into a deep sleep around two in the morning.

The thing about fear is that it's another way we tell ourselves stories. A security consultant my family has worked with for many years told me something that I have returned to time and again. The blaring alarm of your lizard brain that keeps you alive does not tell stories. Rather, it shouts in declarative sentences. *Run! Stop! Fuck!* Anxiety, on the other hand, loves a story. Anxiety tells you, *There's someone who has been watching you for hours and he's just been waiting silently in the dark for you to finally turn off your headlamp and the moment you do, the moment you're finally nodding off to sleep, that's when he'll attack.*

I am acutely aware of my surroundings. I'm often not only the only woman in a space, but the only person on my own. In the bar, at the restaurant, at the gas station, I'm alone in being alone. I avoid streets that have groups of men milling about, same as I would do in Los Angeles. I never drive at night, and only once during the whole trip will I stay in a random chain motel off the interstate. These are the usual precautions a woman takes when alone. The only time I feel genuinely at risk on my trip is later on, walking through Juárez, Mexico—because it's one of the most dangerous cities in the world, and I am at risk. The only time I hear my lizard brain telling me to do something loudly enough for me to listen is in a city named for a game show.

Truth or Consequences, New Mexico, once upon a time was just named Hot Springs. Sometimes Palomas Hot Springs. Before that, before the Newlands Reclamation Act took over the land to build the Elephant Butte Dam and Reservoir in 1912, it was just the land near John Cross's ranch where the first baths were built over the natural hot springs in the late 1800s. But in 1950, Ralph Edwards, the host of NBC's popular radio program *Truth or Consequences*, dared a city to rename itself after his program on its tenth anniversary. Edwards would go on to visit Truth or Consequences, New Mexico, the first weekend of May every year for the next fifty years. The program would go on to become a television show that ran into the late 1980s, while in T or C the city, you can still enjoy Fiesta the first week of May.

As I pass a long train of national guard trucks headed either to or away from the border, I spend some time meandering through local radio. There's a lot of Norteño music, and also Christian pop songs, instantly recognizable thanks to the cloyingly earnest pitch of the mostly male singers; they all sound like love songs.

I've been consulting a handy app that describes BLM camping spots, like a Yelp for the great outdoors. The Bureau of Land Management, begun in 1946 and now part of the Department of the Interior, maintains 245 million surface acres of American land, primarily in the West and Alaska. That's about one out of every ten American acres, or 12 percent of the American landmass. This land is used as common ground for grazing animals, oil, natural gas and mineral mining, and recreation—you can camp on BLM land for up to fourteen days for free. It's the common land, the shared-experience space, that is one of the defining characteristics of the West. While I fill up Minnie, I take a gander at my app, and read some reviews about a BLM area popular with campers not too far away. I glance at my watch—I always want to be wherever I'm going to stay, whether it's a camping spot or an Airbnb, well before sundown. I've only got two and a half hours or so to find a place, get settled, eat dinner, and hunker down.

Off the main highway and several miles down a service road, it's all high desert scrub. It's strange how the land can seem so barren, empty, and flat, yet things can still appear, not even on the horizon but *bang* right in front of you. Suddenly before me is a very old, janky trailer hitched to an old, janky truck, parked right where I was planning to camp—so many miles past a cattle guard, according to my odometer. I figure there might be another spot for a safe fire, so I continue to approach what even I, who have never seen the show, can casually identify as a *Breaking Bad* camper. As I pass the rig, a rangy, thin man with choppy hair and ropy arms stares me down from the doorway of his camper. I raise my hand in a silent greeting, but there is no response. Just dark eyes staring out of sunken cheekbones, a jutted chin.

I continue down the bumpy dirt road, getting farther and farther away from the highway. The land is not dipping at all, so the camper is still visible in my rearview mirror. I go about another mile, but there are no more turnouts. It doesn't seem like a good idea to park so near this other camper. To be alone in the desert is one thing, but to be so close to such a sketchy setup feels like sitting down in a nearly empty movie theater directly next to the only other person there. I turn the van around, and head back. Passing the dodgy-looking camper again, I see only a quick, angry glare and the door to the camper slamming shut. Message received. So, where do I go now? I open my app again, which recommends a spot on a beach on the Rio Grande, part of Elephant Butte Lake State Park. Dusk is coming, and I'm anxious to get settled in a spot before it's totally dark.

On the banks of the Rio, everything is an ashy beige. The brownish river, the sand, the small hills on the other side of the river all blend together with the overcast sky. The wind picks up and I take cover in the van, risking spotty reception to check in with friends back home. Suddenly I feel like I exist again. When you're alone in a totally new place, it can feel as if you've dropped out of the main story line, and the moment you're recognized by someone you know, or better yet love, you exist again. You're reminded of your consequence, of being tethered to people, somewhere back in the world you know.

Twilight is just giving over to darkness when I hear the truck coming. Peering out of my window I can see the tail and cabin lights of a butch pickup truck. It's an extended-cab, extended-bed, extra everything sort of a truck. It parks down on the water's edge. Four or five men stumble out of the truck, all yelling loudly. Loud music starts to play, and two of the men start wrangling something big and unwieldy from the truck bed into the river.

It's a body! A body in the river! one part of my brain screams.

The other part of my brain reminds me that I grew up on rivers: many hot summer nights began by putting the cooler in the river to keep the ice from melting too quickly. These are probably just a bunch of local guys who come down to the river to get rip-roaring drunk. Is this particularly dangerous to me? Probably not. Chances are they don't even see my dark van back higher up the beach, closer to the road. But if they do notice Minnie . . .

I didn't see much life going on in the residences on the access road. I don't want to deal with five drunk men anywhere, but certainly not out here. And on top of that, the music is loud. Even if I do decide to stay, it'd be a miserable night's sleep. Most important, from my body comes a clear, plain instruction:

Move.

So: I crawl into the front seat and, keeping my headlights off, cross fingers on both hands that I'm not too deep in the sand.

A moment of heart-stuttering wheel spinning but then I'm back on the state park road, literally singing the praises of Minnie the Wonder Van. I consider just pulling over on the side of the road to get back to sleep, but that strikes me as an invitation for a window knocking, so I decide to default to my backup plan all along: the Walmart.

Many Walmarts all over America offer overnight parking in their lots, which are lit and sometimes have security around. Of course, they're hoping that you wake up in the morning and wander inside for breakfast, or a new set of jumper cables, or leggings (which, in the morning, I do—well, two out of three; I also make good use of their restrooms for washing my face and brushing my teeth).

I hunker down inside Minnie and listen to an episode of *Alright Mary*, a podcast entirely dedicated to RuPaul's Emmy Award–winning *Drag Race*. The only disturbance in my sleep is around eight thirty the next morning when a fairly methed-out-looking man trying to hitch a ride starts to play a bongo drum.

I swing by the saucily named Passion Pie Cafe, clearly a meeting place; I hear a lot of first-name greetings as people meander in for some very good coffee but not very good breakfast tacos. After my meal, I start walking. It's only April but already the sun is punishing by midday, bleaching the nearly empty streets a yellowy gray. I pop into several thrift stores, most of which are only half-full of loose ends and odd bits. There are a lot of mostly empty shelves. Milling about, I keep seeing the same eager folks around town. I think we're all wandering around looking for something lovely to do or eat, or a charming shop to spend some money in, but on that day, nothing was doing in Truth or Consequences. With some time to spare, I park Minnie beneath a tree by the river, and set up The Chair.

Back in Los Angeles I'd bought a small collapsible camping chair. Tidily designed, it (hypothetically) folded up into a tiny bag whenever I wasn't using it to sit outside the van. It was so well designed, in fact, that I could never get it to either lock into place or fold back up and fit into the bag it came in. It was small, came in a nice print, and was totally useless. While in Albuquerque, my father spent a large chunk of his time off at the chain outdoor store Cabela's. Need a water bottle?

Need a bowie knife? How about a crossbow, a rifle, a handgun, some dehydrated enchiladas? Go to Cabela's.

"You're gonna need a chair, you should get this one," my dad said, parking himself in an expansive, foldable rocking chair, nearly wide enough for me to sit next to him.

"Dad, that thing is huge, no way. I've got limited space."

"Then this one. You're gonna need a place to sit. Might as well be comfortable." He pointed to a smaller version of the same chair. "You've got to get this chair. This is *the* chair."

So here I am, beneath a tree in Truth or Consequences, enjoying a cup of tea in my rocking chair, listening to a woman speaking French who won't shut up. About thirty feet away, a couple has parked their SUV. The husband is still in the car, with the engine on and radio blaring, while the wife is walking around on her iPad, showing the view and a scowling American with a *great* chair. She keeps on for about thirty very loud minutes, every moment of which I debate asking her to move or moving myself. I also think about all the people who asked me, "Aren't you going to get lonely on your trip?" How am I in the middle of nowhere and still being annoyed by people?

I'm saved from making some sort of decision by my date with the hot springs, just down the road, past houses with dirt yards and fences festooned with found art, mosaics, sculptures of doll and motor parts. I wait in a little gazebo with a group of fellow bathers—mostly couples, but also a group of teenage friends, who keep earning glares from the harried employee giving us all the lay of the land. We're all to keep to a respectful hush so as not to disturb anyone else's bath.

I've splurged on a private bath—an open-air space with three walls, and a view onto the river and the desert beyond. Two plastic lawn chairs, a pull for a cold shower, potted plants, all very tidy, with a deep Jacuzzi sort of pool at the center. As I sit in the comfortingly hot waters of the spring, a surprisingly cool breeze picks up and brings in an urgent spring shower, rippling across the river and causing the fish to jump. In the heart of the desert, I am surrounded by water.

I did not grow up camping. The one Girl Scout trip I went on with my mother was disastrous. She stayed on the periphery of the other mothers and chain-smoked the entire time, praying and whispering to herself. I've camped with friends in upstate New York and started camping regularly once I moved back to Southern California, but until this trip my most memorable camping experience was in the Lake District of England near Windermere, where Wordsworth and Coleridge lived, wrote, and wandered the hills. It was the summer of 2005. I'd graduated from Vassar and met up with friends from my year at the University of St. Andrews in Scotland. Not too long before, bombs had detonated in the London Underground and a city bus, killing fifty-two people, and making a war-weary Britain even more edgy.

Our campground was isolated and not everyone had arrived, so two of the group meandered to the entrance to flag down any headlights in the encroaching darkness, so that no one would miss the turnoff.

Meanwhile, the rest of us were enjoying some boxed wine by our tents. I had come from Paris, arriving with an actual *suitcase*; this had earned me plenty of scorn, and needing to borrow a sleeping bag and pillow had only added to the low-range ribbing from the Brits. Trying to defend myself, I just made everything worse by saying I'd compensate for my mooching by taking care of the bear bag (the one thing I'd learned as a kid about camping was how to secure food in either a barrel or bags that one slung over a high tree branch to avoid bears rummaging for snacks). Someone had brought a bear bag, right? Blank looks were all I got in response to my generous offer.

"Hanks, there's no bears on this island," my friend Mary pointed out before pealing into laughter. This wasn't Tahoe: no black bears, no cougars, no bobcats, no major predators of any kind.

I was still getting it from every direction when a stranger walked up to our fire.

I had noticed the solitary single-person tent as we were setting up our own, and the tall, dark-haired man, midthirties maybe, in head-to-toe Gore-Tex. Camping, like everything else in Britain, can get quite soggy. He'd struck me as a man who knew what he was doing.

"I've got some wine here, can I share your fire?"

David, Mary, and I said of course and moved over, and we all refilled our cups. It seemed to me that maybe he'd already been drinking for a while. He asked how we all knew each other, and we talked about school and Scotland. I got made fun of a bit more for being American, and there was some talk about the bombings, the wars. I can't remember who asked him about camping alone, but by that point we'd all been in our cups for quite a while.

He was recently returned from Afghanistan, which at that point was going as badly as possible for the "Coalition of the Willing." Being home wasn't any easier. He'd only just gotten married before he left, and now he and his wife were not getting on. She wanted him to tell her what "the war was like," what he had seen. What he had done. She wanted him to tell her that he hadn't done anything bad, and he couldn't.

"You ever see that show *Band of Brothers*?" the camper asked. David and Mary looked at me for direction. They weren't going to say anything about my dad being the producer behind the series.

I told him, "I've seen it, yeah."

He told us that the show got a lot of things right, but maybe more than anything, it got the randomness of it all right.

"When you start off," he said, "you don't know the guys you're with. You probably don't have anything in common. But by the end, you've got more in common with them than with your own wife. They know things about you that she should never know. My wife wanted me to tell her I was there to do good," he said, poking at the fire. "And I can't tell her that. It's been real bad. She told me I must get myself sorted out. So. I'm here. Trying."

From down the path in the now pitch-dark came the sound of the rest of our group arriving with giddy laughter.

"That show really got it right," he said.

Billy, Lori, and Allison emerged and we all hugged. There were jokes about bears and fancy suitcases from Paris. The man excused himself; we obviously had a lot of catching up to do.

I've thought about that man many times since we crossed paths in 2005. I have no idea what became of him, his wife, their marriage. Truth or consequences, indeed. Whenever my mother talked about her family, her parents and three brothers, she would tell me that they lived by a core tenet of southern culture: *Don't talk about it.* Whatever "it" is, don't talk about it. The way she described it, what wasn't discussed was her father's alcoholism and his violence, which I'm sure was true, but to this list I add what must have been early signs that my mother was not like others. Though I don't actually know if there were signs, early or otherwise, as I've never known or spoken to anyone who knew her when she was a child. I only met two of her brothers for the first time on the 10 in 1996, and I haven't seen or spoken to them since, not even when she died. I have not decided whether I'm going to get in contact with them. The idea makes my insides clench with anxiety.

Maybe this is one of the things my mother and I have in common—beyond pale skin and the ability to read three-hundred-page novels in a single sitting: we have lived in fear of the consequences of the truth. Never did I ever say to my mother, "It's not normal that you sleep with a revolver next to your bed. It scares me that you might shoot me when I come through your bedroom to use the bathroom in the middle of the night." Never was it mentioned how strange she could be in front of strangers. The repercussions of acknowledging the surreality of life with her would have too high a price. It was unthinkable to speak the truth. It feels illicit, dangerous even, to acknowledge it now, turning over all these rocks and unearthing all the squirmy worms of my childhood. I don't remember where I read it, but somewhere I did: the truth ends all conversation. I believe that. But I also think it can start whole new conversations if you give it a chance.

Back in the verdant green of the English Lake District, so far from this dusty place named after a game show, the lone camper vanished in the morning. His little tent was gone, and the green grass there was flat, still holding the shape of his body.

Chapter Eleven

White Sands

Always keep landmarks in sight—don't get lost!
Carry water, even when walking a short distance!
Do not tunnel into dunes; they can collapse and suffocate you.

—WHITE SANDS NATIONAL MONUMENT BROCHURE

The sun is setting in New Mexico, and I'm pretty sure those people are lost.

The first thing any official (or unofficial) guide to White Sands National Monument will tell you is how easy it is to get lost. It made enough sense in theory, but now that I'm standing in a sea of white sand dunes that all look the same, and now that the sun has sunk, I really get it. In June 2019, a male hiker died out on the alkali flats.[1] In September 2018, a man's body was discovered on the same hiking trail after a ranger noticed a car without a backcountry camping permit. In 2015, a French couple died while hiking, but their nine-year-old son was found alive.[2] Four people have died at White Sands in as many years.

All the White Sands guides mention the neon-orange pylons that mark the two-mile hiking loop around which there is camping—

pack-in and pack-out camping, meaning there are no facilities. No bathrooms, showers, trash cans, or water. Everything you're bringing in, or any trash you have, you carry back to your car with you. The rule about the orange pylons is that if you can't see the next marker from where you're standing at a current marker, turn around. The changeability of the sand dunes, the glaring sun on the white sand, the faraway mountains—the San Andres range on the west and the Sacramento Mountains to the east—mean it's very easy to get turned around.

When I pulled into the visitors' center and museum, multiple signs warned that this was the last place to get potable drinking water in the park. The temperature was already in the high nineties during the day, even as early as April. The official website for White Sands recommends that one does not start hiking if the temperature is eighty-five degrees or above. An informational film discussed the sort of wildlife that survives in the pure desert landscape and harsh conditions of White Sands, 275 square miles of gypsum dunes. Each as white as this page, rising and falling with the winds and looking overall like a landscape from *Star Wars.* At night, foxes and the rare large cat might make an appearance, while bleached earless lizards and Apache pocket mice blend in during the day with their nearly white camouflage. Reading warning after warning about overheating and the tendency for campers to get lost, not to mention multiple signs about the last potable-water spigot, I spooked. The interlude with the loner British veteran camper in the Lake District wasn't too dissimilar from my usual experiences: not too far away from a car, always with friends, never far from civilization. I've never hiked out from a trailhead and camped in legit wilderness, and I've never camped in the desert backcountry, or alone. The fact that White Sands abuts a missile range as well as Holloman Air Force Base did not make me feel any safer.

Back in the van I join a long caravan of cars and SUVs ranging from midsize to behemoth to enter the monument. I like that it's called a "monument." There are picnic spots, an area for horses, a hiking loop through the alkali flats at the far end of the main road closer to the base of the San Andres Mountains, an interdune boardwalk for those who can't climb the sloping sandy peaks, and a 2.2-mile hiking loop for campers in the backcountry. Alongside the road, which only penetrates 8 miles deep, diminishing from a large, paved road to a smaller, rougher one over which the white sand flows like tidal waters, families pull over for summertime sledding.

The gift shop sells bright plastic sleds for the sandy slopes that remind me of the cafeteria trays we would use when winter laid its heavy hand on my college campus. In fact, the sand looks so much like snow that my brain hiccups at the sight of kids squealing and grabbing hold of their parents as they toboggan down the steep white dunes in shorts and tank tops.

I pull over in the parking lot at the base of the camping loop and decide to see just how scary the path out to the campsites looks, as if I could eyeball the likelihood of getting lost. Slathered in SPF, wearing my supposedly sunproof long-sleeve shirt and a substantial hat, I climb to the top of the first dune, barefoot.

It's clear why all the van lifers whose blogs mention White Sands mention footwear. The sand is not actually sand but gypsum so fine heavy boots sink through it. Millions of years ago, the Permian Sea receded, leaving a vast expanse of gypsum behind. When mountains arose out of the basin, the gypsum would travel down with rainwater and melted snow, returning to the basin and the ephemeral lakes. Wind and sun separated the gypsum from the water, creating selenite crystals; then strong winds worked the sand into finer and finer granules, creating the dunes. This particular dune field has lasted so long due to the moisture—water is just below the surface, keeping the dunes from blowing away. It also means you can hike barefoot and not burn your feet. It feels decadent to this California girl, who is used to needing flip-flops to navigate burning beach sand.

I climb to the top of the first dune at the head of the backcountry loop. There's no wind, not a cloud in the sky, so I can see a long line of neon-orange pylons, marking the trail. Seems like it would be difficult to get lost if I don't deviate from the marked trail. I decide I don't have a good enough reason not to try camping, so I go back to the ranger station to see if there are any sites still available; it's first come, first served. It turns out that on this Sunday evening, there are many spots still available—it won't be crowded out there tonight.

"Is this your quiet season?" I asked the helpful young female ranger.

"No, actually. Spring is very busy for us, before the heat really comes."

Then I remember: tonight is the season premiere of the last season of *Game of Thrones*. The ranger takes my license plate information and reminds me to pack in more water than I think I'll need—so I buy an extra water bottle and fill up.

Back in the hiking loop parking lot, I pack up my gear: a tent, my tiny propane heater, inflatable pillow. All so new and gaudy I'd be outed as a greenhorn the moment any experienced camper looked closely enough. I also have two gallons of water and protein packs, per the recommendations of the park's official website. And then I start out for my camping site—one of the farthest out on the two-mile-ish loop, a tip I picked up from a van life blog. This way there won't be anyone in between me and the sun setting behind the San Andres Mountains. I arrive at my site a sweaty mess, agog at the beauty. The dunes aren't white, but a glowing, pearlescent white tinged with pink. I pitch my tent on the sandy flats between dunes, per instructions. I've forgotten a mallet for driving in my tent pegs, but I'm not sure how helpful that would be anyway, given that the gypsum isn't hard-packed enough. Camping out here in a high wind would quickly become miserable.

I spend the afternoon writing and reading on the top of a dune, and soon enough the light begins to change to dusk. As I eat another dinner of surprisingly good rehydrated enchiladas—which of course I got at Cabela's (thanks, Dad)—I begin to hear other campers popping up on top of dunes to watch the sunset. A group to my south is rambunctious, and loud. Sounds carry oddly over the dunes—sometimes I hear whole sentences as if the speaker is right beside me, and other times I hear a murmur behind me.

Actually, behind me is an older couple who know enough to come prepared with some back-supporting folding chairs. I watch the loud campers wander away from the main dunes near their campsite, going farther and farther west from the marked loop in search of better photographs—I can easily see the phones held up in outstretched hands, extended from their bodies like appendages. I don't blame them; it's ridiculously beautiful out here. I'm watching them get farther and farther from their campsite, and while the margarine sunset lingers, the moon brings its own befuddling effect on the dunes. They flatten and become even more indistinguishable, while seeming to glow from beneath, rather than reflecting moonlight.

Now the group is turning around on a dune; I see a lot of hands raised to foreheads, hands pointing in different directions. They're lost. I take out my phone and start waving it in the dark, like we're friends who have gotten separated in a movie theater. They start down a dune in my direction and eventually pivot south to their campsite. I have no idea if I helped or if they even saw me—I'm a little distracted by the beetles.

You wouldn't think that in a sea of white sand a large black beetle could sneak up on you, but a couple of times while reading, I caught, just barely in my peripheral vision, a spindly-legged black beetle scuttling toward me. This is a darkling beetle, which when frightened will stick its rear end in the air and emit a horrible stink. The idea that beneath all this gypsum are untold numbers of these bugs, jostling and scurrying? Not my favorite.

I read by moonlight for a while before tucking in to sleep. The only thing I forgot to pack was a pair of thick, cozy socks, and the temperature is beginning to drop. That's a rookie mistake from someone who lives in a desert. Even in the summer, LA, from oceanside Santa Monica to the eastern reaches of the city in Boyle Heights (originally known as Paredón Blanco, White Bluffs) and beyond, cools down significantly at night, which is the joy of that "dry heat" people are always talking about. Humidity, after all, is not remotely affected by the sun setting.

It takes me a while to fall asleep, because the flats between the dunes are not particularly comfortable, and because—the quiet. It's so deeply quiet. No crickets, no birds, no trees to rustle in the wind. In the morning, though, there is a slight scratching sound. When I glance outside the mesh, there's more beetles than I could ever be comfortable with, jockeying for position against the bottom of the tent, I think because of the slight condensation that has collected outside.

I eat my oatmeal and enjoy my PG Tips tea on the top of the dune, watching the milky alkali salt flats wake up in the pinkish air. Even this early, though, the heat is waiting in the background. I can see why all the guidebooks suggest packing up and hiking out as early as possible. (They couldn't have mentioned the bugs?)

Back in the parking lot, there's a real van life setup. A couple dressed in a lot of khaki are organizing their gear in what is obviously a customized van with a blond-wood-paneled interior. They have a cool logo on the side of their rig, along with their Instagram handle. Their dog lounges happily on their custom-built bed while they pack up. In comparison to this couple, my setup is bare-bones, but you won't hear me speak badly of Minnie. I've got one big bag full of clothes, toiletries. There's a bag with a set of sheets and a towel; the rocking chair; my "office bag" with my laptop, passport, and daily diary. I've got several two-gallon jugs of water, for fear of breaking down on a lonesome stretch of highway in the desert. Then there's my camping pack, which also has all my first-aid materials, cooking gear, and head lamps. Also, a lot of books. I don't really have any storage, so during the day this is all just on the bed, which is simply a wooden platform with a twin Ikea mattress. I don't look so much like a cool van lifer as I do a hoarder.

I drive about an hour back to the 10 and Las Cruces, where I go to a twenty-four-hour gym to shower and change, and end up chitchatting with two more van life folks. One is an older gentleman who asks how it went at White Sands, since that's where he's headed. (I tell him about the bugs.) And the other is a woman, around my age, in a regular hatchback. It's hard to tell if she's living "van life," or just driving across the country. The line between modes of van life pivots on privilege. There are people who choose to step out of the usual nine-to-five job, the property ladder, hallmarks that defined success for the generations before us; they've decided to bypass the dictates of capitalism. Then there are folks who feel like their only choice is to live in their vehicle. For every souped-up Mercedes Sprinter van I see with decals of an Instagram account and an Etsy shop (and I see plenty), I see twice as many vans that look like they're being held together with duct tape and crossed fingers.

There's still a little gypsum between my toes when I park Minnie in the Franklin Mountains State Park on the outskirts of El Paso, Texas, and climb into bed. Sleeping in the tent made me feel particularly vulnerable, but in here I feel like a swaddled baby, comforted by the van's compactness. When I close my eyes, I see the sea of pinkish dunes, and no buildings at all. This too is a comfort. Since setting out I have seen too many stroads, too many of the same fast-food chains over and over, the same strip malls and nondescript buildings in a blur of sprawl that makes my eyes go gray. The buildings in these places feel like an insult to the landscape; they are drowning out the hymn that we would be able to hear otherwise. Usually when LA starts to wear me down, my instinct is to go running to a green place and drink it in like a parched woman; but here in the desert, I'm surprised to find emptiness just as comforting.

My brain revs up like a heaving machine, trying to get me to think about Emptiness and America, or My Mother and Mother Nature, but my body is so exhausted, I *can't* think. The constant warnings about safety, the hike, the tremendous heat have all wrung me out. I don't *want* to think, either. My brain is sloshing around with information and research and questions. I hold the scenes of the day in my vision: the peachy light, the mountains on all sides. There's no roads, no people who I can see and eventually none who I can hear. The gypsum holds on to the sun's last rays, and then there's the moon's light. It is soft to the touch, cool. The desert is still surprising me.

Enjoy it, my body tells me. Enjoy being tired, and safe, and in the middle of nowhere. Buildings and traffic and questions will all be there tomorrow. Don't think about your mother, just feel. I hear the sound of pages turning, her constant cough. There's the taste of the water from the sink in her bathroom. The way Momma snored. I sleep.

He grew up watching "The Magnificent Seven,"
My brother that I thought was god.
He dressed like the american idol of the 1950's;
In his black leather jacket,
cigarets, sports car, hair brill creamed,
his rolled up white t shirt sleeves
he looked like James Dean.
[. . .]
he moved to the west Texas town of El Paso.
He dreamed of joining the mexican revolution
with bandoleros criss crossed across his chest,
as in the days of Emilio Zapata.
But he grows roses now in his backyard.
Struggling with a past not of his own making
that will not let him go,

—SJD

Chapter Twelve

El Paso

¡Chinga tu muro!

—BUMPER STICKER

Texas is a very complicated place," a new friend will warn me. "And it's a place of many possibilities and many different existences. I've lived three very different lives in the same state."

I had thought that entering Lone Star territory would feel like a seismic shift, but El Paso feels like more desert. El Paso, it turns out, is definitely *in* Texas, but it doesn't feel particularly *of* Texas. Edwin Delgado, an American who grew up in Juárez and now goes back and forth over the border, will also tell me, "I like to describe El Paso as 40 percent Mexico, 35 percent Texas, 15 percent New Mexico, and 10 percent Arizona. Yes, I'm a Texan. But most importantly, I'm from El Paso."

Some 85 to 87 percent of the Texas population is east of the north-south interstate that runs through Austin, San Antonio, Waco, and the larger Dallas–Fort Worth area. This means that only 13 to 14 percent of the state's population lives west of the 35, in the vast space of west Texas—the part that in 1996 made me feel like I was losing my mind. To El Pasoans, empty west Texas? That is considered the east.

It's kvetching about February in Maine, to someone who lives in the perpetual winter of Newfoundland.

Location is destiny, and where El Paso is defines its relationship with the rest of Texas. As someone told me, "It's like they say, closer to San Diego than Dallas, El Paso."

To most Texans, it's west; to Californians, it's east; and to New Mexicans, it's . . . south? I had to confirm this multiple times to convince myself of it, but it's true—El Paso is mostly south, rather than east, of New Mexico. At least, on the 10.

The cute park ranger comes back with a map. The sun was going to be setting soon and when he'd stopped by to confirm that I was intending to camp in the Franklin Mountains, he told me that the ridge hike was the best place to catch the sunset. The only other person in the park is a woman in an RV much closer to the entrance off the Transmountain Drive. El Paso itself curls around the southern tip of the Franklin Mountains, hemmed in on its southern side by the Rio Grande. From the ridge, he said, I'd see El Paso and, beyond that, Juárez, just on the other side of the river.

On my hike, I think about the last time I was in El Paso, with my mother. We stopped to spend some with her eldest brother, Michael, the one who gave us Fern the dog. As a teenager I thought he was a bit curt. Once, when my mother, the Jack Russell, and I were on the sofa together, he joked, "Look, three bitches on a couch!"

I remember my mom rolling her eyes, like a little sister would. I was mortified, but he also gave me my first Anne Rice to read (against my mother's wishes), so I called it even. Michael teased me about tarantula migration season, and all these years later I'm fighting off the conviction that the moment I turn around, my sleeping bag here in El Paso is just going to fill to the brim with spiders.

Spider-related fears aside, waking up in the Franklin Mountains and hiking in the early morning before the sun and heat get too intense is exhilarating. For the next four days I'm alone, and the quiet is so complete, I feel it inside of me. Unlike at White Sands with its caravan of people entering, I hardly ever see anyone besides the park rangers who drive by in the mornings to check on me and let me know where the park's lone cougar has been spotted.

Many El Pasoans don't seem to know about the campsites available in the Franklin Mountains—unless they're the sort of people who spend their days off mountain biking. I get a lot of blank stares when people ask me where I'm staying and I tell them I'm camping outside of the city in the state park.

More than once I get asked, "Is that out past Abundant Living?" AL, as I hear it called a lot, is a very popular megachurch in the suburban sprawl of El Paso. Its proper name is the Abundant Living Faith Center, which strikes me as a sort of Goop-ified evangelicalism. It's almost Easter weekend, so I briefly consider seeing when AL's Sunday services might be, but decide against it.

Besides the campsite, my favorite thing about El Paso at the outset is its streetcars, which are so beautiful: straight out of the 1950s, in hues of deco jadeite and cream, but with the modern conveniences of air-conditioning and Wi-Fi. The streetcar system in El Paso dates back to before the turn of the twentieth century, but really got going when Mandy the Mule, who pulled a wooden trolley on the streets of this town, was retired and replaced by electric cars in 1902.[1]

On the other side of the Franklin Mountains from my campsite is the National Border Patrol Museum. Earlier in the year sixteen arrest warrants were issued after immigrants' rights protestors affixed stickers with the faces of Guatemalan children Jakelin Caal Maquin[2] and Felipe Gómez Alonzo,[3] who died in the custody of the Border Patrol. When I walk in and sign the visitor's log (admittance is free), a woman welcomes me. Her young son is in her office behind us, watching cartoons on a desktop computer. In another office, a large white man is also watching a television and glaring at me. He doesn't seem convinced that I'm not there to cause more trouble.

America's borders include 1,900 miles of the Mexico border, and 5,000 miles along the Canadian border. The original Patrol consisted of 104 officers who had no authority to arrest anyone or "actually patrol the border," and 24 percent of them were Texas mounted guards of the Chinese Division, responsible for enforcing the Chinese Exclusion Act, a law that "provided an absolute 10-year ban on Chinese laborers immigrating to the United States. For the first time, federal law proscribed entry of an ethnic working group on the premise that it endangered the good order of certain localities."[4]

There is no one here, besides me, looking at old jeeps and broken mannequins with old BP uniforms. As austere as the outside is—1980s beige concrete—the interior is similarly flinty, like a warehouse with random things plopped around. It's echoey and feels temporary. There's a miniature Statue of Liberty and dioramas of how drug smugglers build tunnels. There's a picture of the last Border Patrol agent killed in the line of duty, Rogelio Martinez, who died November 19, 2017. I zero in on one plaque in particular:

> . . . Men quickly became hardened by their experiences and mistakes were sometimes made, but it also led to the camaraderie among officers that became the backbone of the Patrol.

> . . . It was a different time then and many of the things that happened there were reasonable under the circumstances and guidelines and policies of the time.
>
> They were the "Old Patrol."

After the museum, I head to Savage Goods café, and as I'm eating I notice a girl, probably in her early twenties, surrounded by laughing friends, wearing a cheery turquoise shirt that reads *Inmigrante También* (Immigrant Too). I'm in a completely different universe, functioning under different rules, than I was just an hour ago. How can these two places exist in the same city? It feels like something is missing, some context clue or bit of information that would bring everything a little more clearly into focus.

As I'm climbing back into my van after lunch, I notice a young Black man crossing the street, shielding his eyes with a folder. I offer "Afternoon!" and he says, "Howdy." I think we're done, but soon he's knocking on my window. Turns out, he just got discharged from the hospital and doesn't have his phone on him. Any chance I can call his aunt so she'll come pick him up? Why not? Only, when I explain the situation to his aunt, not only is she not surprised that a total stranger is calling on behalf of her nephew but she's also nonplussed.

"Tell him he can walk his ass home. I'm at work."

When I pass some version of this message to him, he sighs. Not today, not that aunt.

"Any chance I can grab a hat from you?"

He's got his eye on the cowboy hat on my front dashboard. Instead, I offer him a baseball cap. To be honest, both hats have good memories. The cowboy hat was a gift when I was fourteen, from a boy who rode horses back when I also rode horses. The cap is from a trip to Baton Rouge when I tagged along with my father to scout the USS *Kidd*, a retired World War II destroyer that is now berthed on the Mississippi, as a location for a film that would go on to be *Greyhound*. The *Kidd* is now a museum and part of the Louisiana Veterans Memorial. On the day we visited the ship (one can get in a lot of trouble calling such a vessel a "boat"), we met many local veterans, mostly in their sixties and seventies, who volunteer as educators and docents. But there was one gentleman, in his late eighties, whose family had driven him halfway across the state to come and meet my father. He was dressed in his formal uniform—the blindingly white one. While the prospective film crew was on board the *Kidd*, I sat with this man drinking coffee and listening to his stories about waiting for the rain to take a shower on deck in the Pacific. Later, he insisted that we go to the gift shop and pick something out. I grabbed a simple cap.

"How about the cowboy hat?" the man in the glaring El Paso sun asks me.

"No can do. But how's about this?" I hand him the *Kidd* baseball cap. He's visibly disappointed but takes the hat and checks his look in my side mirror.

"Can you give me a lift?"

"Nah, dude. But I've got, like, ten bucks in cash if you wanna grab a taxi?"

He shrugs no and ambles off, shaping the brim of his new hat.

Spring storms have rolled into town and sent me indoors. I get an Airbnb on the far side of El Paso, on the other side of an old refinery. It's a little casita behind a 1920s adobe house. There are some chickens who meander around, a cat who lounges in the window of the big house, and a little dog named Coco who wanders into my kitchen every now and then to say hello. By the time I meet up with Edwin Delgado, the wind and thunder are epic. There are warnings about flash floods on the radio, and I'm glad I gave the camping a pause. The coffee spot where we meet is in a converted metal storage container, and occasionally it's so loud we have to pause our conversation.

Delgado is a local freelancer who covers immigration issues and is frequently published by the British newspaper the *Guardian.*

"My final year of elementary school is when they were starting to find all these bodies all over the place," Edwin says, sipping from a very large, sweet-looking coffee beverage. He was born in America but returned to Juárez with his family. After his parents' divorce, and with cartel-related violence running rampant, Delgado came back to the States to live with his sister and her husband. His mother, who owns a hair salon, still lives in Juárez.

"When I went into journalism, my plan was to do sports," he explains. But with his background, and immigration issues on every front page across the world, it seemed clear that sports was out. Edwin seems a little nervous; I'm not sure he's been on the other side of an interview often. He fiddles with his straw. I ask him what it is that most people don't understand about immigration policy in America, and he shrugs. Essentially, no one understands immigration policy, because we don't really have any. We have fingers in the proverbial dam.

"Our immigration policy is—actually, our border enforcement policy, I should say—is deterrence," he says. "If there is a doctrine, it is 'Make it so bad that people won't want to come.' In whatever way it is. Make it a logistical nightmare, make it a literal life-threatening nightmare. But all of this is rooted in grave perpetual misestimation of what people are fleeing. No matter what version of hell you implement at the border, no matter how hellacious you make the journey or the crossing or the domestic immigration enforcement, people are going to fucking deal with it. When there's certainty about what they're fleeing.

When they're fleeing certain death? How can we not put two and two together?"

This is the end of my time in the Southwest, and the beginning of the Lone Star State. But I know now not to trust maps, as they cannot really tell us where something starts and another ends. Roads. Mothers and daughters. Cities. El Paso is funny in this light, because while everyone here has told me how Texan they are, this city and the stories it's been telling me are not American. They are of the borders—the in-between. Even the name of the place speaks to its identity as in-between: El Paso, from *El Paso del Norte*, Passageway to the North. To Americans, El Paso is the point, because we always think the point is within our own borders—but the point is that El Paso is only half a whole, balanced on the other side by Ciudad Juárez.

When I was here in 1996, I remember my cousin telling me that he would hang out with his friends in the parking lot of the local Walgreens.

"What do you do there?" I asked.

"Just . . . hang out."

Now, as then, El Paso strikes me as a town *hanging out*. In LA there are people who just "hang out" because a lot of them don't have regular nine-to-five jobs. It doesn't feel like that here. When I drive around El Paso, I see a lot of people just . . . hanging out. It feels like people are . . . waiting. Looking. For something to do, something to happen; there's a listlessness, a sense of anticipation. Hot streets bake in a stillness that pervades even the angry traffic stuck on the interstate. I feel like I'm holding my breath. The word that keeps coming to mind is *liminal*, the effect of simultaneously being just on either side of a threshold, of transitionality. But here is a nuance to *liminal*, though, that I think applies to El Paso beyond its existence on the thresholds of two countries.

But first, let me explain how much I love "long-ass YouTube videos." This is what happens when I watch something, like a two-hour-long video on how a meme stock craze became an apocalyptic financial cult, or an hour-long piece on why there are so many biracial couples on television: I find them fascinating, and I text a link to a friend, and they always respond, always, "Is this another long-ass YouTube video?"[5] And it always is. I like watching smart people talk about things that interest them, especially if they do it stylishly. Enter: ContraPoints.

Natalie Wynn, who publishes her video essays under ContraPoints, is a former piano wunderkind, PhD candidate in philosophy, and Uber driver. She now makes highly produced, thoroughly researched, wonderfully glamorous videos on subjects like Opulence, Canceling, Envy, and Justice, not to mention a nearly four-hour video breaking down the *Twilight* phenomenon that went into St. Augustine's philosophy of lust, the politics of BDSM, and the nihilism of Team Jacob. If the "YouTube" of it all is making you doubt her intellectual bona fides, she won a Peabody.

In one video, Wynn describes a nuance to the liminal that is often overlooked: the *hauntological*, or "the haunting echoes of a lost future." Perhaps when you were old enough to realize that *Back to the Future* lied to you and you were not ever going to get a floating hoverboard, you felt a pang of disappointment. Maybe as your biological clock wound down and your future as a parent faded out of possibility, you had to mourn something that never happened. Hauntology.

At this point, I've lived in Los Angeles longer than anywhere else, yet when I think of home, my Proustian sense-memory is instinctually the afternoon light in my Sacramento bedroom, the hum of the ceiling fan, strains of classical music coming from my mother's room, the way the old house sighed and settled, creaking in the wet winters and dry summers alike. Yet now when I come home, it feels like I'm trying to revisit a dream, the edges of which are starting to fade from memory.

It seems to me that El Paso and Juárez are stuck in the hauntological, mourning a future of reunion that seems, if not totally impossible, deeply improbable, surrounded as they are by a demilitarized zone and separated by politics. If these two cities are supposed to be one, then I wonder if even the people milling around their own hometown are never actually *home*.

The next morning, I am getting dressed in a rush because I'm running late. I shove my foot into one of my tangerine espadrilles and know instantly that there is a huge bug in my shoe. On my toes. It's wriggling. I'm too panicked to scream but focus on getting my foot out as quickly as possible without flinging the shoe from me. If it's a scorpion and it stings me, I need to know what kind it is. Only in the desert would I be relieved to see that it's only a huge, mostly dead cockroach smeared all over my toes. So that's how the day starts. It can only go up from here.

Right?

Chapter Thirteen

Juárez

"¡Pobre México! Tan lejos de Dios, y tan cerca de los Estados Unidos."

—ATTRIBUTED TO PORFIRIO DÍAZ

I have made a stupid mistake.

I have dressed for church, but not for the walk to the church. I blame Budapest. The last time I was in a place of worship, it was the Dohány Street Synagogue. It was summer, and I was wearing a sleeveless silk blouse. The tour guide told me I couldn't enter with my shoulders showing. I could either use a sort of tissue paper bolero that looked too much like a toilet seat cover for my taste or dip out to buy something. Outside the temple there was a stand festooned with colorful shawls. The old woman working the stall gestured that a black-and-gold-paisley wrap would match my hair, and I paid too much for a cheap shawl that became one of my favorite possessions.

Since it's the Great Sabbath, the Saturday before Easter Sunday, and since I am going to church, I thought I should dress appropriately. So here I am in a floral dress, shoulders covered, thinking about Budapest, and drawing way too much attention to myself when all I want to do is blend in. Budapest has been on my mind a lot since I got to El Paso, but more on that later. There's a dog about to tear my leg off.

Getting into Juárez is easy. Fifty cents and you're over the bridge, walking over the river past cars idling trying to go in the opposite direction. While I cross over, I don't know to look for an open-air pen holding women and children beneath it. Moving down Avenida Juárez, down to where the old open *mercado* used to be, is a balancing act. My guide, George Salon, is an El Paso real estate businessman and the kind of person who knows everyone. He is descended from Juárezeños, from a line of Lebanese Mexican immigrants.

"The Syrians and the Lebanese are like the Jews of Mexico," he says to me.

After WWI, Mexico, fresh from the revolution, "the first true social revolution of the 20th century and one of the bloodiest wars in North American history,"[1] opened its doors to those the global conflict had left in the diaspora. The Lebanese, among others, came to Mexico bringing their food, culture, education, and orthodox faith. Generations later, George crosses into Juárez multiple times a week, though not many join him.

I met George in his office near the border. It's solidly seventies fare with a lot of brown marble. There are stacks of paper everywhere, and George is the sort of man who has a lot of keys on a lot of key rings. He's a little apologetic—we were supposed to be in a much larger group. George, a devout Catholic, usually spends the Saturday before Easter walking to light candles at San Lorenzo, the church his family from both sides of the border attends.

Turns out, it's just George and me crossing—everyone else has canceled, possibly because of general concerns, possibly because this weekend there's been a spike in cartel-related violence. Before departing, George asks if I'd be comfortable praying with him. We both close our eyes, and George prays that we be blessed with safe passage to and from Juárez. He thanks God for the opportunity to show this place to a new friend, and for all our blessings.

As we head out, George asks about my religious history. The best way I can describe the depth of my mother's evangelical fervor is to explain that I once asked her why the date 1066 was important, and her response began, "Well, when people don't have the light of Jesus in their hearts . . ." The tepid Episcopalian faith of her childhood was not enough, I think, to guide her and provide comfort as her mental health declined. My mother's faith was the bedrock of her every moment—she frequently prayed out loud, a constant conversation with Jesus, and the battle between God and Christ on the one hand and Satan on the other was the lens through which she perceived life. Bad nightmare? Satan needed to be cast out. I got over a cold quickly? Jesus blessed me. She saw her premenopausal acne as God having a laugh at her prayers for her children's skin issues to be cleared up.

The great miracle of my mother's life was that she got clean and sober. This marvel was tainted by the fact that, as a sober sponsor, my mother often invited people in the midst of serious addiction, sometimes in trouble with the law, to come into our home. It was common for me to wander into the kitchen, wondering what was for dinner, to find my mom holed up with a group of rough-looking men, walking them through the Big Book.

Not only did my mother bring addicts home but she would also host twelve-step meetings, and in the heyday of her working the program, rather than get a babysitter she would bring me along to Alcoholics Anonymous, Narcotics Anonymous, and Cocaine Anonymous meetings. I cheerfully wiped down the whiteboard, set out snacks, and organized Styrofoam cups for coffee and to use as ashtrays into tidy lines. Anyone who has had anything to do with the twelve-step program knows that while a large component of its guiding path includes addicts acknowledging "that a Power greater than ourselves could restore . . . sanity," that Power is described only as "God, as we understand him"[2] —the program specifically stipulates that no one in attendance is to make statements about which God, from which faith. I don't know who or how my mother was exposed to the specific theology of evangelical Christianity, but it's clear to me that her newfound faith replaced substance abuse as her coping mechanism.

One of my friends from high school is now a therapist. We were in a discussion about addiction, and she pointed out that substance abuse as self-medication works—to the detriment of the rest of your life, eventually dissolving all your other coping mechanisms—your friendships suffer, your work, your physical space and emotional state all begin to crumble, giving way to this one tentpole barely keeping the circus going. I believe that the only way my mother was able to get clean and sober (and, to the best of my knowledge, never relapsed) was that she replaced one obsession, drugs and alcohol, with another: her evangelical fervor.

Evangelicalism is loosely the idea that a general belief in Jesus Christ as the son of God does not quite cut it. You can't simply go to church on Christmas Eve, say grace before a meal, and call it a day. My mother was "washed in the Blood of the Lamb," as they say, which meant that Jesus wasn't merely a faraway figure she prayed to when times were tough but present in her everyday life, her every moment. She looked to him in all matters, large and small. When I told her I had a crush on a boy, her response was that the relationship was a dead end unless he had a love for Christ in his heart. I was twelve. You must invite Christ into every facet of your life, and you must proselytize to convert as many people as possible, and you must remember that this life is fleeting. What truly matters is the eternity you spend in paradise (or the other place).

The course of world history, and current politics were, according to her, determined by whether or not people had accepted Jesus Christ as their "personal Lord and Savior." *Personal*—that is the most important word. Evangelicals do not believe that the Bible or the teachings of Jesus need to be translated for lay Christians by an official emissary of God; a member of the clergy, as the Catholics believe. Nor do they believe that a childhood baptism is enough to protect your soul from satanic intervention, as some Protestants do. Choosing "what would Jesus do" is a twenty-four-hour task, and spreading the good word, converting non-Evangelicals, Christians and non-Christians alike, is the priority.

This is how you get to a place where the question "Why is the date 1066 so important?" has an answer that includes whether someone has brought Jesus into their lives as their divine savior.

I don't have any clear memories of my mother when she was still using and drinking. I was young enough that those early years in Sacramento are mostly shrouded in a disquieting fog. I knew that I'd missed a lot of school and done very little of the work I needed to do, and so had to repeat the first grade, but I hadn't put it together that the reason was that there was no one home. Literally—my mother would vanish for a night or two, leaving my older brother to watch over me. This was explained to me only last year. By the time I was old enough to recognize that there were some classmates who were not allowed to come over to my house, Jesus had moved into our home and never left.

Although evangelicalism played a huge part in her life, my mother never belonged to a corresponding church. We never attended services at a "megachurch," worshiped with anyone speaking in tongues, or witnessed faith healers. The closest we ever got to something along those lines was when we drove a couple of hours to see a rainbow reflected on the wall of a church that I was told was an outline of the Virgin Mary. I only remember the very long line to get in.

In fact, the only church my mother visited with any regularity was Episcopal. We attended in fits and spurts, the longest stretch being when I was rushed into baptism as a six-year-old and was briefly in the choir. When my father married my stepmother in the Greek Orthodox church, my mother panicked, anticipating that I would be drafted onto another team, and it suddenly became very important that I become officially not–Greek Orthodox.

I accepted Jesus Christ as my personal Lord and Savior when I was around eleven years old, when my mom was driving us home from a twelve-step meeting. I was devout enough that while out bowling, I felt compelled to approach a grown woman whom I was sure the Lord wanted me to preach to. I happily filled plastic bags with candy and added a proselytizing comic strip made for children to hand out on Halloween. I completed Bible study workbooks published by the ultra-conservative Focus on the Family and spent recesses at school highlighting my pink Bible.

My adolescent faith was snuffed out by reading the Bible cover to cover. As a good Evangelical, I had read the Gospels, but at around twelve years old, I decided to read the whole book. There was the story of the ten plagues of Egypt: wherein Moses tells Pharaoh that, unless he frees the Jews from bondage, God will inflict a series of increasingly dire plagues—water turning to blood, everyone being covered in horrific boils, and finally the death of all the firstborn sons. In the story, the Jews are instructed to paint their doorways with the blood of a lamb; that way the angel of death will know to spare that family and pass over their home. All the firstborn males of all the families, of all the animals, of all life anywhere, die, including the heir of Pharaoh. Broken, he frees the Jews, and Moses leads them to freedom.

This story flummoxed me. God killed all the firstborn males? What bad did a bunch of babies do? What evil had all the animals committed? Come to think of it, why sons—wouldn't anyone be sad if their daughters were randomly slaughtered? Troubled, I asked my mom about it.

She told me that was Old Testament God. We didn't have anything to do with Old Testament God, as Christians; ours was the God of the *New* Testament, and as born-again Christians, Jesus Christ was the crux of our faith. Old Testament God was about law, sin, obedience, and shame; New Testament God gave us his only begotten son, who died for our sins on the cross, so our faith was about grace, love, and forgiveness.

My response to this was: Let me get this straight . . . God changes?

And that was the end of my time as a born-again Christian, though I never announced to my mother that I had, in evangelical parlance, "lost my testimony."

Like many who grew up with zealous faith, my following years of skepticism were just as strident. My history as a born-again has also come in handy an odd number of times, such as when I was a student abroad at the University of St. Andrews in Scotland, and some of my schoolmates were evangelical, as rare in the United Kingdom and Ireland as it is common in the United States. Wonderfully kind, thoughtful young women, they were utterly flummoxed by someone who had heard "the good news," knew Jesus Christ and the respite he offered from sin and damnation, had read the Good Word, and said, "Thanks, but no thanks!" Over dinner one evening, I was simultaneously eating and working on translating an Old English piece, "Dream of the Rood," an extremely strange poem that tells the story of the crucifixion of Christ from the perspective of the tree that becomes the cross Jesus is nailed to. ("They snatched that almighty one / hefting him from hard heaviness. / Fierce to fight, they've forsaken me / to stand there, made to drape blood, / put through with piercing."[3]) One of my roommates, wearing a lavender Eeyore sweatshirt, finally admitted how much my lack of faith upset her.

"Ach, Liz, it's so sad."

"What's sad?"

"That you're going to hell. Aren't you scared?"

"Well, no, because I don't believe in hell."

"Just because you don't believe in it doesn't mean you're not going there," she explained patiently, with stereotypical Scottish fastidiousness. I believed her—that that idea of me going to hell was upsetting to her, that is, and I'm sure it seemed perverse that I had chosen to forgo eternal life in paradise. Ending up in hell because of ignorance was one thing—but choosing it? She was baffled.

When my mother was undergoing treatment for her cancer, she was living in an apartment in Los Angeles, too weak to walk the big dog she'd brought with her from Sacramento, wearing little wigs and still smoking a pack a day. I visited her, I wrote down the local radio stations, and I read romance novels sitting next to her while she read her Bible. We never talked about her impending death; I never asked if she was scared—in fact, I don't ever remember her seeming frightened. Maybe she was sheltering me, or maybe her faith allowed her to face her death without any fear. I wonder what she would say about me going to a Catholic church. Nothing good, probably.

The truth is that nowadays, what I value over specific faith or general doubt is I think best described as curiosity. I'm curious about other people's faith the same way I'm curious about Juárez. If someone wants to tell me about their beliefs, I'm all ears. If someone offers to walk me through Juárez, I'm there. I don't think I've inspired any confidence in

George with my short-version explanation of "I would say I'm spiritual, rather than religious." He can smell the distinct odor of California flakiness on me.

As we walk, I ask George in turn about his faith. After an adolescence of punk shows and "whole cemeteries full of skeletons" in his closet, George is a father and husband with graying hair whose T-shirt and sneakers out his teenage roots. He has the serious faith of the reformed. His intensity reminds me of a shorter, less tattooed (that I can see) Henry Rollins. The only time I get him to really warm up is when we're talking about his son and my nieces.

Directly across the international bridge is the Avenida Benito Juárez. In 2015 after the drug cartel violence supposedly peaked, the government flushed the wide avenue of businesses it thought would deter tourism and painted everything white. The hope was that a clean façade and clean businesses would bring Americans back over the border for fun nights out. At eight thirty in the morning, nothing about Avenida Juárez seems all that clean. Most places, I am aware how walking with a man changes my experiences moving down a street, but never more so than today. George's daunting presence seems to be warding off anyone from harassing us. I have never stuck out more. Here in Juárez, I look like a clueless white woman come to look at How Bad It Is on the Other Side. Which I suppose I am.

And it is bad. Along the avenue of white shop fronts, now as dingy as four-day-old New York City snow, many of the buildings more or less function as brothels, George explains as we pass a bored and very young woman, at most seventeen or eighteen, slouched waiting in a doorway. Her girlish flip-flops stand out. A shirtless man, his hairless stomach protruding with gargantuan growths and a wound oozing along his side, stumbles up to cars already queuing up to cross over into the States, mumbling and merely holding up his hands.

"Just don't look," George urges as we walk on. He shares stories of a cocky friend of a friend who lingered behind while on a walk; while the guy swore he'd just asked someone if they'd seen his friends, he came back bruised and with fingernails missing. George suspects the kid had tried for a quick score and thought the main drag there was safe enough. It is not. By 9:30 a.m. there are already people standing in doorways, watching, waiting, and others walking back and forth along the street, offering unlicensed Disney blankets and wilting plastic fans. It feels like an aquarium, its denizens just circling and circling, the sharks on the outside, keeping track.

We turn onto Avenida 16 de Septiembre, named for the day of Mexican independence, and pick up the pace, even though the sidewalks are a real high-wire act. Every now and then there are cavernous holes, three or four feet deep, showing exposed pipes, and very little is level.

We walk past a hot dog restaurant, wrapped in police tape. George looks chagrined almost, and tells me that several hours before in the early morning, a man was executed in this parking lot. That's how you know it's a cartel-related death—people aren't just murdered, they're executed. Over the course of this extended holiday weekend, twenty-six people will be executed, with an average of six executions a day.[4]

George asks me if I want to keep going, and says he wouldn't blame me if I pulled the plug. I say I want to keep going. A little farther on I see someone pop out of an office in a ramshackle strip mall to pick up a late breakfast from an Uber Eats delivery guy on a scooter.

Down the road we pause for a moment to admire the façade of the Cine Victoria, a beautifully ornate movie theater from the early 1920s whose walls used to be covered in murals from Mexican cinema. Over the decades, unpaid taxes added up and the cinema swapped hands a number of times, becoming a pornography house for a while, before being abandoned. Soon enough squatters moved in and there were fires. From the street you can see through the façade of the tower to the blue of the clear sky. We pass by a number of beautiful deco homes from the twenties and thirties with large gates around them, mostly empty, though some are event spaces.

There's a large park—it's very easy to squint and see the Juárez from before "all the trouble."

This is when I begin to think of Budapest. It wasn't until I was in Hungary that I learned it's actually two cities: Buda and Pest, divided by the Danube. It's hard for Americans to understand that for a long time the border was a porous place, when folks went back and forth between El Paso and Juárez the same way people go back and forth between Buda and Pest.

At some point George points out a large, abandoned hotel where drug lords threw big parties and weddings. Now, like so many other places, it's a hollowed-out ruin. We're peeking through a ramshackle gate, two pieces of plywood loosely chained together with a gap between, into a roofless banquet room when a dog—in my memory it is the size of a horse—throws itself at us, snarling and barking. Chains rattle and I nearly scream.

Eventually we come to the church, and the first thing George does is call his wife to tell her we've arrived safely. We pop into the church's shop, which is jam-packed with candles and Catholica—statues of various saints, of the Christ, and many of the Madonna. Before I left for the trip, a friend lent me her St. Christopher medallion, him being the patron saint of travelers. While talking about all the various saints represented in the shop, I show George the necklace, but again his response is a bit like a grand slam champion responding to someone bragging that they go to the batting cages every now and then. He buys us both offering candles and we head into the church. It reeks of spray paint.

Up near the altar there's a group building and painting a cave that, during tomorrow's Easter services, will be the stage for a re-creation of Jesus's resurrection from the dead. Teenagers are spray-painting crinkled-up paper bags silver to look like rocks. In a small side chapel, George and I light our candles and find seats to be alone with our thoughts for a moment. A steady stream of older folks join us. One couple shuffles in, the man with legs so bowed he walks with canes. His heeled boots clack on the marble floor. He lights his candle and goes to kneel in front of the altar. When his wife moves to help him, he shoos her off, determined. On his knees, he crosses himself and begins his prayers while his wife greets another woman in the pews.

I'm exhausted. The walk was long, and I've been up for hours, but then it dawns on me that I've been truly scared since we crossed the bridge. I'm reminded that Edwin told me that while he spends more time in Juárez than in El Paso lately, he doesn't spend much time out on the street.

"If I'm gonna go out, I have a purpose. So, I'm gonna go do A, B, C, and come back."

I'd asked Edwin if he worried about his mom living in Juárez.

"Yeah. Especially since she has her own business."

"Right. Her salon. How far into the city is she from the border?"

"It's pretty in."

"Is that safer?"

"It's hard to know, like, what area is safer."

I've turned off my phone and haven't told anyone at home that I was going to Juárez because I didn't want to explain to my family that I was going to the "most dangerous city in the world."

* * *

Eventually I finish my prayers and meet George back in the main area. He suggests we get lunch. George, the eternal fixer, had someone drive his car over the border earlier and park it at the church; so, off our feet and safely (maybe?) in the vehicle, he points out the pristine Church of Jesus Christ of Latter-day Saints temple, which opened to its faithful, both American and Mexican, in 2000. It is as tidy as the rest of the neighborhood is in shambles. The Mormons believe that a temple includes a "celestial room," a sort of representation of and precursor to paradise, or heaven. It's a place to contemplate the eternal, to feel hope. As we park alongside the tall iron gates and I look onto the beautiful garden beyond the bars, I think of Señora Crawford.

In high school I had a wonderful Spanish teacher who attempted to infect us all with the same fascination and passion she had for Latin culture. As a senior in her Advanced Placement class, I watched the original *Ugly Betty* (a telenovela called *Yo Soy Betty, La Fea*), read Pablo Neruda, memorized Shakira lyrics, and studied famous and infamous sayings. Standing there outside the temple, one comes to mind: "*¡Pobre México! Tan lejos de Dios, y tan cerca de los Estados Unidos.*" Poor Mexico, so far from God, and so close to America!

Lunch is tacos and Topo Chico, exactly what I eat for lunch most days back home in Los Angeles, and soon enough it is time to cross back into El Paso. In the long line of cars waiting at the border, women walk up and down the lanes selling beverages, children's blankets, and fireworks. I ask George how often he comes over alone, and he tells me that his family sometimes comes over with him, but not many of his friends will anymore. Yet it's important to him that his son knows where their family is from, that life exists on the other side.

* * *

Back on the American side of the river, people are bustling around, there's chitchatting, and maybe I'm just so relieved, but it seems like everyone is smiling. I thank George for everything, drive back to the Airbnb in silence, and fall asleep so deeply I don't wake up until midnight. The only time I've felt adrenaline leach out of my body like this was after I jumped out of a plane to celebrate one of my brothers' birthdays.

A fact that has come up again and again in my conversations about El Paso is that a big part of being from El Chuco ("the tip") is that you grew up in a safe city. To be consistently rated one of the safest cities in America, across from the city infamous for being the murder capital of the world, creates a schism in the center of what had been one community longer than it's been two cities. El Paso/Juárez is a simulacrum of the Southwest itself: not really America, and not really Mexico. No. That's not right.

It is both America and Mexico at the same time. It's liminal, as I said; nuanced. But we want good guys or bad guys, America or Mexico, when for a very long time, it was fluid. The border was fluid, identity was fluid, language was fluid. Outside of Spanish and English, there are three hundred dialects of Native American languages in this land. More than anything, I've learned that, to understand that Southwest, you've got to make peace with the flash flood—the sort of torrent that comes from hours, or even mere minutes, of intense rain after months of dryness. These floods tear through the desert and city streets alike, sweeping everything along in their path.

Campers in the desert, including myself, are inundated with warnings about how fast the desert can change on you, told to keep a skeptical eye on the sky. Here, you've got to understand both the dry arroyo and the rushing tide. You have to understand the catholic, as in the adjective.

It's perverse, but sometimes I wish that rather than swinging between good days and bad, my mother would have just picked a side, even the bad side. It was confusing that sometimes she would be up at four in the morning to drive me all over the state to compete at horse shows, and other times I was late every day for school because I could not get her out of bed to drive me. For my third and fourth grades, bang in the middle of my most ardent love for Jesus, I attended a strict religious school that, unlike my previous school, did not have a bus I could take. My grades, never very good, got even worse. I asked my mom how I could get her up to get me to school on time. Her answer was that while I was making my breakfast, I should make her a cup of coffee, bring it to her, and tell her, "It's a bright new day that the Lord has made us."

I kept being late, and eventually begged to go back to my old school. My pink Bible, embossed with my name, sat on the shelf and began to collect dust while instead I pivoted to books like *The Egypt Game* and *The Secret Garden.*

Easter Sunday, I wake up bleary-eyed and lie in bed a long time, watching shadows on the ceiling. I can't shake the images from the day before: the pink flip-flops of the girls waiting in doorways, the smiling Disney princesses on the blankets being sold in stalled traffic, the pristine yard of the Mormon temple behind high bars. What are frozen pictures for me are other people's lived reality, day in, day out, in a place that's been divorced from itself. El Paso and Juárez are like conjoined twins who might be able to exist separated from each other but can't ever thrive.

I'm leaving El Paso soon, and I want more time here. I make a list of things I want to do when I'm back in town on my way west, unaware that when I return to this place, the safest city in America, everyone will be in mourning because twenty-three people will have been murdered in yet another mass shooting.

Down in Texas in the Big Bend country
whose green expanse
is cut and traced with wide ravines
and with small creeks
"Hollering Woman Creek"
"Cracker Creek"
people here in Texas have an unacknowledged sense
of humor.

—SJD

Chapter Fourteen

Marfa

> I think the sheer fact of women talking, being, paradoxical, inexplicable, flip, self-destructive but above all else public is the most revolutionary thing in the world.
>
> —CHRIS KRAUS, *I LOVE DICK*

Before I left for this trip, I met with a medium. Why not? He was wearing a simple black button-down, work trousers, and heavy boots. In a warehouse partially used for theater storage, we sat in two fat, comfortable chairs facing each other, each with a glass of water beside us, and a discreet box of tissues nearby. It was the same setup (minus the puppets) as my therapist's office. I sat across from him while he closed his eyes, said a prayer, and then began to describe to me what images my chakras were inspiring him to see. It was extremely Californian.

"You are going into the desert," he said. I kept quiet. "You're going into the desert and you're walking a very long ways. Actually, that's not right. You're not walking, because you're a snake. You're a rattlesnake, so you're slithering, but on your forked tongue there is always a blooming rose. Wherever you are in the desert, whenever you stop, make sure to bury something sweet in the sand, otherwise the bitter ghosts will haunt you."

I had no idea what to make of this, other than to be oddly flattered by the idea that I was a rattlesnake with a rose on my tongue. A friend drew me this image, and I've got it up in Minnie, another little talisman to meditate on either while stuck in traffic or on the long stretches of empty road. At one point, a glossy truck blasting music revs up loudly behind me, annoyed I'm only going five over the speed limit. It swerves around me and passes. As I watch it angrily speed on into the impressive dark, my eyes catch on my rattlesnake drawing.

It feels perverse to associate this image with my mother, who would have no other reference for snakes beyond the devil tempting Eve. I have her Bible, marked up with as many notes in the margins and tucked-in index cards as my copy of David Mitchell's *Cloud Atlas*. In between some of the wafer-thin pages are stray pieces of her hair. The big book still smells like smoke, nearly twenty years later. I'm not surprised, the hours she sat in her big bed, poring over this worn book, smoking, always smoking.

In her Bible, as notated as it is, the margins around the story of Adam and Eve are naked—in fact, she doesn't really start marking up pages and making her own commentary until the book of Deuteronomy, although like all good Evangelicals, the overwhelming majority of her attention was clearly focused on the New Testament, rather than the Old. I don't know if my mother literally believed women were responsible for sin in the world. Even the question brings her voice to my mind, telling me not to worry about sin because anyone who believes in the power of the Lord, who has accepted Him as savior, has been washed in His blood and lives in grace. That's what my mother would think when looking at this snake. When I look at it, I think of Joseph Campbell:

> Sometimes the serpent is represented as a circle eating its own tail. That's an image of life. Life sheds one generation after another, to be born again. The serpent represented immortal energy and consciousness engaged in the field of time, constantly throwing off death and being born again.[1]

Ouroboros, the snake that eats its own tail, is supposed to represent wholeness, infinity. When I think of my mother, of her mother, I see the same snake trying to learn the same lessons, over and over, shedding skins into new generations, attempting to end the cycle. All these miles in Minnie, I'm slithering along, trying to find my own tail.

The thing is, I don't know when else I'm going to be driving through west Texas, and I want to see Marfa.

Marfa, Texas, population 1,775 or thereabouts, is about two hundred miles east of El Paso, along US Route 90—south from Van Horn. Once you're off the 10, you see a lot of signs that most city dwellers won't recognize: FM, RR, RM.

"So the Texas Highway Department was started a hundred some years ago," explained Jennifer Wright, a public affairs officer for the Texas Department of Transportation whom I met in El Paso. (With her honeyed blond locks, I couldn't help but instantly think of the iconic and beloved Tami Taylor, Mrs. Coach, of *Friday Night Lights*, played by Connie Britton.)

"It was just farm-to-market roads, so that the farmers could get their trucks and wagons out of the mud. That's why they started building roads, so that they could haul the carts, drive the trucks. That is what all the FM, RR, and RM roads are." They stand for farm-to-market, ranch road, and ranch-to-market.

It's a desolate but lovely drive to Marfa. I remember how Jennifer and her husband, Bob, gave me pointed advice about gassing up before I left El Paso and carrying a lot of water.

"You don't want to break down in west Texas," Bob said, knocking on the table for emphasis.

"Girl, the buzzards will have you. Do not let your gas tank go below half a tank," instructed Jennifer.

The land looks flat, but there are dips. I keep thinking that I should be able to see Marfa from a hundred miles away, but it is beyond a dip and on the other side of a wee hill. It's somewhere along the 90 that there's a Border Patrol stop. Traffic slows to a crawl, and eventually a young officer signals for me to roll down the window. Am I an American citizen? Am I traveling alone? Why am I going to Marfa? I don't know what I'm supposed to say in this situation, or why I have to answer these questions. In my nervousness, I answer all his questions earnestly.

For most of its existence Marfa was just another cow town in west Texas—and there are still a lot of cattle around. Then, in the 1980s, sculptor Donald Judd decided to make it an art town. He bought a defunct army base complete with empty barracks, moved his entire body of work there, and called it home.

In the wake of Judd's flag-planting in Marfa, more high culture followed. Now along with Judd's collection, Marfa is known for a Prada store that never opens, a television show that only lasted one season called *I Love Dick*, and the mysterious Marfa Lights. Locals and tourists alike report that on certain nights, large balls of white light zoom around, or hover, fading in and out of luminescence. No one really knows what they are—and that's my favorite thing about them.

The Prada store that never opens is art. The creation of artist duo Elmgreen & Dragset, Prada Marfa was meant to be a "pop architectural land art project."[2] It's a small square shop with a collection of Prada wares—ruthlessly expensive shoes and purses—on display. If you're planning on robbing it, you're a little late. In its first iteration, an adobe that would eventually disintegrate back to rubble, the windows were smashed and the designer goods were looted. Now the building has a security system, much stronger glass, and only right-foot shoes.

These days it's a place where passersby take selfies. In fact, when I pass by it, on the outskirts of a town named Valentine, there's a group of three or four women posing for pictures in front of it. I will see this group of women everywhere I go for the next three days.

My first day in Marfa I discover that in a town that is only 1.6 square miles, no one walks anywhere, unless you're a tourist. The wide-open streets, often just gravel, are empty when I meander over to the much-lauded Marfa Burrito for scrambled eggs wrapped in a tortilla. I mention this subpar breakfast situation to someone later, lamenting that I'd probably ordered incorrectly. "Nah," they say with a shrug. "You're not gonna get the best of anything in Marfa."

Meandering around, I duck into an expensive shop, Communitie. There are bandannas for $95 or a cotton canvas tote for $1,350. There is a hip-looking dude with long hair, low-slung Wranglers, and jangled teeth. I strike up a conversation, and he seems like he could take it or leave it. While I work too hard at small talk, a gaggle of women, all wearing hats I don't know that they've ever worn at home, walk past—and his eyes go right to them. They're all dressed like they're going to a hipster country music festival. There's a lot of fringe. This is when I realize that the men of Marfa have a plum situation working for them: a constant stream of young women, usually from Los Angeles, pass through town looking to have a good time. As one woman put it to me, "The men in this town get to have their pick." The one thing this dude does say to me is that my hunch is right: only tourists walk in this town.

"You're still in Texas. We like our trucks."

It's so quiet and so still as I walk the couple of blocks to my rental. The little houses with chairs on the porches, the patchy lawns—the light softens the parts of this town that are ragged. In this light, Marfa feels like that perfectly worn pair of jeans that are so soft they are just on the verge of fraying. I like it here, and I don't have anything pressing on my schedule, so I decide to stay the full week.

The Chinati Foundation, on the former army base, houses a permanent collection not only of Donald Judd pieces but also of Dan Flavin, whose work involves neon light. There are different tours you can take of the works Chinati has in permanent and visiting installations, and I opt for the all-day affair.

Joining me on the tour are an older couple from Dallas who look like they're straight off the golf course and show a deep knowledge of contemporary art, a single man from Brooklyn who is a baker and returns to the Marfa area whenever he can, and a couple from Manhattan who are both reporters for the *New York Times.* We trade people we all know, including my editor from when I recapped television shows for the *Times* website. First stop on our tour guide Jessica's agenda is an exhibit of Judd's hundred boxes of milled silver aluminum. Housed in two former artillery sheds (which still have signs in German from when they were also used for prisoners of war), each of the boxes has the same dimensions (41 x 51 x 72 inches) and exterior, but the interiors differ. The only thing I think is beautiful or interesting about this art is the Texan light that falls on them. While we walk between buildings and hear more about Judd, I think about everything that was going on here before Judd decided to move in, since humans have been in this area for ten thousand years. In fact, there's a cave nearby, the Spirit Eye, which has Native artifacts at least five thousand years old.[3] The Flavin light installations, on the other hand, are lovely. And yet what I'm specifically in awe of is how wonderfully awkward it is being in a large, empty space with strangers, all aimlessly wondering how long we're supposed to look at colored light on white walls. What I like most about the day-long tour is when Jessica tells me about the party in the river.

Before the events of September 11, 2001, the border between the United States and Mexico was treated differently. People in the Big Bend area of Texas, south of the 10 and right up next to Mexico, crossed the river daily, between Boquillas and Paso Lajitas and the American town of Lajitas. After 9/11, the border was closed, and the closest port of entry was fifty miles away. The music festival Voices from Both Sides, also known as the Fiesta Protesta, was created to have at least one day a year when everyone congregates in the river itself to celebrate the duality of border life. People drive from as far as Houston to visit with family who live on the other side of the border. I'm in luck—the festival is coming up.

It takes me about three hours to drive from Marfa, through a landscape that is a bit desert, a bit mountain, a bit prairie. First I pass through Alpine, where most of the people who work in Marfa actually live. A motel sign reads GLUTEN-FREE BEDS AVAILABLE. There's tension between the two towns. Alpine looks on Marfa as an enclave filled with rich, entitled hipsters, and Marfa looks on Alpine as a busted town filled with a lot of cantankerous hippies.

"I never go there," one Marfa guy told me about Alpine. "Never."

As I get farther south from Marfa, I realize I'm in a bit of a hinterland. West Texas is the demarcation between the West and the South and is so far from Houston and Dallas that I feel like I'm on an outer rim planet; the vast emptiness I find so comforting could very easily strike someone else as boring or, in this heat, deadly. "I mean, one of the things I loved about being in west Texas was that everybody hated it," Dan Flores said to me, back in New Mexico.

Lajitas is a blink-and-you-miss it spot, but beyond the town I start seeing cars and trucks parked on the side of the road, so I know I'm getting close, plus I can hear the tubas. Any social gathering that has a bunch of happy dogs roaming around is probably going to be one that I enjoy, so I'm heartened when, in the jammed, makeshift parking lot, there is already a pack of them, tongues lolling, meandering around and greeting newcomers. People have set up tents with barbecues and coolers. Blankets are spread out; there are folding chairs and the sound of beer cans cracking open. I follow the sound of music down to the riverbank. The Rio Grande is not very grande at the moment; at this little bend in the river, it's barely waist-high, but that hasn't stopped someone from bringing a impressive rainbow unicorn Pegasus pool float, covered in a gaggle of kids screeching joyfully in both Spanish and English.

Across the river is a small stage where a band is cranking out tunes over a rickety sound system, but no one here cares. People are standing in the river, crossing back and forth. The smell of charcoal and lighter fluid, the perfume of summer, wafts over everyone. I was expecting to be able to buy lunch, but there aren't any food vendors, only one table selling stickers and T-shirts. I buy a set of stickers and think about putting them on my bumper—could make the drive back to Marfa interesting.

"You know what it means?" the woman behind the table asks me, eyebrow raised. It feels a little bit like a test.

"'Fuck your wall,'" I say. *Chinga tu muro.* She hands over the stickers, grinning.

Back down at the river, it's time for everyone to join hands. I see my tour guide from the Chinati Foundation, Jessica. She is wading through the river, wearing a straw hat on its last legs, smiling hugely as she photographs the kids on the river floatie. A lopsided circle of Americans and Latinos and those in between forms in the river, and everyone starts to sing—I don't recognize the song, but I make a note to try to figure it out.

An hour or so later, after the Mexican stage quiets down, it's time for the Americans to take over the late afternoon's entertainment. By this time mostly everyone is either sunburned, drunk, high, or some combination of all three, and I've got a long drive back to Marfa. Headed home, I hit another Immigration stop, and once more the agent who questions me looks younger than I am. I'm alone, but so many people driving home tonight will be in a caravan of vans, filled not with books and a mattress but with kids asleep in the back, the dog snoring in the way back, everyone smelling of the river and sunblock and with sand between their toes. I wonder how many people's last memories of Voices from Both Sides will be a flashlight in their face, and barked questions.

A couple evenings later, when I show up at the Lost Horse Saloon, Julie Pham and I are wearing the same exact thing: army-green jumpsuits and sneakers. Julie and I met at the river party when she noticed that I was taking notes and asked me if I was a journalist. Julie has been in Marfa for about four years, covering west Texas for radio and print outlets. While she loves it here, she misses the one thing that no one in a small town has: anonymity.

"Is it possible to keep a secret in Marfa?" I ask.

"No. Unless you tell nobody nothing at all. No."

"I imagine that if you have a bad night out—"

"Everybody knows. Everybody knows. I got rid of all my slutty clothes when I moved here."

On the back patio, nursing drinks and watching a rainstorm take a long time coming in, we talked about her Texan life. When I get out my ear pods and phone to record our conversation, Pham laughs and tells me that she hadn't seen ear pods until she visited New York recently. Rainstorms move faster than technology in west Texas (but not as fast as gossip). Born in Houston, one of the largest Vietnamese enclaves in the country, and Texas-educated, Julie has lived her life almost entirely in the bluebonnet state.

"Did I identify or see myself as a Texan growing up?" she says. "Not really. It wasn't something I really thought about. It wasn't until I left the state that I realized how Texan I was. The things I identify as being Texan are a sort of openness. A generosity. And it's not always like that, but there is a sort of baseline friendliness here. A friendly vibe you get from people. Whereas when I went to Massachusetts for a few months . . ." She laughs.

Likewise, I'd never felt more like a Californian than when I moved to New York and met actual WASPs. In my first roommate tiff with a friend who could trace her lineage to the *Mayflower*, I was baffled by the line: "Yes I *am* annoyed with you, but the last thing we should do is *talk about it*." As cold as a fresh gin and tonic in August.

I tell Julie how I noticed that the guy working in the expensive store was also working at Chinati, and my tour guide there also being in Lajitas; the roaming hordes of tourists I keep seeing in the same general goods store, and at the pricey restaurant that most locals can't afford to eat in. Part of that is how small-town life is, but there's something else at play: no single job pays well enough for locals to be able to afford how expensive everything is getting, so most people work multiple jobs. This comes up when I ask Julie how she feels about the influx of newcomers in the past several years.

"It seems like before, people who came here sort of knew why they were coming here," Julie says. "They chose this place for a reason. For the art or for the space or for the light. Often because of the art. But at least they had a knowledge of this place. People come here now for the brand."

It's the bachelorette parties that tip me off to what it is I think I've been trying to understand about Marfa. It's not all that different than Las Vegas—they are both destinations that serve a lifestyle fantasy to those passing through, and whose local populations depend on that tourism but exist outside of the story.

Las Vegas was developed and rose out of the desert in a manifestation of commercial will. Marfa too only exists because someone thought it should, and not because it was near water or a rail line. Rather than glitzy lights, swanky cocktail lounges, and the whiff of desperation that Las Vegas offers, Marfa provides a different sort of enticement, a coming-together of the physical (life in cattle country Texas) with the intellectual (high modernist art). It's big money and big art and big men, literally. The first of Judd's works to be installed at the Chinati Foundation was *15 Untitled Works in Concrete 1980–1984*, featuring large concrete blocks outside along the perimeter of the property. Chinati, I should add, does feature female artists, some visiting, and in the permanent collection there is a piece by the sculptor Roni Horn.

"There's this weird thing of respecting what he did, but also wanting to dismantle it. Because all of this"—that is, Marfa itself—"exists because of him, this very masculine, macho move," Julie says of Judd. "But the town was dying on the vine; people will say over and over again: Marfa only exists today because of Judd."

It's the art world of Marfa, the legacy of Judd and his ilk, that Julie feels tension with.

"There's the local Hispanic population here, and then there's this art world. And then transplants, newcomers. And a lot of that world is being invested in literature, poetry, and contemporary art. And I am interested in all these things, to a degree. But I don't feel like I belong in that world."

"Is that a class distinction?" I ask. Earlier in the week I had asked Julie if she wanted to join me for a poetry reading by visiting poet and professor Kaveh Akbar, and she had gracefully declined.

"In some ways. I don't know why. I don't know why I feel sort of unwelcome and uncomfortable in that space. No one has said anything, no one has made me feel this way. But I just always feel outside."

Listening to Julie, I'm reminded again of the liminality of El Paso, and how often I think of Sacramento as *home*, even though I wonder if I belong there now. These eerie in-between spaces can feel cold or off-putting, but perhaps there is something hopeful, even optimistic about those spaces and times in our lives: between childhood and adulthood, or the couple of years you live in a weird art project village in west Texas. "Liminal spaces are a refuge for people for whom nostalgia has lost its sweetness," Natalie Wynn says in her long-ass YouTube video. "If going home is lonely to you, the liminal is a refuge for you. It's comforting. I feel like a renter in this world; home is always an improvised situation. And sometimes liminal art makes me feel like that's an exciting way to live. I'm not stuck in some delusion of the past. All my longings are in front of me."[4]

Being comfortable with change is akin to being comfortable with liminality; and to have grown up with perpetual change, with Circus Life, as I call it, is to flourish when and where others are uncomfortable. As a teenager I felt the strain of being born in Southern California, formed in Northern California, then only feeling my westernness when I went east; but as I delve deeper into this trip, into the liminality inherent in any journey, I realize that the unsettledness of my life has been its own sort of gift. I'm like a green purse that matches everything because it matches nothing; if I belong nowhere, maybe I can fit in anywhere.

"I have my people," continues Julie. "A small group of people who are all kind of outside those things. I mean, I live in far west Texas, in the middle of nowhere. I'm a Vietnamese woman with no other Vietnamese people."

Soon enough Julie will have to head west on the 10, back to El Paso to cover a mass shooting, but for tonight we just hug, and I drive less than a mile to the rented apartment I've stayed in much longer than I expected to. When it's finally time for me to get back on the road, I'm sorry to go. As odd and small as Marfa is, I'm drawn to the beauty of it, how empty it feels, and the train that goes right through the middle of town.

Back in Sacramento, in my bedroom in the house on Forty-Fourth, I would lie awake at night and listen for the sound of the train horn in the distance. In Marfa, the train is so close it can be deafening, but I still like it, especially when the horn echoes from a distance and, in that sleepy in-between twilight, it almost feels like I'm twelve again, in my room with horse posters on the walls. Trains will be with me the entirety of the trip, as the 10 haunts old rail lines. Before I leave town, I go for a walk, even though only tourists walk. A sun-shower just passed through town, and the hot concrete doused with rain has its own perfume. I wander down to the train tracks and sit for a moment, thinking about maybe coming back. I'm grateful to have met Julie, to have danced by the Rio Grande, and I'm confident about moving on into deeper Texas. I have no idea that I'm about to have the worst day of my entire trip.

Chapter Fifteen

The Bad Night I

It was clear that it was going to be a bad day. As usual, I didn't see my mom before school. Except for my brief adventure going to a religious school, since earliest grade school, I'd been getting up and out of the house either by myself or with Colin. When I got home, though, I heard her banging around in her bedroom. At some point she announced that we were going to the grocery store. In the produce aisle, she stood still, blocking the plastic bag dispenser, praying in her normal mumble, eyes rolling. She was a bit louder than usual, and a woman waiting to peel off a bag stood awkwardly, taking in the scene. I tugged on my mom's sleeve to move her out of the way, and like a provoked snake she hissed and grabbed at my forearm. She squeezed me hard enough that I made a noise, and she got very close to my face. I remember the other woman watching us, her worried expression. It was new for Mom to be this unsettled in public. She'd pulled my hair, grabbed me by the neck, but it had always been at home, in private. This public display was off somehow.

"Sorry we're in your way," I said to the woman, who waved me off, no worries, and my mom dropped my forearm. Her eyes seemed to clear for a moment before they took up rolling again. I put things in the cart while she pushed and prayed, talking to herself even while paying the cashier, who wasn't so much concerned as freaked out.

At home, I turned off the car radio as we pulled into the driveway and smiled at her, my usual strategy for diffusing tension. She sucked air in through her teeth and pulled her hand back as if to lash out. I apologized, fumbling for the door. I tried to explain I was just turning it off because we were home, not to cut off whatever she was listening to. She made a dubious sound. I brought the groceries in while she went back to her room. The sun set. The noises from her bedroom started sounding like she was moving furniture.

As on most nights, I called a friend to help me with my math homework—I couldn't do it on my own. Twice my mom came in and yelled at me to get off the phone, and I showed her the papers spread out on the bed: "It's for school!"

Around ten or eleven she came in, vibrating with anger, slammed the door, and started yelling. It was hard for me to understand what she was saying. Sometimes she was screaming at me, and sometimes she was screaming at God, begging for help. The gist was that I "didn't respect her" and I was ungrateful. She screamed that I had shamed her at the grocery store, that everyone could see what a monster I was.

I very clearly remember thinking, *If she hits me, I'm moving to Los Angeles.*

Chapter Sixteen

San Antonio

> Deep within my heart lies a melody / A song of old San Antone / Where in dreams I live with a memory / Beneath the stars, all alone.
>
> —"SAN ANTONIO ROSE"

I have done what the heavy San Antonio sky could not: cracked open into uproarious waterworks. Outside Minnie the air is dense, and inside there is a danger of a flash flood. Nearby, an obese woman wearing a wonderful bejeweled purple shirt with matching leggings is smoking and watching me warily, which tells me I am approaching a loud sort of wailing. I have spent a large part of today crying either on the phone or in front of real live Texans, which nobody enjoyed.

I am sick, with a low fever, and have spent the past three days in my lumpy Airbnb Ikea bed, trying to sleep, but my whole body aches and I can't stop shivering.

It all starts so innocuously. On the 10 from Fort Stockton, I remember Jennifer's advice in El Paso, and gas up the van and pick up more water—I'm about to enter the long stretch of the 10 most infamous for being big, empty, and flat. Many of the "towns" I stop through seem to have only a gas station for all their needs. Out here there's more semitrucks than cars, and I spend a lot of time gripping the steering wheel in fear watching speeding drivers cut off truckers, slam on the brakes in front of them, or attempt to pass them on the right. Over the course of the whole trip, I saw multiple burned-out carcasses of semis, like the one still burning by the side of the highway I veer around outside of Junction, Texas. When I was sixteen, I worked at a public relations firm for a summer, mostly on a safety campaign for the California Trucking Association. I had spent hours looking at numbers of fatal accidents involving semitrucks. The horrific stats imprinted so deeply in my brain that I find myself obsessively making sure I can see semi drivers in their side mirrors—it's the only way I know they can see me.

Trucks make up most of the traffic along the 10 (2,459 miles) as it is the only all-weather west-east transcontinental interstate. I-90 from Seattle to Boston (3,085 miles), I-80 from San Francisco to Teaneck, New Jersey (2,906 miles), and I-40 from Barstow, California, to Wilmington, North Carolina (2,554 miles) all have to deal with real winters, while the 10, being the southernmost route, only really has to deal with rain. Now that many Americans are shopping exclusively online and deliveries are constant, truck traffic along the 10 has skyrocketed, and the road is crumbling beneath the weight of all that freight. When I am not keeping an eye out for truckers in their sideview mirrors, I am gawking at the green.

Somewhere between Junction and San Antonio, I've entered a totally different dimension: one with humidity. From here on out, my days and nights will feel totally different. Suddenly everything is green, with a level of lushness that approaches jungle. I pull over to fill up the gas tank, buy some DayQuil for this tickle in my throat, and text back people who wish me a happy birthday. I am now thirty-seven years old and I celebrate by playing the new Beyoncé record very loudly. When I get out of the van, the wetness in the air hits me like a wall. After months of the dryness of Arizona, New Mexico, and west Texas, the humidity feels exotic, otherworldly. I have crossed over; I am in it now. What is it? I think it's the South.

What does that mean to me? It's Harper Lee's *To Kill a Mockingbird*, and Billie Holiday singing "Strange Fruit." It's the grits my mother would make with cheese, butter, and black pepper, and New Orleans Square in Disneyland. I don't know anything about the South. Since talking to family, I know that my mother lived awhile in both Virginia and Florida, but I'm not sure for how long. Did she live there long enough to have a particularly southern view of things? I don't know. But I know my grandmother was as southern as it gets, and that's who raised my mother. Could her southernness have been passed down to me? What are the lessons my mother taught me when she was able to teach me things? She taught me how to lay formal table settings, and how to serve tea. She taught me to either smile when someone insulted you to your face or knock their fucking teeth out and make sure other people saw you do it. She taught me men were to be either feared or pitied. Above all, she taught me, "We don't talk about that." Are those things especially southern? *I don't know.*

All I know of San Antonio is the Alamo and *Still Breathing*. The former was the site of the 1836 battle in the Texas Revolution and the latter is a 1997 film with Brendan Fraser, who figured largely in my burgeoning sexual awareness. If your first thought is *The Whale*, in which he plays an obese recluse, remember that nineties Brendan Fraser includes *Encino Man*, *George of the Jungle*, and *The Mummy*.

The plot of *Still Breathing* is simple enough: Former artist, now cynical con artist Joanna Going mistakes Fraser's Manic Pixie Dream Dude for her latest mark. The man she thinks is a wealthy Texan oil tycoon is, in fact, a charming street puppeteer who sometimes sleeps on top of his piano in his aesthetically cluttered Victorian mansion and, like all the men in his family, has visions of his one true love. At some point Fraser waxes poetic about San Antonio in such a way it makes me think that writer-director James F. Robinson, himself a Texan, has had his own love affair with the city.

> "It's like an old woman who's lived long enough to know who she is. There are ghosts there. . . . Most people who go there would just see the mini malls, potholes in the streets, and a lot of lawns that need watering. The really cool stuff is hiding out and you really have to know where to look for it."

That sounds like a lovely place, a place I would like to explore. All of it, however, the mini malls and the cool stuff, has missed me nearly entirely because from the moment I arrived in San Antonio, I've been sick. Really sick.

My days in this Airbnb are up, and I've seen nothing, gone nowhere. I decide to check into a proper hotel, in the hopes that some real sleep and food will get me back on my feet so I can avoid a trip to urgent care. It's Memorial Day, and I somehow manage to snag a room in a hotel near the River Walk, a meandering park that hugs the San Antonio River as it dips right through the center of town, and the Alamo. Head throbbing like an overfilled balloon, I start to pack up and load the van. I've just lugged the last of my gear and hauled the door closed when I turn around and see a white dog looking up at me. It's a pit bull, flea-ridden and skinny, with a face that says, *Help me.*

"Fuck," I say out loud to the dog and no one else.

* * *

It probably started back in Tombstone. Just because you have experienced grief before does not mean you know what to do the next time Death visits your house.

It's been nearly twenty years since my mother died, and I think of her all the time, dream of her often, but rarely do my thoughts carry the salty weight of grief. My feelings are more about regret and nostalgia. Her death does not feel like a trauma anymore, but a sad fact. Since her death when I was a freshman in college, I have comforted my friends when their parents or loved ones died. When I'm asked for advice, I say things like: It doesn't matter how lucid you think you are, how bizarrely hyperreal things may seem from time to time, you will lose the entire first year after a death. It will be a blur, whole weeks, months gone. Perhaps if you keep a notebook more will stay with you, but I have found that visiting that notebook is like going back to a strange island no one wants to visit again.

I say that they have to forgive themselves for the days they feel all right, or hungry, or eager to do something fun. I say that they may pivot from a Buddha-like level acceptance of the evanescence of life, to eating, fucking, working, or shopping as if the last sands of their hourglass are about to run out. I say: It will not occur to you that this orgy of action and anger might have something to do with the fact that someone just died. I know this sounds nuts, but it's true: you will not be able to make the connection. You would only know this if you had been paying attention to the tide slowly rolling in.

For two decades I have given this advice, each time more sure that I have reached a deeper understanding of what it means to bury someone. So it should surprise no one that what was happening to me, what started on the streets of Tombstone and really began to blossom when I got sick after my birthday, had nothing to do with me wanting to avoid fake cowboys, or one evening drinking too much, but everything to do with my lizard brain using this goddamn dog to make a point.

First, I get him some water. He laps at it with little interest, then goes back to a collection of bricks beside the building, trying to keep in the shade. After thirty minutes of waiting on 311, I start calling veterinarians. It is 11 a.m. on the Friday of Memorial Day weekend. No one wants to pick up the phone, let alone speak. No one will take a dog off the street pro bono, and none will hold him. Also, no one can confirm for me whether, if I managed to get Animal Services on the phone, the dog will go to a kill shelter. I eventually find a vet who will at least check to see if the dog is microchipped. The moment he notices that I've opened my passenger door, the dog simply moseys over, gingerly climbs in, and curls up on the floor, sighing.

Once I get to the vet, the ladies there are friendly and kind, and offer me some Advil—I must look like I'm sick and stressed. The dog, who has started wagging his tail and licking my hand, meanders off with one of the nice ladies for the microchip inspection while I try to find a no-kill shelter that is open and has space for a medium-sized dog. Most of them are closing early for the holiday, and the others ask me: Is the dog a pit bull? I lie to the couple of people I get on the phone and tell them I don't know what kind of dog it is. It is definitely a pit bull. I call the hotel I'm supposed to be checking into: no, they do not allow dogs. The nice veterinary receptionist, who is looking forward to a barbecue with her whole family to celebrate the holiday, calls the San Antonio VCA (Veterinary Centers of America); they have the space to flea-dip a larger dog and also the space to shelter him. I can bring him over soon. A bit later, the vet tech and the dog, whom I have named Blanco for the street I found him on and for his white coat, come back,

Blanco's tail wagging. The good news is that the dog was chipped, and we have a phone number for the owner. The bad news is that the owner was recently murdered.

I don't know how to write about Scott. I don't want to. I only know that I can't write about what happened in San Antonio without writing about him. I thought that because I had buried my mother it meant I knew how to bury him. I even have a problem with that sentence. I didn't bury him. Many people, his family, his friends, we all buried him. We are all still burying him, a year later.

I have underestimated how different it is to lose a friend, rather than a parent, and the biggest difference of all, suicide. Cancer makes a sort of sense; it is a natural disease. A horrible accident makes sense, as accidents happen. Suicide makes no sense to those who have not danced with their own darkness right up to the edge, and it is because of how senseless it seems that we, those left behind, have worked so hard to create narratives that restore order. In this way too, we need stories. Last year I spent my birthday flying to Scotland because they'd found his body.

An hour or so later, my clothes feel like steel wool on my skin, and my head is pounding. One of the receptionists calls me over: There's been a misunderstanding; the VCA does not shelter dogs and cannot help me find one. Once Blanco's flea dip and visit with the doctor are over, I have to take him. I ask if she can put me in touch with someone at a local no-kill shelter. She doesn't say anything, but her face says, *Lady, that is not my job.* Then I get a text—it's a response to the text I sent earlier to the number associated with Blanco's microchip.

Hi! I have found your sweet dog! I am sure you have been missing him. How would you like to proceed?

Ok I'm sorry I'm not home but my boyfriend takes care of him but now my boyfriend just passed away in couple day ago. I'm cannot make it home can you please Return back in San Antonio or Paul please

My boyfriend just died in Couple day

I'm so sorry for your loss, that's horrible. Would you like me to return the dog? To you or your boyfriend's home?

Yes please so you know how long my dog 🐶 runs out side

I am in San Antonio and will happily drive him to you.

I'm not sure how long he's been on the streets, but I am with him at the vet making sure he gets treated for fleas.

No my boyfriend get kill in Couple days ago

He'll be healthy and happy to see you

Where should I deliver him?

Sorry I'm For away from home
I am at I am in Arkansas City
I am working right now

Is there someone here who can watch
him until you get home?

My boyfriend love him a lot
No my boyfriend died.

I understand. Do you want the dog?

Can you please return him back in the
Paul for me please

I don't understand what the Paul is.
The pound?

Yes

So you do not want him.

I just lost adopting him for two months.

Would your boyfriend's family want to adopt him?

They are living in Houston.

I am going to Houston soon.

If you want to ask them, I would drive
him there.

Anything to avoid him ending up in the pound.
Then she sends me two pictures of the boyfriend with the dog.

This is a my boyfriends. Love him Alo.
And thanks very much to keep the dog
for me.

I'm staring at the picture of this man, who is apparently dead, when my phone rings—the woman is now FaceTiming me. I answer, but I can't see her face. Her accent is thick, and she speaks quickly. Her boyfriend was a gangster, and he was murdered. She's not home; she can't take the dog. It was her boyfriend's dog; he was a gangster. He was murdered and she cannot take the dog. My head is pounding, and I feel like I might throw up all over the linoleum of the waiting room. I tell the woman I'm sorry for her loss again, tell her I'll figure out what to do with the dog, and get off the phone. I've enough time to go to San Antonio Animal Care Services to see if they've got room (no one is answering the phone at 3 p.m. on a Friday), but before I do, I text my therapist and ask if she has ten minutes to talk.

A devout dog lover, my therapist calmly asks: What kind of dog is it? Have I seen him interact with other dogs? How big is he? Is he older, or a puppy? A lot of these answers I just don't know. She asks me about what I have next on the trip: more museums, interviews, and a trip to Austin to spend the day at the Texas Department of Transportation library.

"So, you don't know if you can leave this dog anywhere, because there's a chance he could tear up the room?"

"That's right."

"And you can't leave him in the vehicle, because it's so hot."

"No, of course not."

"And you can't bring him into libraries, museums, and restaurants, and that's what you've got lined up for the next couple of weeks."

"I don't think so, no, unless I get him made into a therapy dog."

"But you don't know if he'd be good in those spaces, because you don't know this dog."

". . . I guess."

"So, let me ask you something: Why do you feel like you have to save this dog?"

"Well, I found him, so I guess he's my responsibility. And I can see how cool it could be, to have a dog on this trip."

"If it happens to turn out that he's nonaggressive, a good traveler, and doesn't chew on anything."

". . . Yeah. . . . And, I guess I'm aware of how much people would love it. You know, on Instagram."

"And?"

"And . . . because if I don't, who will?"

"Salute the magpie!" Scott told me once when we were in a forest near Glasgow, rain misting down on us. Being American, I had no idea what he was talking about. He told me that if you see a solitary magpie, you salute it, and if you have the time you say, "Good morning, Mr. Magpie, how fares thy lady wife?" (or some version thereof), but he didn't know why. I looked it up later and told him: Magpies mate for life. If you see one alone, it's thought to be bad luck. We salute the magpie to ward off the bad luck of being alone in the world.

Scott and I first met briefly in 2009, when his band Frightened Rabbit played a gig in Brooklyn at a bar that later on became a children's gym. We met again in 2013 when the band was on tour in Los Angeles, and I invited everyone to my favorite taco place, Guisados. Suddenly I had hulking Scotsmen in my tiny Fiat bombing down the Sunset Strip.

I was embarrassed to be as big a fan as I was, but the coterie of Frightened Rabbit friends in Los Angeles was a good group of people, a great hang of Brits and Americans. I had just moved back to the city, and since no one loves Los Angeles like an expatriate Brit (all that "midday sun" Noël Coward went on about), the times together were of mutual romance with the city. I never forgot how much I loved Scott's music, but I am well suited for getting over someone's fame. I also enjoyed reminding him, he wasn't *that* famous.

There were road trips to see the band play Red Rocks, and drinks when the band was passing through town. I had posted something on my blog, an invitation for anyone who wanted mail—if you sent me an address, I wrote you a letter, and included whatever else I thought might suit: a sticker, a funny business card left on my car window, a Polaroid. This was when I was having trouble writing, so I was looking for an exercise in pointless creativity. Scott, reminded of the times he and his bandmates would earnestly send out demos, sometimes with a biscuit, to record companies, was tickled by the idea and asked for a letter. We became pen pals and wrote to each other for the rest of his life. Letters, emails, flurries of texts. It was an epistolary friendship, an indirect but deeply felt intimacy, that waxed and waned according to how available Scott was. Sometimes I heard from him all day every day, and sometimes there would be silent months, but I couldn't help but collect things to share with him: a strange moment I happened to photograph, a perfect lyric I heard somewhere. He could be drily funny; he could be a pill. He told me he was afraid of boring "that big brain of yours," and that all he wanted to do was live in a hut somewhere and draw all the time. There was a brief period when Scott lived in Los Angeles, but it was a dark time for him, and we hardly saw each other.

The night he went missing in Edinburgh I sat on my sofa at home in Los Angeles. I texted with people in Scotland and friends in Los Angeles, waited for news. It made sense to me to ask my mother to watch over him, to guide him, either back to us, or across. Across to what, I don't know. I only know what I hope: That when we die, the energy that makes us returns to a collective pool. That we were never made, and so we can never be truly unmade; that as Scott moved from one state of energy to another, there was someone there to guide him.

It also made sense to me to light a white candle. I could not sleep until either I heard news or that candle burned all the way down. While waiting, I read a book of Georgia O'Keeffe writings about her paintings. I was only just beginning to pay attention to her. The book had been a birthday gift, as mine was coming up. Perversely able to focus and dead set on staying awake, I turned the pages slowly and read O'Keeffe's own words about her work. I stared at the open desert landscapes she'd painted with the eyes of a woman set loose, the flowers that she refused to let others define for her. It's human to want to make a narrative to attempt to explain what we don't understand, though. A story is a form of control, even a story that allows for ambiguity; those are merely the things a storyteller chooses to keep blurry.

Some chose to tell a story that Scott knew the whole weekend what he was going to do. Others thought it was planned for an entire month.

Some felt if they'd only managed to get him on the phone, they could have stopped him. If only he'd stopped drinking, if only he'd gone to therapy. If only. A never-ending list of silver bullets.

At first the woman at the shelter tells me that they do not have room for a big dog.

"He's not that big, he's only a pit bull, he's not a mastiff."

"He's a pit bull?"

I've made a mistake. I feel like shit, and I don't want to cry in front of a stranger. I panic, and go back to the VCA to pick up the dog, whose real name, apparently, is Cletus. The vet told me earlier he is relatively healthy, minus the heartworm, for which he gave me a prescription, and the fleas, though the flea bath would take care of those. He urged me to adopt the dog, even when I tried to explain my situation.

Later, woozy and sitting in the van with the dog, air conditioner blasting, I finally get someone on the phone from 311's animal control department. Through a haze that is really beginning to feel like a bad dream, I listen as she tells me she cannot help me find a shelter to take the dog, nor can she confirm whether San Antonio Animal Care Services is a no-kill shelter. At some point I start crying—no, bawling—on the phone and confess: I just don't want to send this dog to its death. What do I do?

I have to submit the dog to the ACS via a website because the shelter does not admit drop-off dogs. You must reserve a spot and confirm with someone via email that they can take a dog. I just so happen to be lucky: when I check, there is one space for a large dog, and I have an hour and a half to get back to ACS and check him in. I race to get across town in the holiday Friday traffic, constantly checking my phone for the confirmation email.

Again I am confronted with a skeptical receptionist who, once she has my reservation in hand, is very gentle with me. I must look insane: fevered, clearly having cried recently, rambling about murdered gangsters. The last truck to the larger shelter facility is already outside and is just about to leave. Suddenly, after some paperwork, an employee, just trying to get out of there to start the weekend, asks me for the leash.

I'm hugging Blanco hard, while also handing the staffer the heartworm medicine I bought earlier, feeling like a mom trying to ensure that the lunchbox makes it onto the school bus. And then Blanco shuffles off, and I walk away, not wanting to watch him be put in a crate. I do not make it to the van before I start crying, but sitting behind the wheel is when I really let it rip. I realize, *I've just seen my monster.*

Joseph Campbell wrote about the hero's journey: the call to adventure, the descent into the underworld, resurrection and atonement. Campbell has his critics, but the journey he describes is universal: we all have some monster in the center of the maze waiting for us, one that reflects us back to ourselves. Our shame. In this journey that I'm on, who or what is the monster that is tailor-made to suit me? It's not that hard to figure out. Even the most casual observer of pop culture knows that the thing Superman is vulnerable to is Kryptonite—chunks of his destroyed home planet, the childhood he was forced to abandon all too soon.

Maybe someone else, like so many children of addicts, would be susceptible to alcohol or drugs, but I dodged those bullets. My downfall has never come in a bottle. It has always been love, love defined by absence. While summers and weekends were spent with my Los Angeles family, the day-to-day reality of my childhood was that my father was not there. Months would sometimes go by without me seeing him, though he called frequently, and would record himself reading books and then send me the tape and the book to read along with.

My mother, down the hall, was just as unreachable in her own way, behind the drugs and alcohol, and later her psychosis. I grew up to be someone who loves those who are not available because of distance, because of their anger, because of their girlfriends, or their wounds. Especially their wounds. I grew up thinking that to love someone was to heal them. That if I loved someone enough, they would be happy, and near.

The last thing I texted Scott was a piece of music. It is incandescent, airy, bright. It is hopeful.

This music is so beautiful, I want it in my bones, I said. I'd talked to him only days prior—giddy stories of vacation with friends, of platters of seafood and good wine. I wonder if he ever listened.

In the wake of his death, in a soggy Glasgow before the funeral, I resented everyone wondering what *they* could have done to stop him, as if they had superpowers the rest of us lacked. I watched people vying to be close to tragedy and wondered with disgust if I was guilty of the same.

Could it be that what I was also angry at was that these people could express remorse and I could not? I'd let myself forget all the advice I was so good at offering to others, lost track of the fact that in grief we are all ducks: working so hard below the water to seem as if we're gliding along effortlessly. Anniversaries, arbitrary and Hallmark as they may seem, serve as the fulcrum on which all that unconscious work relies. After saying good-bye to the dog, I realized that the day I had started crying "for no reason" in Tombstone? That was the anniversary of the last time Scott and I spoke. My birthday, when I started to get sick? I'd been on a plane, on my way to witness his burial. This day, the bad day in San Antonio, is the day I finally let myself acknowledge how guilty I feel that I had not figured out how to love him enough to keep him here with all of us. As if any of us hadn't loved him enough.

I feel guilty that I could not see a way to keep the dog and continue my journey. I feel guilty that I wasn't able to find a better shelter situation. I feel guilty that Scott is dead. After I calm down enough to be able to drive, I make my way to the hotel by the river, get in bed, and start emailing pit bull charities in Texas. I post on Instagram and Twitter that I will pay the dog's medical and food costs. A friend offers to cover all adoption fees. I get a steady stream of comments and emails and texts, from strangers and friends alike, asking, "Why can't you just take the dog?" It's as if my guilt has become embodied by this bodiless internet chorus: *Why can't you just take the dog?*

Eventually Alamo City Pit Bull Rescue gets back to me—they will help me find a foster for the dog, once he's released from the mandatory hold the shelter places on all animals in case their chipped owner changes their mind and wants them back. Relieved and exhausted, I fall asleep and don't wake up for fifteen hours. The next day I make fliers about adopting the dog, and the hotel concierge kindly posts them in the staff workroom. The day the dog can go up for adoption, I call the shelter to ask how he is doing, and if they have worked with Alamo City before.

"Oh yeah. All the charity people are pretty intense," the woman on the phone tells me. "But you should know, the dog was adopted this morning." I burst into tears, yet again, but this time in relief. I ask if the adopters might be interested in emailing with me, and the woman says she will pass along my offer, but I never hear back. I trade texts with another pit bull charity worker and tell them the dog was adopted.

> Well, that's what they told you. They could have just put him down. You can't trust the VCA.

I decide that I have to believe the dog was adopted. I don't know if it was someone from the hotel who saw the flier, or someone who saw any of my myriad tweets or Instagrams, or, more likely, someone who had never heard of me or read anything I posted, but just a dog lover who would provide a home.

Eventually my fever drops enough that I get restful sleep and I can enjoy San Antonio. I walk by the river, meander through neighborhoods of slightly run-down Victorian mansions I would like to buy, and eat the best Vietnamese bánh mì I've ever had. I'm still anxious and shaky, and feel weak.

I know that the story would probably be more interesting if I'd kept the dog. I could have posted a lot of pictures, #whorescuedwho, and finally had a response for all the people who keep telling me how dangerous it is for a woman to be driving across the country alone. I could have been Natty Gann. It would have been a good story. But that would also be the story of a woman who purposefully put her own foot in the bear trap. That would have been me acting out of guilt, out of duty, thinking it's my responsibility to get Mom to come out of her room or make Scott better. The dog was not a dog: he was my monster. I got him some medicine, I tried to help, and I sent him on his way. I am still on this path. I am still headed east, and there are more trials, maybe more monsters waiting for me.

Chapter Seventeen

The Bad Night II

When I got up to show her the math homework I'd just finished, she rushed me, grabbing my hair at the roots. We struggled a bit, and she dragged me across the bedroom. She shook me, and the room rattled with my teeth. When I saw her arm cock back, I raised my hand to block her, and her fist and my hand smashed into the left side of my face. I collapsed, not from the impact, but because my legs just stopped working.

The rest of the night, she went back and forth between my room and my older brother's. I could hear her screaming while I hid under my blankets. She'd storm back in, threatening me, then put her hands on me to pray, and then leave again. I don't know how long it went on, but eventually she slammed her bedroom door, and I finally fell asleep.

Understand, before this night, my brother and I kept a fairly respectful distance. As kids we fully brawled. My dad once compared me to the blow-up toy clowns with sand in the bottom: I'd get knocked down and merely pop right back up again. On the airplane rides between

Sacramento and Los Angeles, I believe we traumatized a generation of young flight attendants with our squabbling; but as teenagers, we had a general sort of separate peace, especially because at this point, Colin had basically moved out and was living with a family nearby. With two sons around Colin's age, this family had opened their house to a phalanx of teenage boys from East Sacramento and brought my brother into a tribe of neighborhood families who loved unconditionally and lived accordingly. They saved our lives.

The pack of boys only occasionally came by our house. One of them told me once that I had always spooked him, opening the door, my hair very long, and always silent. To hear him say it, I was always in a dark corner, reading. Looking.

The next morning, as usual, my brother and I drove to school, but unlike other mornings, we talked.

He turned to me. "So. Last night was rough."

We compared what she had been yelling at us about. I think I started crying. I told him she had hit me. He asked me if I wanted to go home after school, and I said no. My brother told me he would take care of it. And he did, as he has always taken care of me.

Not halfway through the school day, he popped his head into my French class, and brought me to sit in someone's office. A teacher who had taken my brother under her wing, another generous soul, asked me to tell her what had happened the night before. Soon enough I was telling the same story to my father, on the phone. I told him I didn't want to go home.

Between Colin and my father, helpful teachers, and threatening lawyers, I ended up spending the next few weeks with the family of some of Colin's friends. Days blurred, and while I went to school, I spent most of my time in one office or another on the phone with lawyers, telling the same story over and over: the bad day turning into the bad night, and my sudden understanding that it wasn't my imagination: my mother wasn't normal.

Eventually she came to fetch me away from my hideout, and a scene played out in this family's driveway while I cowered inside. We lost the fight when she threatened to call the cops and claim this family had kidnapped me. I got in the station wagon, terrified I was being driven home to suffer a real beating.

Instead, my mother was soft, pleading, confused. Why was I telling everyone such horrible lies? What did I mean I wanted to move to Los Angeles—how could I do that to her? Did I want to abandon my life, my friends? Didn't I understand that without me, she wouldn't get any more child support payments? She'd be destitute. Back at the house, Colin made me a bed on the futon in his room, and we watched silly movies. Mom came in, mystified why I wouldn't sleep in my own bed.

"Honey," she said, and I could see the hurt and confusion in her face. Her big brown eyes. "I would never hurt you."

Chapter Eighteen

Houston

"Houston, we have a problem."
—SOME GUY IN A MOVIE ONCE

Driving into Houston, the 10 swells into a monster, and the interchanges are snarled, angry. Flicking on your turn signal indicates that what you want is for everyone in your desired lane to speed up and not let you in. "Southern hospitality" doesn't mean shit on the freeways of Houston. I grew up learning to drive my mom's manual Volvo station wagon (she was a very good driving instructor), and she was generous, or dumb, enough to let me borrow the car once to drive to The City—San Francisco. I've had a teenage meltdown trying to drive a stick up and down the hills of the East Bay and have years on the open-season highways of Los Angeles under my belt, so I'm a fairly unflappable driver. However, Houston has even me cursing a blue streak as I rush to get to the airport to pick up my friend Brandon.

It's all these goddamn trucks. I don't mean semitrucks, I mean glossy, extended-cab Fords and Chevrolets that look like they've never hauled a thing. I get a lot of joy checking out how many have trailer hitches—hardly any. Since I could drive, every highway I've been on, Fancy Trucks have always been a nightmare: 'roided-out aggressive driving, swerving between traffic, tailgating, barreling up middle lanes expecting everyone else to get out of their way. Like my father and brother Colin, I am a tediously law-obeying driver; I've had my license for twenty-three years and only ever had one moving violation, thanks to a brand-new traffic sign posted overnight in the hills over Malibu. I am one of those puritanical drivers, moralizing hardnoses who believe bad driving reveals psychological truths. I want to conduct a study on the number of pathological narcissists who never use their blinkers.

Every single accident I saw in my months on the road all involved a Fancy Truck, and most of them were in Texas. Perhaps this shouldn't surprise me—Texas buys more trucks than any other state,[1] but I wonder how many of them are being used for ranch work. I knew a one-handed cowboy named Lefty who used to dismiss lesser men by saying, "All hat, no cattle." I hate to step on Lefty's line, but I think it should be "All truck, no cattle."

On the outskirts of Houston, I see the wreckage of an accident that must have happened within the hour—a Fancy Truck is pulled over on the side, a man beside it screaming into his phone. Ahead, sitting on the ground beside her totally demolished sedan, a woman is weeping, her head in her hands. Above her is a billboard for a Houston outpatient plastic surgeon: "I make sexy bodies! FREE BOTOX!"

I watch Brandon as he climbs into Minnie, taking in everything.

"Does it look insane? Do I look insane?"

"No, not at all. I mean, it definitely looks like you've been living in this van, but it seems good." He eyes me up with a slight moue of discernment. "You look good."

We've been talking about Houston for months, but now we're both finally here and the reality is stupefying.

"It's so huge," he says as I ease back onto the interstate.

"Massive. This must be how people feel when they come to Los Angeles for the first time. I'm not sure how to attack it. It's like looking for the front door of the Death Star."

Brandon is my hero. A professional travel writer, he has been to every continent minus Antarctica, and more than 125 countries. He's written Lonely Planet guidebooks and countless articles. Now he writes two very popular travel columns for Bloomberg. From the world's finest hotels to Airbnbs that ended up just being a mattress in a corner, Brandon has seen it all. More than that, he is one of my favorite people in the world, and we have a lot to discuss.

Months ago, I asked Brandon if there was anywhere on the 10 he'd like to see. In part because I miss him, but also because I want to see him do his job; there should be a word for the joy you get from watching someone you love be good at their work. Also, I've been thinking a lot about the difference between a traveler and a tourist (if there is any), and I know Brandon has very strong feelings about this. His traveling skill set is usually employed in places like the most remote island in the world, Pitcairn (home to the descendants of the HMS *Bounty* mutineers), or Uzbekistan, but I want to see him apply his skill set to an American city—to look with a foreign eye on a domestic place.

Brandon is a Francophone French Canadian, and our first conversation of substance was when he walked me through all the differences between Anglophone French Canadian, Francophone French Canadian, Quebecker, and Quebecois. He finds himself looking for English translations of French words that have too-subtle meanings, like how there are many different ways of describing being full from a meal. Hearing him discuss being Canadian, and French, with an outlier American Jewish grandfather (similar to John Raymond Dillingham's Jewish mother), I learned that he was a person who thinks about place, identity, and history very deeply. I think it makes him the sensitive, perceptive writer and traveler that he is. He cuts a trim, short figure, and his only extravagant trait is his gold school ring—on others it might look gaudy, but for him it just looks comfortably refined. He exudes a tidiness that one might equate with Japan, which makes sense because he has lived there and returns often so he can stay on top of all the new spots and continue learning about the place. When I asked what city on the 10 he'd like to see, he didn't have to think.

"Houston."

"Really? Okay. Why Houston?"

"Zoning."

Who the hell cares about zoning? Texans, that's who.

Our first point of entry is, I suspect, both a gross stereotype of this city and a very real slice of Houston life: our hotel. Brandon has put all his PR connections into play, which has netted us several nights at the Post Oak Hotel, touted as "Houston's only five-diamond" hotel. It feels extremely Houston in that there is a luxury car dealership in the hotel, right off the lobby. This means that the looped driveway is usually clogged with Bugattis and Bentleys, including a white one perpetually parked in front of the entrance, with the license plate MR. PO. If your idea of luxury is a hotel that is also a car dealership, this is the place for you.

Our first night in Houston starts a pattern for our trip here: eating a lot of simply delicious food. Once we get settled at the hotel, we head out for the old-school Houston Mount Olympus of Tex-Mex: Ninfa's. It's named for Ninfa Laurenzo, a struggling widow with a failing tortilla business, who is credited (somewhat controversially) as the creator of fajitas.

Ninfa's fajitas are predictably incredible, but I'm particularly fond of mole sauce, which is popular in Los Angeles thanks to a large contingent of Oaxacan immigrants. The Ninfa's mole poblano sauce is so good it nearly makes my eyes roll back in my head, as if I could taste every single ingredient in it, but the whole is more than the sum of its scrummy parts. Before I left Los Angeles I was going to Guisados, where I took Scott, for their perfectly light fish tacos or velvety mole poblano nearly every day, afraid that I wouldn't have access to the good stuff for months. I'd forgotten completely that all through the Southwest and Texas, I'd be blessed with some of the best Mexican and Tex-Mex in the world. Well, until I get to Louisiana, anyway.

Brandon and I feast until we couldn't possibly eat another bite—*on avait les dent du fond qui baignent.* We talk Texas and writing. Like all writers, we love to talk process, and Brandon wants to know how I'm taking notes. His notebooks terrify me with their precision and order—they look like the killer's notebooks from *Seven*—whereas mine are likely to be tea-stained and illegible even to me. I walk him through the events of San Antonio and am so grateful when he doesn't look at me like I'm a girl undone.

"You're on the cusp," he says to me. "You're about to figure it all out."

"Well, I'm definitely on some sort of hinge," I say, shredding a straw wrapper. "Houston feels like the gateway to the real South. Texas is a literal republic. But Houston is where humidity kicks in. I'm leaving the desert, and I'm headed into the green."

Brandon nods. "The Southwest is behind you. Maybe this place is the fulcrum of the trip."

"Yeah, but fulcrum for what? What's the story behind the pivot?" I wonder. I partially expect him to have the answer.

"That's the thing about a trip: you can't count on when it'll reveal what it's really about."

* * *

I can tell Houston is mocking me. I keep waiting to arrive, even though I've been in this city for days. Yet every day I feel more lost than before. I wonder if this has something to do with what piqued Brandon's curiosity about this place: zoning. Houston is one of the very few American cities, and overwhelmingly the largest, with no zoning laws whatsoever. Basically, anyone can build anything, anywhere, except for in the historical districts. This is a legal legacy from Cold War hysteria that considered zoning socialist. LA may have its eccentricities, like having a storybook cottage next to an "Italian" mansion, but at least we have houses next to houses. Brandon points out that there's a tattoo parlor next to an elementary school. The lack of zoning here means no neighborhood feels cogent; walking is difficult and unpleasant with so many stroads. Brandon and I keep meandering around looking for people and only finding empty streets. It's easy to imagine that all the buildings I can see out my hotel window are actually as empty as this car dealership/hotel feels.

Texas has not happened to me. Besides a few reminders in El Paso about the city being technically Texan, and a joke or two about trucks in Marfa, I haven't seen, heard, or smelled anything that has struck me as particularly Texan. Jennifer Wright explained to me that the majority of Texans live crammed into its eastern reaches. These weeks in the west have felt like more desert—arid and epic. Perhaps I missed the start of Texas because I am viewing it through a particularly hostile lens: that of a Californian.

Ask someone from Timbuktu or Vienna to draw you a Texan, and they could do it, easy: boots, jeans, cowboy hat, voilà! A Texan. Ask the same people to draw you a Californian, and they will once more have no problems: flip-flops, board shorts, a surfboard, presto! Good luck drawing someone obviously from Rhode Island.[2] Yet plenty of people in California ride horses, and Texas has its own beach culture, thanks to miles of shorefront on the Gulf of Mexico.

A Californian is uniquely unsuited to write about Texas, as we are two different expressions of the same idea, a republic within the Republic, each vying to define America in the eyes of the world. Physically and existentially, these two states dominate America, and with all the space we've got, there's still barely enough room for the two of us.

Can Texas be as easy to understand as *Friday Night Lights*, a rack of ribs bedewed with sauce, big hair, and Buddy Holly? (He was born in Lubbock.) Maybe. Because I couldn't honestly say that a carnitas burrito, a pair of Uggs, the Sierra Nevada, and *L.A. Story* don't, in some important and partial way, explain California. We are simultaneously much more than these and exactly these.

I didn't know how Californian I was until I left for college, and I didn't realize how much of a chauvinist I am until I found myself hating a city that has more in common with Los Angeles than it doesn't. I am not understanding this city. That is okay. My body is inside Houston, even if I feel perpetually outside, and my job is to listen.

I don't think that there's one group of people who know a place better than another—it limits the reality of a city to just one perspective. My own city of Los Angeles, nearly as ungainly as Houston, has taught me that some cities have many faces, and not everyone meets all of them—and even fewer will understand them all.

When I was very young and living in Sacramento, on the weekends I visited my Los Angeles family, I would play a game: What if I lived here? Where would I go to school; what would my room look like with the detritus of the stuff of actual living, rather than clothes I only wore twice a month and Christmas stocking stuffers still unopened in April? Would I dress differently from my current uniform of Colin's old Stüssy shirts and baggy shorts? Even though I visited LA on the weekends and in the summer, the idea of actually living there was exotic to me. I knew what a Saturday was like in Los Angeles—a weekend spent with a divorced dad trying to keep his kids happy and busy meant hockey games for Colin, and theater for me. What was a Tuesday like in Los Angeles, though? It boggled my mind. Then, quite suddenly, I did live in Los Angeles full-time. There was a scramble to find me a school to begin attending in the middle of the academic year, and my room looked like I'd tried to decorate a hotel room to feel homey. I was halfway through the seventh grade, but by the time I was halfway through my freshman year of high school, a funny thing had happened: now I couldn't imagine living in Sacramento.

Sacramento took on its own otherworldliness, a space stuck in a time warp of my adolescent self. This switch unsettled me. How had this happened so quickly? So much of my life, and my identity, had been built around being from Northern California, and in only a handful of years I'd switched allegiances between devout rivals. Visiting my mother on the weekends, I drove around and tried to remember what it was like to wake up in Sacramento on a cold, damp school day in the winter. What high school would I have gone to? Who would have been my friends? My bedroom looked like a time capsule of the thirteen-year-old who'd lived there, with horse show ribbons proudly displayed, clothes that no longer fit, and dusty school projects. It was a reliquary of a girl who didn't exist anymore, no matter how hard I tried to hold on to her. When exactly had I lost her? Was it when I stopped saying "hella," or when I gave up wearing Colin's old skater shorts? Was it when I began to notice how bad all my Sacramento clothes smelled, and was embarrassed? I was like Wendy, horrified by how grown-up she's become when Peter comes to ask her to fly away one last time.

I was a much more investigative resident when I moved back to LA in my late twenties. My new life in Los Angeles didn't look anything like my cloistered existence as a high schooler, when I wasn't allowed to (or, honestly, all that inclined to) explore anything beyond the comfortable and close. As my thirtieth birthday came down the pipeline, I worked at a bookstore in downtown Los Angeles, akin to being a bookslinger in the Wild West. There was a lot of human excrement involved.

Inspired by the writing of food critic Jonathan Gold, I ate things I couldn't identify in the vast and delicious San Gabriel Valley while neighborhoods like Boyle Heights, Koreatown, and Little Ethiopia also drew me in with the promise of good meals. I made a point of exploring the hindered wilderness of my neighborhood green space, Griffith Park, and beaches I'd never heard of turned out to have the best swimming spots. When I first moved back, the Eastside of Los Angeles was so foreign to me, I had to use my car's satellite navigation system, just as if I were fresh off a flight from Kansas City—it didn't matter that I was born in Burbank and thus counted as a local. I'm from this place, and I still don't know it all, so you can imagine how I feel when someone who tried walking down Hollywood Boulevard announces that they "don't like Los Angeles." I smile, I nod, and I think: *Less traffic for us who are busy exploring.*

The fact is, Houston has completely eluded me. It's as confusing to me as a car dealership inside a hotel. I'm hesitant to write it off entirely, but there's a quality to Houston's opacity that makes me wonder if the fact that it has intentionally been built with no cogency means that it would be silly to attempt to understand the whole of the place. Brandon has been off to meet people on the tech innovation front, while I catch up on sleep. I feel safe with my friend, after so long in the wild. We've also enjoyed more delicious meals, but I feel like Houston is a bit like its most famous patron at the Breakfast Klub, a chicken and waffles spot that has earned its prestigious reputation: Beyoncé. Houston is larger than life, it is impressive, and, to my eye, it is completely untouchable. Unknowable. I keep trying to get close to things that maybe I was never supposed to be close to.

I'm ruminating on this as Brandon and I once more finagle our way through a snarl of traffic, rushing to arrive before sunset. Our target is the Turrell Skyspace, a permanent installation on the campus of Rice University. James Turrell is an American artist who builds light installations, but unlike what I saw in Marfa, Turrell's work exists beyond mere aesthetics. The Skyspace, from a hundred yards away, strikes me as a heady place. Rising from a typically collegiate quad with green lawns, the structure is a lopped-off pyramid, its green sides sloping into an upper layer, while dug-out walkways beneath give access to the ground floor. When I tell you what "the Skyspace" is, it will strike you as a dumb art thing, but in a city that has been insultingly hot, it's the only place in Houston I felt warmth.

Above the flattened pyramid is a sort of open-sided roof, white, and in the center, at a slight angle that seems to shift subtly as you stare at it, is a rectangular skylight. Just sitting on one of the benches built into the square walls on the ground floor, watching the hue of the sky change as sunset tiptoes out, is beautiful enough; but soon Turrell's LED lights, hidden away in the structure, begin to paint the white ceiling in hues so soft I barely even notice what is happening, but it's the beginning of the forty-minute-long Twilight Epiphany light sequence.

I understand that what I'm describing to you is some different-colored lights being pointed at a white roof with a hole in it, but what I'm telling you is that it was as beautiful a thing as I've ever seen. I spent four days staring at Houston so hard, it was as if I was waiting for a hidden image to reveal itself and jump out from a collection of abstract data. Now, sitting in the Skyspace, I am able to let my eyes go as soft as possible, and am finally able to see the whole of something.

Brandon and I sit in silence beside each other for a long while, like two parched people finally given water. I sigh.

"I think the dog was Scott," I say.

"Oh, absolutely," Brandon says.

Part II

The Swamp

Chapter Nineteen

New Orleans I

It may be difficult to maintain a town at New Orleans.

—JEAN-BAPTISTE LE MOYNE DE BIENVILLE, APRIL 1719

The silence when you get back into the car alone after leaving a friend at the airport is so particular. Minnie, not even a full-sized minivan, suddenly feels cavernous, and the moan and groan of everything inside her moving around echoes. My diatribes once more are monologues as the drive east continues, and while I wish we could continue together, Brandon has his own trips to make, and I've got to see mine through. Palatka, Florida, John Raymond Dillingham, place and person simultaneously are looming on the horizon. The hours I've spent behind the wheel, I've been thinking about the way my mom would reuse coffee grinds so she wouldn't have to go to the grocery store, and how she would help me dye my hair *My So-Called Life* purple. That is to say, I've been thinking about her, not her father. My thoughts glide over him like a stone skipped on still waters, purposefully. Even dead, he scares me. Better to focus on what's right in front of me. Or right behind me.

Pulling out of Houston, I'm relieved to be leaving this confounding place. It's rich, coming from an Angeleno, but it's too big, too confusing, too off-putting. Its massive stroads are alienating. Stroads don't allow for sidewalks, trees, or smaller storefronts one can pop into. Instead, stroads require big-box stores, with their huge parking lots and towering signage. In Phoenix I marveled at how people would have to slam on the brakes to peel off the stroad directly into strip mall parking lots—Houston drivers are on a whole other level, and as dependable as Minnie is, I fear she can't quite rise to the levels of murderous intensity that Houston drivers manifest. Speaking of Minnie, she's got desert sand in her nooks and crannies, and is bursting at the seams with books. Whenever I travel, my first stop is usually a bookstore, and I have a very hard time leaving without at least one new book. Minnie is starting to resemble a traveling library. At this point, in the segue between landscapes, I'm reading a lot about travel itself. Is that what I'm doing? Traveling? That sounds so pedestrian. I flatter myself that I'm on a journey, a quest. Is there a difference? Sociologist Dean MacCannell wrote in his book *The Tourist: A New Theory of the Leisure Class*: "Actually, self-discovery through a complex and sometimes arduous search for an Absolute Other is a basic theme of our civilization, a theme supporting an enormous literature: Odysseus, Aeneas, the Diaspora, Chaucer, Christopher Columbus, *Pilgrim's Progress*, *Gulliver*, Jules Verne, Western ethnography, Mao's Long March."[1]

Great pillars of literature, to be sure, but all men. Warriors, colonizers, and worse. Is this the grand tradition of travel and self-discovery that I ascribe to?

Clarissa Pinkola Estés, author of *Women Who Run with the Wolves*, wrote, "As [women] leave one life for another, or one stage of life for another, or sometimes even one lover for no other lover than themselves. Progressing from adolescence to young womanhood, or from married woman to spinster, or from mid-age to older, crossing over the crone line, setting out wounded but with one's own new value system—that is death and resurgence. Leaving a relationship or the home of one's parents, leaving behind outmoded values, becoming one's own person, and sometimes, driving deep into the woodlands because one just must, all these are the fortune of the descent."[2]

While this narrative makes a bit more sense to me, it's just as problematic as the MacCannell in my mind—so men travel to conquer the external world, but women travel to explore inner worlds in grandiose experiments of solipsism? This seems reductive and too pat.

I think people travel because they want to touch and be touched by the unknown. The Romantics of the nineteenth century made art about the human desire to experience what they called the Sublime—the feelings we have in moments of awe and sometimes danger. It can be the smallness you feel beside a skyscraper, or the sensation of dancing in tune and en masse, all limbs of the same ecstatic body. Poet Samuel Taylor Coleridge wrote, "No object of the Sense is sublime in itself; but only as far as I make it a symbol of some Idea. The circle is a beautiful figure in itself; it becomes sublime, when I contemplate eternity under that figure."[3] I have faith that, seeking more than an Instagrammable moment, there are people who travel to contemplate the unknown meaning beneath the unknown.

I cross over the Sabine River and the state line into Louisiana, and about five miles in, there's a traffic snarl. I don't see any police lights up ahead, and it doesn't look like an accident. There's a gigantic—I mean, truly huge—carcass of a feral pig smack-dab in the middle of the eastbound lanes, forcing both to slow down and swerve around it. I can almost see the heat lines wafting off it, like in a cartoon, while the gargantuan body roasts in the sun. The highway here is potted and gnarly, the asphalt crumbling. I'm reminded of a drive I took with my father from Berlin to Wrocław, Poland. The German leg of the trip, on the famous autobahns, was akin to being in a jet, gliding over smooth terrain at terrific speeds. The moment we crossed into Poland, however, we had to decrease our speed by thirty miles per hour because the road suddenly became riddled with potholes, bumps, and lumps. The change was instantaneous, as was this one.

In between Lafayette and Baton Rouge I pass through Grosse Tete and by a billboard that reads "Our Tigers Lived Longer 2000–2017 Tony Was Adored and Nurtured" with a picture of a miserable-looking animal. When I pull over to refill the tank and deal with the prodigious amount of dead bugs on my windshield, I avoid the Tiger Truck Stop, but I do give Tony a quick Google. The results are as depressing as I thought: Tony was an "attraction" at the gas station from six months old until he was euthanized in 2017. When people talk about Southern Gothic, there's usual some overripe accent detailing a convoluted murder plot in a crowded parlor. Now I just think it's a sad tiger spending its life being ogled in a cage beside a gas station.

New Orleans and I have a history that never happened. As for many Americans, this place existed for me as a sort of dream. I knew, in theory, about Mardi Gras (literally "Fat Tuesday"), about jazz funerals, and about the importance of Louis Armstrong.

I had been living in New York for nearly a decade, and it felt like my life was getting smaller and smaller. People were getting married and the pool of single people to hang out with had shrunk significantly. After the 2008 recession, bus services in Brooklyn were slashed, and the already spotty weekend subway service gave me the excuse to not leave my neighborhood. I wasn't trying new restaurants; I wasn't going to see live music or museums. I was boring and I'd given up on the city.

Then came the siren call from Louisiana. College friends, either originally from New Orleans or post-Katrina transplants, had been singing about an affordable city that valued artists and where you knew your neighbors. They described a town a bit like Berlin after the war: it was lawless and a little scary, but if you could stomach the chaos, you could flourish there and be part of something. I visited a couple of times, got a feel for the place, and thought maybe it could work. And then I had one magical night, the sort of night that makes people never go back to wherever they live to pack up their shit. Who needs to pack anything, when Soul Sister is spinning Sam Cooke, and the room above Mimi's bar is jam-packed with people dancing, and the light seems to sizzle with sweet alcohol and sweat, as if lightning could strike indoors?

So I decided to move to New Orleans. I spent hours on Craigslist; I corralled promises from friends about going to scope out shotgun apartments.

"You're leaving New York?" Nora Ephron asked me. "But you'll have to live in America."

No, actually, I explained, I was moving to New Orleans.

"Ah," she said, and nodded. "That is not America. You will get very fat, and you will be very happy."

Sign me up, I thought.

In the end I did not move to New Orleans, though not for lack of trying. I was derailed by the news that I'd soon be an aunt. I moved back to Los Angeles, thinking I was only delaying my New Orleans adventure a handful of years. This was not the case.

I've been looking forward to stopping in New Orleans since I left LA, and I feel grateful that I realized I'd need a break midway across the country. I still feel hollowed out from San Antonio and I'm exhausted from running around with Brandon trying to find Houston. When I arrive in town, it's to the news that the musician Dr. John has died. This, right after the death of Leah Chase, beloved owner of culinary institution Dooky Chase, casts a shadow over the city. Soon enough the musician Art Neville will also pass, and everywhere I go people talk about this town, more perhaps than they did before, as a fading thing, a place that is slipping through our fingers. I suspect, however, that this has been how people talk about New Orleans, below sea level and behind the levee, for a very long time.

I've scheduled enough time that I've rented a small guesthouse in the Bywater from Leesaw, a Brooklynite who had a magical time in the Crescent City and never went back. Nearly everyone I meet in New Orleans either knows or has heard of Leesaw, in large part because of the Tigermen Den, a communal space she runs.

The guesthouse is small, dark, and damp if I forget to empty the dehumidifier—but it has its charm, and I'm grateful to completely unpack Minnie for the first time in three months. She's parked outside, straddling the violently downward-tilted gutter to rest partially in the street and partially on the sidewalk, which itself is broken and ruptured like miniature tectonic plates. A bit of advice I was given is to always park on level ground, especially in this neighborhood prone to flooding; otherwise I might not be able to get out of town in a pinch if the weather turns bad. This is hurricane season, after all. My parking job doesn't go over well with a neighbor, who leaves a note on my car in an angry scrawl: "THIS ISN'T COOL! You're forcing old people to walk in the street!" The irony of this is that the street is significantly flatter than the sidewalk.

My first full day in New Orleans is spent settling in—I get groceries for my little fridge, and I go to Target to pick up a couple of lamps and a teapot. I've been settling for plain black tea; being able to actually have milk with my tea feels like a special treat, but I learn very quickly that I can't leave half-drunk teacups everywhere the way I do back home in dry Los Angeles. It doesn't take long for something horrible to happen to milk left out.

My first night out is spent in homage to Dr. John. WWOZ announced that Kermit Ruffins will open the stage of his bar and venue, the Mother-in-Law Lounge, to the piano players of New Orleans to come pay tribute to the gris-gris man who once played with Professor Longhair himself. Not too far from Dooky Chase's, the finest and most elegant eating establishment in the neighborhood, Kermit's is bang in the middle of the Tremé, long considered America's first free Black neighborhood, where Black folks could escape the long shadow of Jim Crow and eat wonderful food in style.

The 10, from California to Florida, is a prime example of "how transportation projects have exacerbated historic inequities in cities across the country."[4] I've been reading about how eminent domain was used to displace Black and Hispanic communities all along the interstate, beginning back in Santa Monica, but it is perhaps easiest to clock here in New Orleans, where the 10 looms ominously over the Tremé like a big bad spaceship from *Star Wars*—huge and never-ending. This elevated extension of the 10 was built in 1968, and as I step out of my taxi in front of Kermit's, I can see how it would have decimated all the businesses that used to dot Claiborne Avenue, once tree-lined and resplendent. That hasn't stopped parades, parties, and cookouts from happening underneath the interstate anyway. Apparently, this stretch of the road is in such poor condition that when it rains, water filled with garbage, oil, and god knows what else just leaks down through the overpass.[5]

When I walk into the Lounge, Leah Chase's funeral service is on the television. Piano player after piano player takes the stage, mostly old-timers, but then a young white man steps up and sends a ripple of concern through the crowd, as if a hundred or so people suddenly leaned back on their heels and crossed their arms. But two seconds in, two seconds filled with real oomph and style, the crowd cheers with delighted surprise—the boy can play! Red beans and rice are doled out and the dancing goes on and on. A woman in Dolce & Gabbana sunglasses and dressed head to toe in neon is selling Jell-O shots, and I dance with the big chief of the Yellow Pocahontas Mardi Gras Indian tribe. He tells me of his divorce, the house he built with his own hands, and urges me to come back for Mardi Gras to see him in all his finery.

"You gonna look pretty this year, Chief?" I ask him.

"Oh, I'm gonna be the prettiest, just you see."

So many things that need to be explained, words that don't make sense anywhere but New Orleans: WWOZ. Professor Longhair. Yellow Pocahontas Mardi Gras Indian. New Orleans isn't a city; it's a universe, a very small one, with its own language, its own values, its own heroes and villains. New Orleans can convert even the most suspicious into true believers, and before you know it, years have passed and you're not just an acolyte in this church, but a priest proselytizing the healing, medicinal qualities of Sazerac.

It doesn't take long before I'm chitchatting with folks on their porches as I walk to the grocery store and coffee shop—always during the day. The other piece of New Orleans advice I take very seriously (because nearly everyone reiterates it) is to never walk anywhere, in any neighborhood, after dark. During the day, however, I'm spoiled by local restaurants like barbecue spot the Joint (always check to see if they've sold out of the burnt ends, and order extra mac and cheese if you know what's good for you), the stupidly addictive Pizza Delicious, and Bacchanal, a wine shop, restaurant, and outdoor music venue that becomes my favorite place to sit, drink, and read, as it's right down the street from me.

By far the best thing about the little guesthouse is Ding, Leesaw's mostly outdoor cat, whom I immediately let inside. Ding doesn't like being touched or petted, but he does enjoy stealing food right off my fork, and at night he likes to sleep with his paw just barely resting on me. When I'm reading on the porch in my rocking chair (the same one I sat in to meditate in the mountains outside of El Paso), Ding likes to lounge somewhere nearby, but never close enough that I can touch him. I'm not hurt, though; I'm too grateful that he keeps the feral chickens and roosters from getting too close early in the mornings. There are feral chickens.

Soon enough, it's Father's Day, and mine is across the globe, but the Perfect Gentlemen Social Aid and Pleasure Club is second lining to celebrate. I've heard many, and read even more, histories of where *second line* comes from, but the short of it is that second lining is like if you combined a dance party and a parade with a full brass band. These events are put on by the more than forty social aid and pleasure clubs, descended from post–Civil War freedmen's societies. WWOZ, the radio station that plays everywhere—and I mean *everywhere*, nearly every business I walk into, be it bodega, bar, or restaurant, uptown or midtown; I basically don't stop listening except when I go to sleep and sometimes not even then (zydeco can make for some odd dreams)—anyway, WWOZ keeps track of second line seasons and shares parade routes so all can join. In this context, the "first line" is the club members and their preferred brass band. The "second line" follows: everyone who comes out to dance and peacock, to see and be seen. I truly love looking at what people are wearing, and I have never seen better clothes, better style and panache than I have seen in New Orleans.

As everyone sets off from the starting point, I notice just how many father-son duos are dressed in their Sunday best, ecstatic in pastels. Just as delightful are the gutter punks with their perfectly thrashed denims (not for the faint of heart in this humidity) and shellacked mohawks that only begin to wilt after a couple hours of dancing. Facial glitter is everywhere, which makes me jealous. Why don't I have any glitter on?

The fathers of New Orleans pose with their arms slung over the shoulders of their teenagers as they dance down the road together, while others hold giddy, hot toddlers. One young boy, maybe eight years old, with white wraparound sunglasses, props his silver trombone like a cane and dances around it, low and loose and so good, passersby stop to watch. Older men especially stop to shine on him, their Sunday suits stained with sweat all the way down to their knees. Hankies come out not just to dab at foreheads, but to flick in the air to egg him on. His mom has no small amount of pride on her face as she films him.

It's been months since I've seen family, but that's normal. Between being a child of divorce and then the circus life of a family in show business, going three, four months without seeing family members has always been par for the course. As a kid, I was more used to not seeing my father, who at the time was on a streak of blockbusters and Academy Awards. Then during summers on location, I'd be away from my mother for months. Being away from my mother, as scary and difficult as she could be, was always much harder. For all her faults, my mother fundamentally understood me. She could use that knowledge against me, but in the good times, being with her meant the comfort of being with someone who truly knows you. Away from our house, with its pet stains and stacks of Shakespeare editions, I felt like I was far from my home planet. I might have spoken the language of the alien world, but by no means did I blend in. I was deeply protective of my mother, aware as I was that, to the eyes of most, she was just "the crazy lady." When I moved to Los Angeles right before my fourteenth birthday, I was still occasionally sleeping in her big bed beside her, the public radio station playing soft classical music, the smoke wafting from her unending packs of American Spirits, a blanket covering us both. I can call her "my mother" hundreds of times, but my muscle memory, my heart instinct is to simply say "Momma." When I did move to Los Angeles, it was as if I'd thrown away our relationship, tossed her aside just like everyone else had. I never slept in her big bed again, but of course I still dream about it, almost twenty years after her death.

I dance alone. I dance with groups of women, and with more than one of the gentlemen who come up behind me—there's no "asking to dance" here (that happens more with the two-stepping Cajuns, I learn). It is the hottest I have ever been, and I'm not wearing a drum kit or tuba. I have no idea how the band is doing this. Dancing is hard enough work. I recognize some of the songs as we continue—there's the stankiest version of the Beatles "Come Together" I've ever heard, as well as standards like "I'll Fly Away" and "When the Saints Go Marching In," but every song might as well be called "Ice Cold!"

Behind the dancers and the band, the hardest-working men in New Orleans today are lugging carts and wagons loaded down with coolers chock-full of Miller High Life, Bud Light, Gatorades of every color, and even some water. Young boys march on their caboose, making sure no one is nabbing what they shouldn't. Perfectly timed, and always on the beat, right when the whole beast of music seems to pause for a collective breath, the men yell out the siren call of life below the Mason-Dixon Line: "ICE! COLD! DRINKS!"

Chapter Twenty

New Orleans II

> The Lovers: You recognize that you are lonely, at the same time you realize that without separation, there can be no connection nor demonstration of love.
>
> —PAMELA EAKINS

I've heard the fact about "disappearing football fields" of coastal landscapes and have assumed this is due to rising water levels. It's about twenty-five miles of land a year that goes under the murky waters of the Gulf, including barrier islands that protect the mainland from hurricane damage and constitute one of the most diverse ecosystems in the world. This landscape originally confounded French explorers searching for the Mississippi River. They couldn't find it. I know that sounds weird, because if you know anything about that river, it's that it's big, right? The "mighty Mississippi" and all. How is it possible to lose a river?

It's easier to find it when you're traveling down the river from the north, as René-Robert Cavelier, Sieur de La Salle, and his posse did in bark canoes in 1681. When they were spat out into the expansive delta, he claimed the area in the name of his king, Louis XIV: Louisiana. The problems started when they tried to find the river from the south. When French traders approached the mainland from the Gulf side, they were expecting a bay but instead saw three million acres of labyrinthine delta marshland.

When you google the Louisiana delta, you will always see it from a bird's-eye view. Imagine, if you will, the point of view from the bow of a ship. What do you see? Miles and miles of impenetrable grass growth, shallows that shift constantly and threaten to ground your ship, swamp that seems to go on forever. No one could re-create La Salle's expedition from the south—or even find this land he'd "discovered" and claimed for the king. Eventually La Salle was murdered by his own crew, and it wasn't until 1698 that the brother duo of Pierre Le Moyne, Sieur d'Iberville, and the younger Jean-Baptiste Le Moyne, Sieur de Bienville, thought to get out of the big ships into some canoes (far better able to navigate the tricky shallows) and ask the Pascagoula Native Americans where they might find this rumored gigantic river. Then the French were able to find the mouth of the Mississippi.

I sympathize with these hapless adventurers. Firstly, unless you're up on the levees around town, you don't often see the river. You just think about it, remember its ominous presence. Up on the levee in the French Quarter, there's a gate festooned with love locks and stickers. Someone has put up a sticker with Scott's picture and perhaps his most beloved lyric, "while I'm alive / I'll make tiny changes to earth." It's the namesake of the mental health and suicide prevention charity begun by his family, Tiny Changes.

Perspective, when you're trying to see big things, vast even, can be hard to come by. Soft eyes help, but when you're trying to simultaneously understand the national, the cultural, the personal, and the political, it's impossible to take it all in. I want to understand how the places I've been to are uniquely American, but we are a big place, and we tell big stories, stories like Manifest Destiny. American Exceptionalism. Mothers and Daughters.

It makes total sense to me that the explorers had to get off the boat; that only by getting lost in the delta did they find what they were looking for. You can't observe the parade to understand it: you have to dance in it, ecstatic and alone, in rapture and en masse so "the armies of those I love engirth me and I engirth them." Maybe then you'll see the river. Maybe then you find America.

Gene's pink palace of po-boys and daiquiris is leaving its home on Elysian Fields, and no one wants to talk about it. It's another culture death in a town that is famous for its ghosts. Can you be haunted by the ghost of a sandwich? If it's possible anywhere, it would be here. When I pop into Gene's for lunch, because I just can't seem to leave New Orleans yet, my sandwich wrapped in extra napkins so the grease won't stain my trousers, I chat with the man behind the counter about rent hikes and the possibility of moving to another location.

"But it won't be the same," he says, shrugging. I have heard a lot of this sort of fatalism from locals—a sense that it's been a really good time, but the water is rising, Airbnb is a bitch, and hey, what can you do? Although I've also heard people equally excited about New Orleans continuing into the next century. There's a lot of ambivalence in the truest sense of the word; that is, strong opinion in opposing but equally compelling directions.

In New Orleans, no conversation sums up ambivalence better than the one I have with Zac Manuel. Zac is a filmmaker I first met when I acted as craft services—cooking—for our mutual friends (and former New Orleanians) Veronica and Nat Moonhill on a short film they were directing. Zac was the cinematographer, and even from behind my trays of enchiladas I could see that he was immensely talented. He shot *Time*, which would be nominated for best documentary at the 2020 Academy Awards, and would go on to direct the documentary *Lil Nas X: Long Live Montero*.

Zac is warm and relaxed and suggests Ethiopian for our dinner. On his arm is a tattoo that reads NOLA, in the style of the blue-and-white tiles of the street names inlaid in the sidewalks of the city, a practice that reportedly started for the convenience of horse-drawn carriages in the Vieux Carré ("old square").

"I think it's hard to watch something decay. It's hard to watch something die. Really slowly," he says to me over a tray of varied deliciousnesses that we scoop up with injera, a sort of flatbread.

"You think the city's dying?"

"Gene's Po-Boy is about to close at the end of July. I mean, it's easy to say 'Oh, things change. Times change.' Not to sound like an old fart, but the times have changed and it's terrible. It's an intentional choice to be like, 'Do I want to live with that change, or do I want to disconnect from the space and have it be something that was once very beautiful?' And still will be."

Zac's family is very New Orleans, generations going back with Creole roots. His father, Phillip, is a well-known singer around town.

"There's nothing wrong with change; I'm not an anti-change person," he continues. "But I think it's symptomatic of something else. Which is that in order to sustain a city, you've got to bring industry to it. And industry means money. And we're not a city that's had a lot of money, and our culture has come from that lack of money. It's come from ingenuity, and it's come from creativity. It's come from having to work a shit ton, and having to work in shitty conditions, and blowing all your steam off and creating something that's beautiful and something that's unique to you and your community and your friends. And the more that we need to be sustained, literally to survive, the more that we need big industry, the further culture is going to go from the city. It's just going to go away."

"So in order to survive, the city has to destroy itself."

"Yes," he says, laughing. "Kind of."

Before I left for my trip, friends gave me things for luck. I mentioned the St. Christopher medallion I wore in Juárez. One friend gave me a slew of greeting cards: "When you're hungry for a food that is not available where you are," "When you wish you filled up your gas tank yesterday," and the incredibly specific "In case you are bored and have a TV stuck on ABC in the middle of the day" (that one had a detailed rundown of what was happening on *General Hospital* that week).

I was also gifted a copy of *Tarot of the Spirit* by Pamela Eakins, PhD. Tarot was something my mother considered "dark-sided," not of the Lord. I remember being entranced by a large, very 1970s wall hanging of the Sun by David Palladini from his popular Aquarian deck. It was in the living room of my godmother, another person who loved my mom and who was banished and invited back into her life seemingly on a whim. I was told explicitly that the wall hanging was not Christian, and we didn't go to my godmother's house for a couple of years.

A tarot deck consists of seventy-eight cards, fifty-six of the Minor Arcana (earth, air, fire, water), twenty-two of the Major Arcana (the Empress, Death, etc.). What do I think happens when I pull a tarot card? Is the universe, or some other unearthly power, guiding my hand to choose a card perfectly suited to reflect the moment I'm in? Or is it utterly random, and the meaning I ascribe to the card merely a reflection of my thinking? To me, it's something in between—and more importantly, it doesn't really matter. The metaphor is the message. The deck is made from the same things as life: archetypes, well-worn stories we all recognize, all of which are worthy of meditation at any given time. I get the eye rolls, but remember that the average deck of playing cards came from a tarot deck without the Major Arcana. So if you don't pull tarot but you've played a game of solitaire, you've used the cards for the same reason I have: to keep your hands busy while you have a ponder.

When Zac mentions that the city must destroy itself to survive, an image immediately flashes behind my eyes: the card of the Tower. Of all the cards, the Tower is the one that usually makes people nervous. It's not Death (transformation) or the Devil (contradiction), but the Tower. In my deck designed by Kim Krans, the Tower is depicted as a stately tree, like the sequoias back home in California, struck by lightning. Its limbs have caught fire, and the top of the tree, its pillar, topples from the sky. It's a good rule of thumb that if you've pulled the Tower card, you may be, as the enlightened put it, in the shit.

Later I'll check my copy of *Tarot of the Spirit*, stacked in the cottage with all of the other books I pulled out of Minnie and read while the dehumidifier stutters. The Tower represents "a series of insights [that] propels you to new awareness; you have outgrown the old structure—physical or mental—you built; you must destroy this structure (or allow it to crumble) in order to make room for the new structures you need; you may have to sacrifice certain things in order to grow."[1]

I have certainly shed different skins so that I could continue growing. If there is a silver lining to the chaos and confusion of my childhood and adolescence, it is that I am unafraid of change, and don't hesitate to drop what isn't working for me. The downside is that I can be brutal about it. I am sure there are some people, particularly some men, who feel that I dropped them very "succinctly."

If a friend comes to me for the umpteenth time kvetching about a car with squeaky brakes, or a boss who emails at all hours, I'm thinking, *Fix the car, learn how to set boundaries, or get out of my way.* I struggle when I perceive people as stuck, when people are complicit in their own unhappiness; there's a bootstrap mentality of a survivor wherein my empathy runs short. I don't wake up afraid or sad, a privilege that's hard to remember when I'm watching someone dig their own grave all the while bemoaning how hard it is to shovel dirt. What I really want to say is, "Well, go spend your one life in a hole, then, and enjoy feeling superior because you really know how to eat shit."

As I'm walking away from a relationship, I see my mother, sitting in her bed, writing poems about the life she could have had—if only—as the small world around her gathers dust. It makes me want to tear my skin off my body, leave it in the wind while I continue slithering away with a rose on my tongue but fangs sharp enough to cut even me.

I've been thinking about the Tennessee Williams quotation "America only has three cities: New York, San Francisco, and New Orleans." And I wonder if it might actually only be New Orleans. Most often a city's culture is defined by its layout and industry. Money-based culture is all the same: nice restaurants, nice museums, nice charity functions. Your primary experience of cities that require you to get in a car to navigate them is of their traffic. Seen through this lens, the differences between London and New York are negligible. Tea versus coffee, black cabs versus yellow. (Actually, most Londoners I know drink coffee. Their parents drank tea.) How different can London and New York be, when you see a Mardi Gras Indian? What culture can be considered "nuanced" in comparison to the Zulu Social Aid and Pleasure Club, whose Black krewe membership parade in blackface wearing grass skirts and handing out coconuts?

Other cities, their culture is top-down. In New Orleans, culture is born and refined in the streets, then travels up through the social echelons. If Los Angeles functioned this way, the whole city's culture would be set by the *abuelitas* selling their tamales on the sidewalk. There is no better example of street-up culture than the way that the entire city of New Orleans experiences Mardi Gras together.

"My understanding is that the biggest difference in experience of Mardi Gras in the city is whether or not you have access to a real bathroom," I say to Zac, thinking of my friends' stories of trying to find open public bathrooms in wealthier neighborhoods.

"Events like Mardi Gras and second lines are class-integrated events," Zac says. "It's poor Black folks, middle-class Black folks, poor white folks, and middle-class white folks, all in the same space. We don't often see that. You don't often see middle-class folk and poor folk in the same place ever."

And I think people are hungry for that sort of cultural experience. They want to experience something original, vibrant, and true. They want transcendence. But the problem is that they're all taking fish out of the lake, and not putting any back in. You can't come here and siphon off the culture, and not put anything back into it.

We settle our tab and, because the sun has set, Zac walks me to Minnie. We make plans to meet up again in a couple of days. I'm thinking about a previous trip to the Crescent City: I'd come down for a wedding, stayed awhile. The morning of my flight home, I got up early and walked through the Vieux Carré to Café du Monde. Café du Monde, smack in the middle of the French Quarter, is where locals and tourists alike get their famous fried beignets covered in powdered sugar and their chicory lattes. Chicory coffee, regular grounds cut with the chicory root, became a wartime mainstay in Civil War–era New Orleans and across the Confederacy during a coffee shortage.

It was early and folks were hosing down the streets, washing away the evidence of night's revelry. There was no line for a latte and a bag of hot beignets, and I took them up onto the levee across from Jackson Square, where in 1803 Louisiana officially joined the Union, right at a bend in the Mississippi. While I watched the Big Muddy and drank my coffee, a saxophone player set up his umbrella and case, preparing to spend the day entertaining (hopefully) generous tourists. Soon enough it was time for me to get going, and I offered him the rest of my beignets. He thanked me but told me the powdered sugar wasn't good for his saxophone.

"Gotta respect the instrument," I said, tossing the bag and wiping my hands. Powdered sugar gets everywhere.

"Ain't that the truth," he said to me, before running scales.

That was years ago, but I remember the smell of that morning up on the levee. Now, driving back to the Bywater, something else Zac said is sticking to me like powdered sugar: "The best days here can be really, really good. 'Cause I think everyone wants to share it. And some of the worst days can be bad because everyone wants to share it."

Back at the cottage, I call a friend who, when she lived here, made theater, trying to put fish back in the lake as best as she could. I tell her what Zac said, and she makes a low sound of agreement.

"New Orleans can give you so much," she says. "But when it takes, it takes big. It takes big, scary bites out of you."

* * *

"Does it feel like I'm leading you to your untimely death?" I ask, leading him through the dark. He laughs and keeps following me, which I suppose means that he isn't at all afraid.

I'd been cooped up all day, trying to write, trying to read, and not getting either done, so at some point I called it and went to get barbecue at the Joint. I lingered over my meal and a Dark 'n Stormy, reading from Jack E. Davis's *The Gulf* and enjoying the late sun, the encroaching porch hours, as the afternoon rain dried out as best it could.

I didn't want to go back to the cottage, with its work, with its too-soft bed. There's a part of me that misses the desert: it's where I was able to sleep most often in Minnie, and I've gotten used to that bed's puritanical firmness and the coziness of being tucked away. So I decided to walk down to Bacchanal and read among the hustling waiters and the tip basket always going around for the band. I park with a glass of rosé and my book, a little too near the trash for actual comfort, but I'm not there for long when a woman, maybe in her midtwenties, and a little tipsy, marches up to me and announces,

"I love what you're wearing!"

Even I can immediately tell that this woman is not from New Orleans. I'm wearing a colorful jumpsuit, which back home in LA I'd pair with both Spanx and a bra, but today I'm wearing neither since it's too hot for either. I thank her, and she asks what I'm reading. I tell her it's about the natural history of the Gulf of Mexico. Her face goes blank.

"Well, I'm here to take a sommelier exam, well, um, I already took it, and I'm here with some other people who also just took it, and we all just ordered a bunch of bottles, would you like to come and join us?"

My lizard brain perks right up. This woman seems way too straight to be flirting with me, but she's cute so I agree anyway, and we wander over to join her table. Suddenly it all makes more sense: she's not looking for tail, she's looking for backup. Her company is two goonish wine bros, roommates from Little Rock who spend all their time performing for each other and bragging about their wine knowledge. It seems that wine is yet another experience that used to be about pleasure, but now is another commodity of performative consumption. I wish Brandon were here.

At some point one of them gets up to use the restroom, returning with a plate of patatas bravas and the news that he found another sommelier from their exam and commandeered his food as impetus to join us. When the fourth sommelier eventually does join us, he takes a breezy seat, and jokes that he's only joining us for the food he paid for. His name is Joshua, and he has a ponytail and a cheeky grin.

I ask the table if anyone has a story of the first bottle to get them into wine. The Goons talk about how they decided (together) that they wanted to work without having to work, and wanted to "wear great suits."

Joshua, on the other hand, tells a story of being in Italy, a night out with a woman, and the silly guitar player beneath Keats's window on the Spanish Steps. He can tell a story, and I like him more than I did at the beginning of the evening. Maybe the Goons have just made him look very good in comparison. Eventually, it's just us at the table.

The next hour or so we talk. About New Orleans, about travel, about the people you meet. The katydids are humming, and while the humidity is still hanging in the air, there's enough of a breeze that there's some relief to the heat. The crowd thins. The lights sway slightly. He has handsome, small hands.

I feel bad for pinning what's about to happen on New Orleans, but I can't say I would have made the same decision in Tucson or Tallahassee. MacCannell the sociologist thinks there are types of travelers who purposely try to engineer authentic accidents: "Certain individuals are prone to the kind of accident that leads to these experiences because they seek out situations in which this kind of thing is most likely to occur."[2] The truth is, I'm a little bored, and I'm a little sad, and here's a would-be sommelier who says things like "It's so great to meet someone who reads."

I discover he doesn't vote. Hasn't. Ever. In any election, local, state, or national. His face shows his equal, opposite disappointment that I have voted, in every election I can.

"We should stop talking about this, otherwise I'm not going to ask you to come home with me," I say.

"We should, or I'm not going to say yes."

We get another bottle to go. Ding the cat seems to know the deal and does not meet me at the gate yowling for leftovers and air-conditioning. We compare recent clear STD checks; neither of us has a condom, but if I felt like being responsible, I wouldn't be attempting to have sex with a twenty-nine-year-old would-be sommelier who has never voted. In for a penny . . .

Joshua and I kiss in a cold shower, washing off the day's sweat, and it's fun, but the moment we're in bed, we lose the momentum built up after hours. He's a child who wanted a certain Christmas toy but is then confronted with a box full of disparate parts and instructions for required assembly. He may not be afraid of me walking him through the dark to the cottage, but in my bed, he's spooked.

"We had all that wine," Joshua says, plucking at the sheets, and I tell him it's all right.

The same thing happens in the morning. Outside the heat is already building up over the dusky, damp grass. The feral rooster woke us up. The light filters through the dusty shutters and the ceiling fan hums.

"You know, you don't really look your age. I mean, you don't look as old as you are," he says to me, his long hair tangled over a thin, limp pillow.

"I'd make you breakfast, but I don't have a kitchen," I say. He at least has the grace to take it as the signal that perhaps it is time to go.

In 1989 my mother took me to see *Peter Pan*, released out of the storied Disney Vault briefly. I was seven years old, watching Wendy fly across Big Ben, Tiger Lily nearly drown, Tinker Bell almost poisoned. I watched the Lost Boys look for a mother. After, I asked my mom if Wendy and Peter were going to live happily ever after. No, she told me. Wendy would grow up, grow old, and as in the books, would be replaced by her own daughter. And her daughter, and her daughter, forever. Peter would never run out of young women to replace old women. He should never have taken Wendy to Neverland, she said—because of Tinker Bell, because of Tiger Lily. This is the first lesson my mother taught me about men: that they are dangerous, fun, and cruel, that they make women compete against each other.

If my mother had a lover or a boyfriend after her divorce from my father, I never heard about them, met them, or saw any trace of them. She had several women in her life who may have been her lovers, but if they were, it was kept secret, and in her later years she discussed homosexuality as a tragic sin, though it's possible this was an expression of self-loathing. Those friendships were as turbulent and confusing as all her other relationships, but if they were of a romantic nature, I hope those women found some joy with my mother, for the chaotic windows of time she was in their lives.

When it came to men, my mother affected a sort of tragic, romantic stance, as if recalling her gentlemen callers from a chaise longue. There were tales of the hunky Irishman she had been with before my father, and how her devastation over that breakup made her complacent enough to let my dad take a crack. That was her revenge on him for all his successes—to write off their history with her as the bored heroine who deigned to let the nerdy theater guy hang around her.

My mother taught me to be Romantic. We read poetry together, and romance novels. She showed me the swoony paintings of John William Waterhouse and his Pre-Raphaelite brethren and urged me to grow my hair as long as possible. She taught me to brush it a hundred times a night—but she never brushed my teeth when I was a child or took me to the dentist. She was forthright about masturbation and female anatomy when I was an adolescent, but when I was a teenager, she told me the most important thing about a man was whether he had the light of Jesus Christ in his soul.

She taught me to be seductive, but also that men who desire me show a sort of weakness. She taught me to both lust after men and sneer at them. Growing up with three brothers has tempered these lessons, made men human to me, but it's taken a lot of therapy to examine the lessons she gave me and begin to dismantle them.

When Joshua leaves, I pour myself a sweating glass of iced coffee. I've been turned on to a dangerous, entirely chemical concoction of highly concentrated syrup that when added to ice and milk (and, according to some locals, maple syrup, which is insane) creates this powerhouse of flavor and caffeine that has my teapot gathering dust, I'm sorry to say. While I get my first high of the day, I'm drawn to the white binder of my mom's poems.

[. . .] you no longer feel love
or need of me, I know
I know my emotions shame you.
For I have grown old,
my clothes are shabby
and my teeth are crooked.

I'm struck by her shame, the way she cannot remember what it felt like to be young and thin and beautiful. And she was beautiful; her cheekbones and paleness remind me of a brunette Meryl Streep. But in the photos I have of her when she is young and thin, her eyes are haunted, wraithlike. Reading her words about her embarrassment makes her so immediately present to me in a way she never was when she was alive. I'm hopped up on caffeine and sugar now, and the heat is manageable enough that I can walk somewhere. I've got an errand to run.

Here's the thing about buying the morning-after pill in Louisiana. Firstly, the box itself has been put in a see-through plastic bin that requires both of my hands to hold, it is so big. I could keep two fish alive in this thing, or one small turtle. Secondly, it's nearly sixty dollars, which seems a bit pricey for what is basically being done out of quite an abundance of caution, and quite a compliment to Joshua.

Thirdly, one never wants to buy only the morning-after pill, so I pair it with some cookies and milk. At the front of the Walgreens, a bored and beefy security guard is always pacing around the entry doors, and the cashier is a man. I head back toward the pharmacy—it's a woman at the till, thank god. While I'm waiting in line, a woman so pregnant I'm concerned she might give birth at any second is sitting in a chair that can barely contain her, fanning herself.

"Wish I'd taken that." She gestures to the pill in a box, in a bin, in my arms.

I laugh. "Would you say the same in December?"

"Shit, I'm so pregnant, I'd be hot at the North Pole." This gets me so good, my laugh disturbs other shoppers, and this moment makes the "sex" I had last night worth it.

It's time to go see some pigs.

* * *

I have doused myself with bug repellent, but turns out there aren't many mosquitos in the Honey Island Swamp. It's too hot even for bugs during the day.

Nearly everyone back home has asked me if I've gone on a swamp tour yet, the kind in the shallow boat with the huge fan on the back, but I've heard that the huge fans scare off most of the wildlife and that we'd be better off with a different approach. Pearl River Eco-Tours promises to leave tourists with "a true sense of what this life is all about."

It's impossible to not think about the swamps when you're in Louisiana. For one thing, it means that New Orleans, for all that it is surrounded by water, feels a bit landlocked—there isn't much interaction with the nature around you. You can't (or shouldn't) get into the water, thanks to gators and water snakes. The land isn't much better, as it's mostly jungle filled with enough snakes and spiders to make the Amazon blush. There are wild pigs, mosquitos, people with guns—take your pick. Of course, Indigenous peoples were able not only to navigate these spaces, but to flourish.

Zac Manuel told me he believed that the perilousness of the landscape here had something to do with how, from the very beginning, the people of Louisiana have been mixed up in each other's business: "I think our foundations are very different. I feel like the landscape here is so fucking nuts, it's a swamp jungle. The ground often isn't ground, and you can't build on it. In the swamps, you're going through bayous and shit like that. The Canadian fur trappers—who became the Cajuns—what the fuck are they going to do? They're gonna colonize and push Native Americans out? They had to work with the Native Americans and figure out how to survive. The foundational spirit of this region was like, 'If you don't work together, you will probably die.'"

The "accidental city," as author and longtime resident Lawrence Powell describes it, is "a state of mind, built on the edge of disaster, where the lineage of three continents and countless races and ethnicities were forced to crowd together on slopes of the natural levee and somehow learn to improvise a coexistence whose legacy may be America's only original contribution to world culture."[3] So it was important to me to see the swamps.

I got a bit of a sneak peek on my way into New Orleans. From east of Lafayette, Louisiana, through to Baton Rouge, the 10 runs over the Atchafalaya (Choctaw for "long river") Basin, nearly a million acres of swamp that, when you're in the middle of it, strikes you as being as expansive as the Grand Canyon. Over the Atchafalaya the 10 splits into two separate bridges with two lanes headed in each direction. While Houston's megahighways had me raging, the only time I was genuinely scared was on these bridges—there's no shoulder, so if you break down or get into an accident, there's nothing to do but back up traffic for miles upon miles. Or there's the nightmare of a semitruck plowing into you and sending you flying into the gators' territory. . . . And then there are the bridges themselves. I don't want to make anyone nervous, but the bridges, 4.4 miles long, they look *busted.* When's the last time these things got spruced up?

On the west side of New Orleans, the 10 passes through (more like over) the Bayou Sauvage National Wildlife Refuge, Lake Pontchartrain, and into Bogue Chitto (from the Choctaw *bok chito*, "big creek") National Wildlife Refuge, which includes where I am headed: the Honey Island Swamp. There's a lot of bees around, so the name suits.

The seventy-thousand-acre Honey Island Swamp is along the Pearl River, named by the French explorers who were mystified by the beautiful pearl necklaces the Choctaws wore. The crew of explorers today are just a friend visiting me from Scotland, myself, a woman I would estimate is in her midfifties, and her adolescent son, who is young enough to have to wear a life jacket and old enough to be embarrassed about it. There's also our captain for the day. The woman is just the faintest degree of flirty with him—there's a lot of "that's so interesting," and "you know so much." She even gushes that she loves the swamp so much, she'd move there. The more effusive she is, the more her son slumps in his seat. My guess says: a post-quasi-recent divorce mother-son trip that isn't going great.

We pass the boat of a competing swamp tour company, whose captain, ours complains, isn't even from the area. Ours grew up sleeping in his skiff and knows every bed in the Honey Island Swamp. He knows where the water is fresh, where the water is salty, and where the water is brackish—a combination of both. The competitors might point out the swamp hogs, feed the gators marshmallows (they look like turtle eggs), but they don't know what the Indian potato is (the tuber found at the end of a three-pointed leaf). They haven't spent boyhood nights camping out with catfish on the tongue and a fear of the Letiche in their hearts.

La Letiche, by the way, is the Honey Island Swamp's answer to Bigfoot. The Cajun version of the story has La Letiche as the soul of an unbaptized baby, haunting the waters. (Catholics, right?) The Native American version involves an abandoned baby taken in and raised by alligators. A more contemporary version of the tale has a local stumbling on a horrifying figure "over seven feet tall, having dingy, grayish hair, yellow eyes, and being accompanied by a disgusting stench."[4]

"What can you tell me about those animals?" I ask, gesturing to the other tourists swathed in cameras.

"Well," says the captain, "the female of the species is more deadly than the male. She'll steal your wallet and your dreams." There are four people on his boat, three of whom are women, but only a coward changes his material to suit his audience, I guess.

"No, no," he says, smiling, "I only joke. I've been happily married for twenty years."

"Congratulations," I say.

"And I've been married for thirty."

The captain explains how the winter freeze will kill off nearly all the green we see—which is almost everything we see. That dead greenery will sink to the bottom of the bayou (Choctaw for "slow-moving water") and slowly decompose, leaving food for all the myriad bottom-feeders, and eventually promulgates the return of all the plant life once the weather warms up again. He tells us that willow bark eventually led to the invention of aspirin, that the original Model T Fords used wood from the cypress cedar trees and nearly wiped them all out. It's astonishing to see just how extensive the captain's knowledge of this landscape is—he navigates the swamp instinctively, seemingly aware of the bird's-eye view of all the paths and bayous of the Honey Island Swamp. He isn't Cajun—they keep to themselves, he says, and I think I detect the faint whiff of disdain.

He tells me that his favorite thing about the swamp is how quiet it is—but it doesn't seem quiet to me at all. The chorus of bugs is constant; there's bird calls, and the occasional grunt of swamp hogs.

Speaking of swamp hogs, this is the summer when Americans will become aware that we have a serious feral pig problem. In what has now become a horrifyingly rote pattern of anger and despair after yet another mass shooting, a Twitter conversation about the uses of assault weapons prompted the question "Legit question for rural Americans—How do I kill the 30-50 feral hogs that run into my yard within 3-5 mins while my small kids play?"[5] The specificity of anyone's yard having "30-50 feral hogs" in it tickled the internet's funny bone, and a meme was born. The thing is, though, many Americans are dealing with 30-50 feral hogs on the regular. More than five million feral swine are running rampant in the US in thirty-nine states (but are rapidly spreading), and they cause $2.5 billion in damage every year. The government is currently spending $30.5 million annually to try to solve this problem, and it isn't working. Soon there will be feral hogs from our southern border all the way to our northern border.[6] The first feral hog I saw on this trip was an absolutely behemoth boar dead on the side of the road in Arizona—it must have totaled the car that hit it. I saw more in New Mexico and Texas. Now, from the safety of our boat that now feels much too small, we get an up-close look at these disgusting, brilliant, horrifying things.

There are only three things I'm afraid of: spiders, lots of small bumpy things like the inside of a pomegranate (it's called trypophobia), and pigs. Pigs will eat human flesh, destroy everything in their path, and scream in that high-pitched wail that makes my skin crawl. I am way more afraid of the pigs than I am of the gators—you can hear the pigs snuffling and rooting around in the water lapping underneath the boat.

The swamp is still unmapped—bayous move constantly as sediment shifts and water finds new paths to the Gulf. If you want to know how to navigate a bayou, you have to log a lot of hours, keeping track of all the changes. You can tell you are getting closer to the ocean as the trees, dependent on fresh water, thin out. While some trees can flourish in brackish water, very few can grow in pure salt. It's upriver, near the fresh water, where the trees grow so dense one can't see through them. But even in the brackish water, they grow so tall that you have no horizon. It is truly a maze, claustrophobic despite being such a vast landscape. It's entirely possible that you could die lost in a boat not twenty-five feet from the open Gulf. If you don't know where you're going, or get turned around, it'll be a very thirsty death.

Every child of the 1980s carries the wounds from watching the scene in the fantasy classic *The Neverending Story* where the hero Atreyu begs his valiant horse Artax not to give in to the Swamp of Sadness. But the beautiful horse can't fend off his despair, and is slowly, painfully subsumed by murky waters. I can't even bring myself to rewatch the clip. As a girl, I wanted more than anything to be called away on an Adventure, preferably with a horse, but I'd settle for a dog (again, *Natty Gann*). Arbitrary beginnings and endings, like state lines, mothers and daughters, "before the trip" and "after the trip," are starting to seem increasingly just that: arbitrary. Like the 10 amalgamating into existence from the 1, like the swamp creeping out of the desert and vice versa. I'm staring at this pig, thinking that I need to change how I understand exactly what it is I'm doing. The trip is just a drive I'm taking; the adventure is a journey. The trip will end. The journey won't, just like my mother and I don't end, like the interstate. What I am hoping for, closure? Peace? I've read enough stories to know that you don't get to choose how the story ends. If I can't get square with that, I'm going to sink like a horse in a swamp.

Our traveling companion, kitted out in a khaki vest that looks brand-new and wielding a ridiculously big telephoto lens, is photographing everything. The only thing that the woman does not take a photo of is the swamp shack we are currently drifting by—abandoned, it still has the search tags left by people looking for bodies left in the wreckage of Katrina. Not that bodies last very long around here.

The last Cajun brunch of the summer starts with a quick note on consent. Leesaw, the owner of my cottage, puts together these afternoons of boozy punches and zydeco and, best of all, two-stepping. The two-step is a bit like the twist: nearly anyone with an iota of rhythm can pull it off. It's a basic building block of nearly all country dances. The Tigermen Den is packed this afternoon with a funny mix of hipsters, country folk, and posh people from uptown. A young woman with short hair, a floral dress, and cowboy boots shows the newbies the basics of the steps as she dances with her female partner and reminds us that, at any point, you can end a dance. The zydeco player and violin player warm up. Leesaw told me that it took her forever to find some Cajun musicians who would make the drive into the city, but these guys are really good.

When the band starts up, the packed room begins happily bopping, couples of every sort grinning. I'm saying hello to a dog with no tail shaking its entire rear end with delight when I realize there's a pair of shiny boots in my eyeline.

"Would you like to dance?"

He's a little taller than me, and his checked button-down is pressed. He looks a bit like the guys I would see in the honky bars I'd sneak into around Sacramento when my friends and I would go to rodeos. Pleasingly thick, with ruddy cheeks, but polite in that southern way. I like it.

"That'd be nice."

There's something wonderful about being asked to dance, and then holding a stranger in your arms and being held in theirs, for a moment in time. He's from Baton Rouge—a city I passed through with the idea to hit it up on the way back to California.

"Don't bother," he tells me, easing me around the dance floor. "Most interesting thing about Baton Rouge is New Orleans."

His family is Cajun, descendants of Canadian immigrants from France; I can tell by the sober slur in his accent, but he tells me he didn't grow up in the culture. His mother rebelled by leaving the Catholic Church and becoming a Baptist, but in his midthirties he started exploring by checking out Catholic services, reaching out to his grandparents, and learning how to two-step. We dance awhile, but I demur a drink and return to sweating outside. I'm leaving town soon, and my heart feels a little heavy.

That night, the entire sky is lit up by lightning, so bright I can read billboards by its light; my favorite is one that feels very Only in New Orleans: a personal injury lawyer with an intimidating scowl, a flashy red tie, and matching red letters that read "Holla at Your People!"

In the morning I slowly start packing Minnie up—it's a little harder to fit all my clothes, because I've made out like a bandit doing some vintage shopping. In this city you can find a Ralph Lauren suede leather pencil skirt in pristine condition for twenty bucks, but a stained, torn Jazz Fest T-shirt from 1987 will set you back $115. Maybe I'm projecting, but Ding the cat seems a little sad, watching me walk back and forth, lounging disdainfully across the white linen sheets I ordered when I rolled into town. My last evening, I'm reading on the porch when an older gentleman passing by on a bike pulls over to explain that he could use five bucks because his wife needs her diabetes medicine, and he lost his ATM card, and the bank is closed, and—I cut off his story by handing him some cash, and he teeters off unsteadily.

When Leesaw swings by to wish me well on my way, I ask her if there's a secret to living in New Orleans.

"Well, sometimes I need to get out of town. I go to Ocean Springs in Mississippi when I need a break. This is a magic place, but it's also a place that can grind you down."

But what is something she wishes people knew about this place?

"Moving to New Orleans is like falling in love," Leesaw says, weary. "It's like those relationships where you completely lose yourself. You didn't like jazz? Well, now you do. You don't eat red beans and rice? Not anymore. You can really lose track of yourself here."

I've been playing house since I've been in New Orleans, pretending Ding is my cat, that this is my neighborhood, that this is my city. Enough neighbors have assumed that I actually moved onto the street to start inviting me to supper. I have not been clear enough that I'm just passing through. I love it here, not because it's easy—it isn't. It's way too hot and too dangerous to ever be described as "easy." It's actually perverse to call this city the Big Easy. I love this place because it's a city that knows exactly who it is. In this, it's a bit like home. LA's drawbacks are so obvious—the traffic, the smog—there's no excuse. Either you can roll with it, or you can't. So it goes in New Orleans as well. If you need businesses to be open when their website says they are, you might be better off in Cincinnati. Wonderful, strange things can happen in New Orleans if you can walk into a room and ask a bunch of strangers, "What's good?" You might have disappointing sex with a himbo barista, but you might also end up dancing in the streets. I don't think it's possible for me to get lost on this journey; wherever I go is part of it. I have gotten complacent, though. I want to stay with Ding on the porch. I have no memory of New Orleans in 1996, only a vague image of the Superdome as seen from the 10. My mother made no special point to stop here, the way she did in Tombstone. Maybe it scared her, maybe the nightlife here worried her, but for whatever reason, it's as if she excised New Orleans from the 10.

The next morning, I don't get far before I realize that I need gas, and I pull off the interstate in the hinterlands east of New Orleans. As I turn onto a side road, a young boy, maybe thirteen or fourteen, riding a bike, slowly raises his arm at me, makes his hand into a gun, and mimes pulling the trigger. He rides off, bike swerving, under the full summer sun.

The farther I go, the fuzzier WWOZ gets. Eventually the sounds of Sidney Bechet's clarinet fully dissolve into static. I guess I'm back in America.

SONGS I LISTENED TO ON REPEAT AND ONE I NEVER LISTENED TO

"Amerika" by Wintersleep
"I can't survive on my Amerika / If the worst is true / Is it just a waste of time? / What am I trying to find?"

"Gris-Gris Gumbo Ya Ya" by Dr. John
All hail the gris-gris man.

"Ride" by Lana Del Rey

"Hold On" by Alabama Shakes
Sometimes you just need to be told to hang in there.

"Mi Gente (Homecoming Live)" by Beyoncé / J Balvin / Willy William
Sometimes you've just got to shake your ass.

"Crash on the Highway" by Hurray for the Riff Raff
From the Small Town Heroes *album by a New Orleans band—the perfect way to wake up on a steamy morning in the Crescent City.*

"Well-Dressed" by Hop Along
I don't know what it is about this song, which is more like three songs in one, but Frances Quinlan's voice makes my hair stand on end. Tender and furious, which is how I feel a lot of the time.

"Hast Thou Considered the Tetrapod" by the Mountain Goats
Sometimes things hit so close to home, you want to live in it.

"Soulmate" by Lizzo

"Go to the Mardi Gras" by Professor Longhair

"Graceland" by Paul Simon
Like every other person my age, I grew up with my mom playing this in the car on repeat. There is no such thing as a road trip without "Graceland."

"California Soul" by Marlena Shaw
I didn't know about this song until my brother Colin used it in his documentary All Things Must Pass: The Rise and Fall of Tower Records. *There are so many incredible songs about California, but this must be one of the best. Whenever I missed home, it was this and Joni.*

Nothing by Frightened Rabbit
Not yet. But soon.

Chapter Twenty-One

Beauvoir

This is America. Don't catch you slippin' now!
—CHILDISH GAMBINO

There is a moment in Ken Burns's documentary *Jazz* that has stuck in my head for years that will strike me all over again when I rewatch it in New Orleans. Wynton Marsalis, trumpet player, artistic director of Jazz at Lincoln Center in New York, and member of a musical dynasty of New Orleans, is asked to comment on an uncomfortable bit of jazz history. Freddie Keppard was a cornet player, arguably the best in New Orleans after Buddy Bolden gave it up when he went mad. Keppard and his band, the Original Creole Orchestra, played in Los Angeles and Chicago, spreading the word of this new music to curious Americans, most of whom didn't know what it meant for someone to be Creole. Along with being known for his ability to play as loud and with as much personality as Bolden before him, Keppard was famous for being secretive. Apparently, he would play with a kerchief over his fingers so others couldn't watch him and steal from him.

In December 1915 it was this fear of being ripped off that made Keppard turn down the Victor Talking Machine Company's offer to be the first jazz band ever recorded. He didn't want other trumpet players to be able to listen to his playing on repeat and figure out how to copy him. Maybe he thought that without him, there would be no jazz recording, but the Victor Talking Machine Company then turned to the Original Dixieland Jass Band, fronted by Nick LaRocca. This band was all white. "Livery Stable Blues" went on to become a smash sensation, selling more than any other record had done before, and catapulted LaRocca and his band into international fame. He would tour the world, introduce it to jazz, and tell anyone who would listen that he had invented it and, furthermore, it could never have been created by a Black or Creole man—they weren't capable of art.

The moment that has stuck with me is when Wynton has clearly been asked to comment on LaRocca declaring jazz to be a white art.

"Race is . . ." he starts, then pauses. He closes his eyes. There's a deep sigh. He wants to get this right.

"Race for this country is like the thing in the story, in the mythology, the thing you have to do for the kingdom to be well. And it's always something that you don't want to do. And it's always that thing that is so much about you confronting yourself. That's tailor-made for you to fail dealing with it. And the question of your heroism and of your courage, and of your success in dealing with this trial is, can you confront it with honesty? And do you confront it, and do you have the energy to sustain an attack on it? And since jazz music is at the center of American mythology, it necessarily deals with race. The more we run from it, the more we run into it. It's an age-old story. If it's not race, it's something else. But in this particular instance, in this nation, it's race."[1]

There are macro stories and micro stories. I got into this van and started driving east because I was beginning to see that there was something at the center of my labyrinth of self that I had not confronted yet: my mother, her mother, Palatka, what might have happened there, and the lessons from that event that became sacrosanct for my mother, and which she passed down to me. As I drive farther into what we call the Deep South, again and again my thoughts return to what happens when we, as individuals and as a collective, cannot look at ourselves clearly, cannot view our histories as dispassionate facts. My mother told me that the most important thing about the South is what isn't said. What isn't discussed. I didn't really know what that meant until I got to Beauvoir.

I don't want to leave New Orleans. I don't want to move on east. For one thing, everyone has been spooking me about Mississippi from all the way back in the desert. "You're not camping in Mississippi, are you?" I was asked in New Mexico. A waitress in New Orleans warned me not to drive through Mississippi at night.

"Body of Missing Pregnant Woman Is Found in MS," "Man Charged in Cross Burning Near Black Resident's MS Home," and "17-Year-Old's Body Found after MS Sound Drowning" are some of the headlines from the local newspaper the *Sun Herald* the week I'm in Biloxi. Not any more violent than what my local papers back home in Los Angeles would report on any given day, but the touches of what to this Californian can only be described as Southern Gothic catch my eye: the cross burning, the drownings.

I find a rental between Ocean Springs and Biloxi, which I learn only Yankees pronounce "Bill-ock-see." Everyone else, it seems, says "Bull-uhck-see." Ocean Springs, right on the coast of the Gulf, was recommended to me by several New Orleanians as their favorite getaway spot, especially when they want to get in the water.

When I pull into Ocean Springs, it's a breezy, sunny day leading up to the Fourth of July. There are ice cream shops and pottery shops and vacationers meandering in their khaki culottes and sandals. There are a lot of flags out. American flags, flags of sunflowers in baskets, flags of American flags. I make my way through the little village and down to the shoreline, with its beach, dappled with tall grass, and bike path. A van is parked, doors opened wide, with good-time guitar music blaring. A girl wearing high-cut shorts and high-top Converse skateboards back and forth. I also notice a couple with lawn chairs parked out in the water. I'm a little surprised not to see more people in the water, given the impending holiday and the insanely beautiful weather.

I still have my big jacket, sweaters, and gloves from New Mexico, from the beginning of the trip when my tent and the van would still be frosted over in the morning. Seeing as how it's now hot enough to break a sweat while yawning, I head to a FedEx to send some things home.

"New here," the man behind the counter doesn't so much ask as announce.

"Just passing through," I say. "Anything I should definitely do while I'm here?"

"Well, whatever you do, don't get in the water."

"That's for sure," seconds his coworker.

And why's that? "There's a flesh-eating algae bloom in the water. All the beaches are going to be closed for the holiday."

"I was just at the beach. I didn't see a single sign. There were people in the water!"

"Well, they're idiots."

The man then tells me about a guy he knew (or his brother knew) who went fishing, got a little cut, but put his hand back in the water, and yada yada, had to amputate his hand. His whole hand. I'm not sure if this is an apocryphal story or at least partially true, but an obsessive Google later proves that the algae bloom is real and there has been loss of life and limb.

Down the street from my rental and across the six-lane avenue is a Waffle House. The chain is as southern as hurricanes, but somehow I haven't been in one yet, so the next morning I pop in for breakfast.

There's one or two occupied tables and one man at the counter, where I take a seat and crack open a book while I enjoy a great cup of bad coffee and wait for my eggs and grits. The other patrons are obviously regulars and chat with the waitresses about the upcoming Fourth of July. There's a bit of a kerfuffle when a man comes in to pick up a to-go order, and then refuses to pay the tab. He gets heated and starts yelling. I assume he's on some sort of drug at 8 a.m., but then again it could just be that he's hungry and it's already punishingly hot outside. The unflappable waitress merely shrugs when he storms out, screaming in the placid, heavy morning. Unlike back home in the desert, where night temperatures plummet from their concrete-melting daytime highs, here the only relief from humidity comes in the first couple of hours after a rainstorm.

"Your tattoos are so beautiful," the manager says to me, as the place quiets down. He looks like he's in his late thirties, with a pale short-sleeved button-down and brown tie. The waitresses share an eye roll as he strikes up a conversation with me. Eventually he asks me what I'm doing in town, and I tell him I'm going to Beauvoir later that day. He's never heard of it. He tells me about his poetry, and how much he likes what I'm wearing. I hurry up, throwing back grits and coffee, give a hefty tip to my waitress, and head out.

In our Sacramento home, my mother's southern life was most evident in the dining room. She ate mostly peanut butter and jelly sandwiches in bed in the middle of the night, and I raided the large freezer she'd had installed in our basement as part of her Y2K preparations. That was the summer my horseback riding barn had moved locations, and I helped assemble new fences around the property. Sacramento summers are hot and dry, usually over 100 degrees. After weeks spent with a post driver in the blazing heat, with only strawberry ice cream in my belly, I melted down to a state of trimness that earned me compliments when I returned to LA.

When my mom did cook, though, I saw the truth of her roots. Whether they were affectations or foods she'd learned to make from her mother and others, the South was on the plate. There were the standards, biscuits and gravy, grits that she served simple with butter and black pepper. I had not believed her when she told me that at some point she grew up around Cubans, but that experience was there in her remarkable ropa vieja. She had a habit of putting oysters in a lot of food, notably her Thanksgiving stuffing, but also many rice dishes, which caused a lightbulb in my head to go off when I was reading about the foods of the Gullah Geechee, descendants of enslaved peoples on the lower Atlantic coast, whose cuisine showcases seafood and grains.

In 1996, our road trip was my introduction to southern chains like Piggly Wiggly, Waffle House, Whataburger (which I still haven't tried), and Cracker Barrel. For some reason, teenage me was convinced that Cracker Barrel was just the best, most delicious food ever. I'm not sure if this was because of the kitschy gift shop, with its rocking chairs and old-timey tchotchkes, but I was sure that this synthetic version of Southern Charm was delicious, and genuinely charming. I didn't understand its cynicism.

There are hundreds of Confederate flags lining the drive as I pull into Beauvoir, the postwar home of Jefferson Davis as well as his "presidential library." This whole area was and continues to be a popular vacation spot due to the breeze coming off the Gulf. Today, the heat is bone-softening. In his book *The Gulf: The Making of an American Sea*, Jack E. Davis explains how the former leader of the Confederacy came to spend his winter years here:

> It had long been the fashion of southern planters to flee the stifling fields of summer to hunker down on the inshore coast in second homes of wide porches and tall windows—a leisure time that, much like that of the ancient Greeks and Romans, was undergirded by slaves. Nearly as soon as Spain ceded lower Mississippi and Alabama to the US in 1811, planters built the first seasonal residences. The patriarch of their culture, former Confederate president Jefferson Davis, came to join them near Biloxi in the centennial year of the nation's birth. Woeful in defeat, the penniless hero moves into a cottage on the grounds of the Beauvoir estate.[2]

The 608-acre estate (now reduced to around 52) was originally built in 1852 by a planter named James Brown, and was eventually bought by Samuel and Sarah Anne Ellis Dorsey. Sarah Anne invited the deposed Davis to Beauvoir to "write his memoir, in the hope of restoring his reputation and his finances." Eventually Dorsey would will Beauvoir to Davis. He lived there with his wife and daughter until his death in 1889, after which his widow and daughter moved to New York City. Varina Howell Davis sold the estate to the United Confederate Veterans, stipulating that the property be used as a home for Confederate veterans of the war, which it was until the death of the last Confederate soldier in Mississippi in 1953, at which time it was turned into a museum. The barracks that housed the veterans are no longer there, but there's a cemetery for them, and the library complex with a gift shop and large theater was completed in 1998. Many cars in the parking lot bear bumper stickers that read "Confederate History IS American History." Bumper stickers can be very informative.

Inside, I buy a ticket, and wander around to kill some time as I'm early for my guided tour. I take the opportunity to enjoy the air-conditioning in the theater, which fits about 150 people. There's only myself and an Indian American family who I later overhear are from Chicago. Soon enough the informational film *Jefferson Davis: American Son* begins. George W. Jones, a kindly Yankee senator from Iowa, looking like an ersatz Mark Twain and sounding like Foghorn Leghorn, welcomes us and urges us to remember the words of his great friend: "When the cause was lost, what cause was it? Not that of the South only, but the cause of constitutional government, the supremacy of law, the natural rights of man." Jones recalls Jefferson fondly and calls him "the most misunderstood man of his time, and I find that vexsome." Everyone I meet working at Beauvoir today speaks with this patter of Dixie drawl—even this actor supposedly playing a northerner.

"Those were good but troubled times," he says, gripping his ornate walking cane with a weary brow. "Jefferson was known as a champion of states' rights. Most people regarded him as a moderate. Gives you an idea of just how hot things were beginning to get in Congress. Well, the debate might have been about slavery, but the real issue here was states' rights."

The mythnotion that the Civil War was a states' rights issue, rather than a fight to maintain the right to own, sell, murder, rape, and degrade human beings, is the backbone of the "Lost Cause" doctrine. That infamous phrase comes from a book published in 1866 by Confederate sympathizer Edward Pollard, the full title of which is *The Lost Cause: A New Southern History of the War of the Confederates: Comprising a Full and Authentic Account of the Rise and Progress of the Late Southern Confederacy—the Campaigns, Battles, Incidents, and Adventures of the Most Gigantic Struggle of the World's*

History. Its main tenets are "that the Confederacy was based on a noble ideal, the Civil War was not about slavery, and slavery was benign."[3] Natural, even.

Outside the theater and library complex and closer to the beach road along the Mississippi coast lies the actual house of Beauvoir, "the estate's main structure, a raised Louisiana-style plantation house. Nine-foot French doors and windows [open] to a white-columned portico that overlooks this particular sound of the Gulf."[4] The house was built so that breezes would come up from under the house and through its large windows, with the kitchen separated from the main house to keep heat from the fires away from the family.

Those of us waiting for the guided tour stand listlessly on the large veranda, all trying and failing to keep cool, waving maps and brochures in front of red faces. There is one family with a baby so young I'm surprised to see they've brought her out into public, let alone into this heat. I ask how old she is (a bright-pink headband is wrapped around her flushed head with its faint pale wisps of hair).

"A week," the mom responds. Everyone coos over the baby's slack red face as the mother holds her against her damp tank top.

Our tour guide, a slightly plump white woman in her forties, arrives attired in a full hoop skirt with part of the hem trailing in the back, exposing the Hula-Hoop at the bottom.

"Oh my lawd!" She fawns over the baby. "Bless my soul, this chile!" She tells us about planters vacationing on the Mississippi coast, about Sarah Dorsey and her empathy for Davis after the war, and a typical day in the life at Beauvoir in the mid-nineteenth century. She points out restored furniture, discusses the damage the house has taken from hurricanes, and describes the role the property played as a home for Confederate veterans. It was here that Davis, broken down and financially insolvent after the war, retreated to write his memoirs.

In the December 2018 issue of *Smithsonian*, Brian Palmer and Seth Freed Wessler set out to discover "the cost of the Confederacy"—how many American tax dollars were going toward the seven hundred Confederate monuments around the American South. "Over the past ten years," they found, "taxpayers have directed at least $40 million to Confederate monuments—statues, homes, parks, museums, libraries and cemeteries—and to Confederate heritage organizations."[5] Beauvoir specifically has received extremely large sums—hence the restored furniture and reconstruction after Hurricane Katrina.

After the tour, I approach my guide to ask some more questions, and she eyes me with some wariness.

"I saw you writing notes during the tour."

"Well, I'm a writer—"

"Oh no!" she moans. She really does, holding her hand to her forehead like a belle in distress. I laugh and assure her I just have some follow-up questions. Firstly, where were the quarters for enslaved people? She does not actually roll her eyes, but she does open her mouth, close it again, sigh, and then explain to me that Beauvoir was not a plantation, not even before Jefferson Davis lived there. It was a vacation home, and so would not have needed the number of slaves to work the land as an agricultural project.

"I understand," I say. "But neither the Dorsey family nor the Davis family were emptying their own commodes or mowing the lawn. There were enslaved people here, and I'm wondering where they lived."

She suddenly drops the accent. "Can I tell you something? This is only my second week as a tour guide. Where are you from?"

"Los Angeles."

"Really? Well, I'm *actually* a voice-over artist."

* * *

While I wander around the cemetery and try to eye how many of the pennies on the tomb of the unknown soldier are Lincoln side down, I think about Jack. When I was sixteen, my oldest school friend, Jack, shaved his head, started wearing white laces on his black combat boots, and was hanging out with a crowd I'd never seen before. Hard-faced, drunk guys who groped me as a "joke" and who I couldn't imagine hanging out with my friend, who balked when I asked him to kiss me while riding the Ferris wheel at the state fair. Suddenly there was a Confederate flag in his room.

"What's that about?" I asked him.

"It's about history. It's about pride."

"History? California was in the Union. What history are you talking about?"

"I dunno," he mumbled.

In fact, troops from California pushed the Confederacy out of Arizona and New Mexico in 1862.[6] By no means, however, does my home state have a clean slate, as Jean Pfaelzer explains in her book *California, a Slave State*. We may have been in the Union, but the enslavement of different peoples is just as much a part of our history. My friend could only give me a chagrined shrug, and that was the end of the conversation and the friendship.

I'm angry with myself and disgusted with this place. I leave without seeing the "Presidential Library." I pull out of Beauvoir and drive back down the Mississippi coast, past T-shirt huts and a barbecue joint called Slap Ya Momma's, whose sign promises BUTTS BUTTS & MORE BUTTS. In Biloxi proper, I meander empty streets with empty business fronts and credit unions. I see no open businesses and very few people. Comedian and writer John Mulaney might have been right when he said, "Biloxi is a place where the outside feels haunted."[7] Eventually I give up on finding something to do and delve into the Hard Rock Casino to eat lunch and watch America beat England in the Women's World Cup. In between chitchatting with the waitress about New York's Finger Lakes, I read up on the debate about what to do with Confederate monuments. In 2017, several statues of Confederate generals were removed from prominent spaces around New Orleans. Subsequently Beauvoir, and the United Sons of Confederate Veterans whose members make up its board of directors, requested to take the statues.[8] The full statement from Beauvoir on wanting New Orleans's Confederate statues: "By expressing our desires for these monuments, we are in no way condoning slavery, which was an evil institution that *has no color or creed and has existed since the dawn of time.*"

I've written it out on an index card. Later, when I'm driving, it's slotted into my dashboard to stare at in traffic. I rewrite it in my journal over and over, as if it will make sense to me eventually. I stare at it while eating dinner in another random diner, Freddie "King" Keppard's "Here Comes the Hot Tamale Man" playing on my headphones. That which "has existed since the dawn of time" is considered intrinsic, instinctive; that is to say, natural. If slavery is natural, the logic is that there are some peoples whose natural state is to be enslaved. *Since the dawn of time.*

Chapter Twenty-Two

John Raymond Dillingham

Most of my mother's poems exist in one of two modes: theological metaphors, or blunt to the point where they are barely poems in the literary sense. An example of the former is this poem, which she wrote several drafts of:

The Enemy

[. . .]
satan is the murderer, not God
satan is liar, not God
[. . .]
satan is the bringer of death upon the world
[. . .]
satan is the child molester
satan is the cause of incest
[. . .]
satan is the cause of addiction
satan is the cause of alcoholism

satan is the cause of depression and suicide
satan is the cause of nervous breakdowns
satan is the cause of mental illness
[. . .]
Satan is the thief, the robber

Again and again her poems return to this imagery of Satan and sex: "When satan and his demon throng invisible, around their bed [. . .] Love's way are changed into hells aping [. . .] love's coupling of sexuality / becomes hate's mauling."

On the other hand, one poem reads simply:

HE ENTERS ME. STABBING ME.
KILLING ME.
SPLITTING ME WIDE.
I'M ASHATTER, SPLITTING.
I'M COVERED IN MY OWN BLOOD, SHIT AND URINE.
MY ARMS AND LEGS FALL OFF.
MY HEAD FALLS OFF.
A BROKEN DOLL.
I'M SIX YEARS OLD.
INCEST.

This poem is titled "Klaus Barbie Doll."

My mother occasionally acknowledged that her father was Jewish. His mother, Renia "Rebecca" Sapira Dillingham, is buried in the Machsikei Hadas Cemetery outside Pittsburgh—known for its service to the Galician community, or Jews from an area that is now Poland and Ukraine.

Her gravestone reads only MOTHER. Beside her is John Raymond Dillingham Sr. Though his marker notes his birthday and the date of his death, in a larger font above those dates are his enlistment in (May 22, 1914) and discharge from the army (October 14, 1920). But while my mother occasionally talked about our Jewish roots—something she never followed up with basics like "Your great-grandmother was Jewish," but rather hinted at a vast conspiracy to cover up some unknown branch of the family, and so I consequently never believed her—she frequently used Nazi imagery to describe her father. Here my mother's imagery is not specifically Third Reich, but militaristic and fascistic nonetheless:

"Black Shoes"

I used to watch my father
spit shine his black shoes
melt the wax, apply it carefully with
a cloth, melt it with a match,
running a burning match over
the whole shoe,
then, buff it until
you could see our smiles in the shine.
on a summer june morning in the south
I watched him wide eyed as he
carved up a young girl
nowadays the psychiatrists
deny recovered memories, recovered memory which in fact was
supposed to be the whole point of therapy
now, they say it was a rape
that felt like a murder,

and I was too young to differentiate reality
but I no longer care . . .
I no longer live my life as if it is a detective novel
in search of the truth
now I hide in my closet and cry afraid
how can I have a present
in Christ when the past won't stay dead
that's why I am afraid of black shoes
green buicks
marines in blue
khaki
men with brass buttons
black shoes that shine with smiles
and most of all fathers who say they love
promises that aren't kept
people who say they love me
people who say they want to take care of me

This poem puzzles me: it seems to hint that at some point someone, perhaps even a psychiatrist, hinted that her "recovered memory" was not of someone else's murder, "I watched him wide eyed as he / carved up a young girl," but her own victimization at her father's hands:

nowadays the psychiatrists
deny recovered memories, recovered memory which in fact was
supposed to be the whole point of therapy
now, they say it was a rape
that felt like a murder,
and I was too young to differentiate reality

Recovered memory therapy—the idea that adults can "recover" accurate memories of childhood trauma previously forgotten, or buried deep in the unconscious—is one of the most controversial topics in contemporary psychology. It certainly left a foul aftertaste for those who will remember the "Satanic Panic" media blitz of the late 1980s and '90s, in which day-care workers and teenage boys were falsely convicted of heinous acts against children. These "satanic ritual abuse claims relied on overzealous law enforcement, unsubstantiated statements from children, and, above all, coercive and suggestive interrogation by therapists and prosecutors."[1] I suspect that in the national fervor about secret satanic groups, my mother took what was a traumatic memory that was not at all forgotten, put a patina of hellishness over it, and projected it onto a different little girl. Still, if her primary experience with therapists was being told that her horrifying memories were probably of her own rape, followed by attempts at diagnosis of mental illness, I understand why my mother was so antipathetic toward the court-ordered psychiatric visits required when I switched custody, even though they were mostly for me.

It has to mean something that what set me out on this trip was the jaw-dropping possibility that my grandfather was a murderer and a rapist, and yet no portion of my attention thus far has been on him at all. It's not that the accusation doesn't shock me, but it doesn't surprise me. I can't separate the nature of the accusation from the nature of my mother: hyperbolic, mad, dare I say it, hysterical. There is also the truth that men rape. They murder. But there's something else, a part of this accusation that I've been purposefully avoiding. It wasn't part of the red journal, but I remember it nonetheless.

It came out because of a T-shirt. The tour merch for U2's album *Achtung Baby* was everywhere in 1992. When my mother saw this shirt, she lost her mind. Screaming, crying, inconsolable. The shirt read "Every artist is a cannibal." We didn't understand, she moaned and raged, her father. Not only had he raped and murdered a little girl. He ate her.

Up until I was nine or so, I was a horrible liar. I mean, I told real whoppers. If you asked me how school was, I might tell you that an FBI agent had visited class and singled me out as clearly the best possibility for a *super*-special third-grade field agent. I kept going in this vein until a family with a daughter a couple years older than me rented a house near my dad's one summer. She asked if I could do a cartwheel, and my response was that I couldn't but only because I'd been in a horrible skiing accident that broke my back and I'd just learned to walk again. I was a literal walking miracle.

"You don't need a reason," this girl told me, after she pulled me aside. "You can just say that you can't, or maybe that you don't want to. You don't have to lie." I was mortified and stayed away from playing with her for a couple of days while I recovered, but this girl had given me an incredible gift. She'd told me, in so many words, that I was enough. When I look back at my lying, I don't see malintent; I see a little girl who didn't know how to ask for help.

Now I can't help but approach this as I approach all things: as an English major, god help me, and the idea of John Raymond Dillingham as a cannibal strikes me as a powerful metaphor. He didn't just molest her, he obliterated the girl child in her. He chewed her up and spat her out. "Cannibalism is an ancient and primal manifestation of predacity."[2] My mother saw her father as a predator, possibly—I am not yet willing to say *probably*—for good reason, and the specter of such a primal, intimate crime drives the point.

He couldn't be just another drunk military man who took out his rage on his own children, because that did not capture the full scope of my mother's pain, her rage. She needed a monster whose size and brutality matched the scope of her ruin, a villain who worked in a major key, who broke not only laws and hearts, but human taboo. *Cannibalism.* The macabre sparkle of that word is thrilling; yet I can only say that if you actually knew my mother, the perverse novelty of that possibility loses its luster. I've taken this part of my mother's story and put it on a shelf somewhere in my mind because, if I'm being honest, it reminds me too much of the lies I told as a kid. It can't just be that I don't know how to do a cartwheel; it's that I snapped my spine in half and just learned to walk again. It can't just be that my grandfather was a mean drunk who molested his daughter; it's that he was a cannibal. Did she not think her pain and fear were enough? Not impressive enough to be worthy of attention? Of help? Why couldn't my mother take to heart that her trauma "was a rape / that *felt* like a murder"?

This is the difference between my mother and me, though: I knew I was fibbing, and I could stop. She didn't and couldn't. It rode her, not the other way around. I don't think of my mother as a liar; how can someone be a liar if they're incapable of discerning reality and fiction? If they aren't even interested in discerning truth from fiction ("but I no longer care . . . / I no longer live my life as if it is a detective novel")? Yet maybe, unconsciously, her hyperbole was also a version of asking for the help, of trying to be worthy of concern. No one told her she was enough.

While my mother keeps coming into clearer and clearer focus for me, my grandfather John Raymond remains a mystery. I know that when my grandmother said, "It's either me or the posting in Japan," he chose Japan. I know that he only quit the service when his eldest son joined the Marine Corps. When I started this trip, I had no idea where he was born, the circumstances of his death, or the true nature of his character. I knew only that a mere mention of him would send my mother wordlessly to her room, where the door would remain closed for days. The only time I saw a photograph of him was in 1996, when we finally reached Palatka, and a portrait of him in uniform, slightly fuzzy the way old photographs are, hung on a wall with floral wallpaper. I was shocked to see how much he looked like my mother. (At that point, I had never seen a childhood photo of her.) He looked like me too. I had never seen my grandmother with any man besides her beloved brother, my uncle David, who was the reason she, and consequently my mother, my brother, and I, ended up in Sacramento. The idea that Grandma Haha had once had a husband was odd. She always seemed content with her flowers, her music, her solitude. What room had there been in her life for a man? I couldn't imagine her, or my mother for that matter, standing beside a man at the sink after dinner, listening to the radio and tidying up before heading off to bed.

John Raymond Dillingham Jr. was born in Pittsburgh in July 1922, and like his father (and eventually his own three sons) enlisted in the armed services. He was in the Marine Corps from 1941 until 1967, and only retired when one of his sons also began serving in the Vietnam War. He was awarded a number of military commendations, including the Purple Heart and an award for Good Conduct—the first of nine. He grew up with one brother, Morton, and his mother, Rebecca. His father, a goy after whom he was named, was often absent, which meant he probably grew up in Jewish Pittsburgh near his mother's family. After he joined the marines and moved away from frigid

Pennsylvania, he was stationed in Florida, which must have seemed like paradise come February. He married Harriet Hall Collins of nearby Palatka, Florida, at the age of twenty-two and fulfilled high school requirements at twenty-three while still in the service, possibly at her urging.

My grandparents, mother, and uncles lived a classically itinerant military life through the 1950s and '60s, living in San Diego; Oahu; Norfolk, Virginia; Twentynine Palms deep in the California desert on the cusp between the Mojave and Colorado Deserts; and Camp Lejeune in North Carolina. At some point John, known to most as Jerry or Jerome, was stationed in Japan, but Harriet was unwilling to haul her four children across the seas, and settled in Miami. The marriage ended shortly after, in 1962.

I now have several black-and-white photographs of my grandfather during his deployment in Japan. It's hard not to project what I think I know of him onto the photographs, but his face strikes me as hard—even his grin. Flinty. When I reached out to my mother's cousin, a woman I have a few brief but warm memories of (particularly of her and her husband's funny Christmas cards, since we didn't get many), I asked her what if any memories she had of "Uncle Jerry."

"I never thought of him as horrible," she said. "He just had nothing in common with Harriet. Except kids. By the time your mom and I were both adults, she was becoming paranoid and was hard to relate to. I visited her once in Sacramento, and she graciously served us eggs. We had come rather unannounced. Another time I invited her to the family gathering in Ashland at the Oregon Shakespeare Festival. She holed up in a dark hotel room."

It's not that I think my grandfather looks particularly ominous, but perhaps he strikes me as a hard man, tough. And why wouldn't he be: a marine who had seen multiple tours of duty, the son of a serious army man himself, and married to a woman who didn't respect him. While he got his high school diploma in his twenties, Harriet had graduated from university already. She enjoyed classical music, and it played in the kitchen. Whatever his music was, it was relegated to wherever she wasn't. No one has told me what kind of music he liked.

After Jerry returned to America and left the service, he resettled in Virginia. Apparently he was married again, albeit briefly (from 1968 until 1973), to a woman named Shirley "Sam" Lewis. I had no idea this marriage existed and was shocked when I came across the name of my grandfather's second wife. For a while my mother had insisted on using a stage name. There was a period of time, very early in my father's burgeoning career, when he was becoming well known while she still was doing the occasional play in Sacramento. The name she took, and which still occasionally pops up on Google, was Samantha "Sam" Lewes. Lewes is a family name, but its uncanny similarity to her father's second wife's name could not have been lost on her.

I do not know what my grandfather did from the time of his second divorce in 1973 until his death in 1981 at the young age of fifty-nine, but I suspect he drank heavily. Here again, my grandfather evades me. Whatever was his actual cause of death, several family members pointed out that, as a serious drinker, he faced a serious health decline in his later years. I was very much surprised to hear that it was my mother who went to Virginia to be with him when he died, given how spooked she was on the rare occasions he was mentioned. I wonder if he asked her for one more drink. I wonder if she filled his glass with water, knowing he was beyond being able to tell the difference. I wonder what they said to each other. I wonder if she was present for his interment at Arlington National Cemetery. I wonder why she never told me any of this. I wonder if, had she told me, I wouldn't be living "my life as if it is a detective novel." All I know is that, according to my father, when she got back to Los Angeles after John Raymond Dillingham's death, she announced that she wanted to have another baby, and nine months later I was born.

Chapter Twenty-Three

Montgomery

"Oh, your daddy's rich and your ma is good-lookin'
So hush, little baby, don't you cry"
—*PORGY AND BESS*

As the road stretches away from Beauvoir, out in front of me and farther into the Deep South, I want to slam on the brakes. What if I don't actually want to know anything more about my mother? What if, when I eventually work up the nerve to contact my uncles, I'll be opening a Pandora's box of acrimony? More than one person cautioned me against this trip: let sleeping dogs lie. The closer I get to Palatka, the bigger and more intimidating those hounds look.

When I first started serious therapy, I was cognizant that I had reached a sort of emotional nook in the mountain I was climbing through my twenties. I had enough breathing room to look down at my childhood, and to look up and gird my loins, as the climb toward my adult life began. I thought I was ready to start the work of the therapeutic process, and yet there was a flurry of canceled appointments, mixed-up dates, profuse apologies. When my therapist gently confronted me, she asked, What are you afraid of? I told her I was afraid that if I acknowledged how much I wanted love, I would never have enough. That once I named my trauma, it would be the only word I knew. My therapist nodded; these were understandable fears. The thing about trauma, she told me, is that we don't get over it. We get on with it, and the only way we do that is by looking at it. Talking about it. Naming it.

The deeper I get into the Deep South, the closer I get to Palatka, all I'm thinking about is trauma. Personal trauma. Political trauma. How do we get on with it? The stories aren't the same, the stakes aren't anywhere near the same, but the process is the same. The only way we get on with trauma is to look right at it, so today I am driving to Montgomery.

Leaving Biloxi, I stop by Ocean Springs again and check to see if anyone has posted signs about not getting in the water over the holiday weekend—none that I can find. I stop at a little coffee shop, Bright-Eyed Brew Co. Two young men in suits are chitchatting with the barista, also a man in his twenties. They all clam up when I walk in, but the shop is small enough we're almost rubbing elbows. I break the ice by asking about everyone's holiday plans. Cookouts and boils seem like the universal answer.

"The other day a guy was telling me I shouldn't go in the water," I say, reaching for the cream. I don't drink coffee at home—just tea by the gallon—but ordering tea in America means you're going to get lukewarm Lipton's with some half-and-half. My version of coffee is basically a hot milkshake: a lot of milk and a lot of sugar.

"Good idea," says a tall man with sunglasses that belong to a sports coach tucked into the pocket of his button-down.

"Well, swimming is one thing, but can I ask, do you eat fish or shrimp or anything else from the Gulf?"

All three men look at each other and nod.

One, wearing a purple gingham button-down, says, "Oh yeah, that's never bothered me."

"So, you'll eat some this weekend?"

All nod again.

"So, you won't swim in it, but you'll eat the stuff that does?"

They all chuckle, a little embarrassed, a little proud.

"It all gets deep-fried anyway. Peanut oil kills everything, I figure."

The thing about Alabama is that it's barely even on the 10. With only sixty-seven miles of the interstate along the narrow appendage that hangs between Mississippi and the Florida panhandle, Alabama has the shortest mileage of any of the eight states along the corridor. Mobile Bay is dotted with oil rigs, but that hasn't had any major influence on beachgoers, according to author Wayne Flint: "Tourism made a 30-mile stretch of Gulf beaches in Baldwin County the state's hottest real estate market even as gas rigs dotted the azure waters that beckoned swimmers."[1] What's driving me to Montgomery is curiosity, but I'm happy to see more of the state than I would if I stuck to the 10—or I would be, but most of what I see on my detour is dense greenery on either side of the road; not the swampy density of Louisiana, but pine trees. At some point I pull over into a truck stop for a rest. Even the dogs sprung from long road trips seem to mosey over the hot concrete here; there's just no hurrying in this heat. After guzzling some water, I try to take a nap on the bed, but I'm nervous about sleeping with the door to Minnie wide open, and even with the windows mostly open, the van is hellish without the AC on. If I were in a proper van lifer rig, maybe I'd be able to have a fan on without completely draining the battery, but Minnie isn't set up for Alabama snoozes in the heavy afternoon.

I give up and continue nearly two hundred miles north of the 10. Montgomery is home to the National Memorial for Peace and Justice, known colloquially as the lynching memorial, and the Legacy Museum, both of which are "dedicated to the legacy of enslaved Black people, people terrorized by lynching, African Americans humiliated by racial segregation and Jim Crow, and people of color burdened with contemporary presumptions of guilt and police violence."

I had no idea "lynching" is actually named for a real person, Charles Lynch, a magistrate and colonel of revolutionary Virginia who would hang Americans for insurrection and selling stolen horses to the British: "Lynch's court was, for all intents and purposes, a court whose judgement aimed to protect America from threat by expelling the enemy within."[2] This is the first time I've understood that lynching was seen as a true justice, a weeding out of bad apples from an otherwise idyllic, sophisticated South.

First I go to the memorial, which is dedicated to the period of 1877 to 1950, from Reconstruction to roughly the beginnings of the civil rights movement, and documents 4,084 lynchings in twelve southern states. This combination of architecture, landscaping, and sculpture comes on slowly; by the time you've walked the memorial's full grounds, you are wrung out like a sweat-soaked handkerchief, exhausted and horrified. Importantly, it's also beautiful.

For each county for which the Equal Justice Initiative (EJI) has found evidence of a lynching there is a long rectangular block, with the names and dates of the murdered. At first these blocks, attached to the ceiling in the open-sided structure, are at floor height, and you walk among them, trying to take in all the names. Soon enough, you're sinking.

Not emotionally; literally. The floor begins to slope downward, and as you move forward, the blocks seem to rise up. It's you who are dropping. It takes your eye a moment to notice that these blocks, so neutral in their geometry before, now hang above you with blood-stilling clarity. The homogeneity of the rectangles becomes something else as they loom over you, not strange fruit, but uniform. The same shape, the same utilitarian metal, over and over, the names that go on and on. One monument commemorates twenty-three people who were murdered by lynching on a single day.

It takes me a moment to find the marker for Harrison County, home to Beauvoir. For every hanging marker in the memorial, there is an identical one nearby on a grass lawn. Each county has the option to claim a copy of its marker. "Over time, the National Memorial will serve as a report on which parts of the country have confronted the truth of this terror and which have not."[3] The day I was visiting, Harrison County had not claimed theirs.

As I walk from the memorial across the wide, empty streets of Montgomery to the museum, I'm thinking about what prejudice and ignorance have been handed down to me. My mother was not a hateful person, but all the same she told me to lock my car door whenever young Black men crossed in front of our Volvo station wagon. I watched *Dumbo* over and over, imprinting on its images, and never did she take the time to explain to me that the jangly buffoonery of the black crows jiving through "When I See an Elephant Fly" were a reference to Jim Crow and minstrelsy. She showed me *Gone with the Wind*, gave me a copy of the book, and never prompted either of us to interrogate the heroism of Scarlett O'Hara. My mother's version of the South was sweet tea, and placid egrets in still water. The scent of magnolias, Spanish moss swaying in the heavy air, and white linen tablecloths. The whitest.

In the Museum's permanent exhibition, the story segues from the work of the civil rights movement to our contemporary times and the over-policing of underfunded neighborhoods. While taking notes from a poster about the number of Black children incarcerated in adult prisons, I overhear one Black man, maybe in his fifties, say to another, "This is where all the white people get pissed and leave. How it's all connected." On that day, I am the only white person I see at either the memorial or the museum. When I start to cry, I duck into a bathroom, because while this is a moment for me, for everyone else in the museum, in the words of Samuel L. Jackson, "This is just another Tuesday."

It's early when I go back to my rented room, and the streets are mostly empty. I order a pizza but have no appetite when it arrives. I try to watch something, but my attention isn't there. I stand under a weak stream of water in the shower for a long time before lying on the bed listening to the ceiling fan circulate and the katydids outside. After my failed nap at the truck stop, I make peace with the fact that I probably won't be able to camp comfortably until I'm on my way west again, out of the realm of humidity. It's strange to think of the trip back, as if my imagination stops at the Atlantic, simply unraveling into its waters and leaving nothing behind to return to California. *California*, even the word sounds like it's from a different planet, as I lie on this damp, lumpy bed in Alabama. I google live music venues I could possibly check out, but fall asleep without meaning to, tumbling into dreams I'm glad I don't remember.

* * *

Driving south, the highway feels hemmed in, claustrophobic. I can't tell if I'm relieved to be going back to my main artery, the 10, or nervous to be finally entering Florida. It feels as though, before I cross into Florida, I can still call this whole thing off, but once I cross over into the parallel universe that is "the Sunshine State," I can't back out. To distract myself, I think about my mom, and all the ribbons that still connect her to me. In this constant state of flow between her and me, between one road and another, I have found more heirlooms, more legacies of hers that have now become my own. She didn't mean to leave me the red journal, she didn't mean to leave me this idea of the South that is so fragile it can't withstand investigation, but here I am, with her small hands, her auburn hair, and her Cracker Barrel ideas of the sophisticated South. Caught between these impenetrable walls of green, I remember when I was very young, and she would cradle me in her arms in the water, bouncing slightly and singing "Summertime."

If there's one song I associate with my mother, it's "Summertime." Even as a child I thought it was an odd choice for a lullaby. *Porgy and Bess* was written by white men, composed by George Gershwin from a libretto by DuBose Heyward (adapted from his book) and with lyrics by Ira Gershwin. It takes place in the slums of Charleston and follows Porgy, a disabled beggar, as he attempts to woo Bess away from her abusive lover and drug dealer. It was originally performed in 1935, and Gershwin always insisted on an all-Black cast of classically trained artists. Its legacy is debated for its representation of Black life consisting of drugs, gambling, violence, and "loose sex," but "Summertime" and "My Man's Gone Now" "remain among the best loved and most performed in the American Songbook."[4]

In all the stories my mother told me about the South, about the life she supposedly lived there, never, not once, did she talk about Black lives, the Civil War, slavery, Jim Crow, or racism. She made sure to show me films she considered important cinema, music and theater she counted as vital to an artist's growth, none of which were made by, featured, or told stories of Black life. She sang me "Summertime," but never told me it was from an opera that featured only Black talent. There were no people of color in her orbit that I was aware of, or in my childhood.

I wish I could say that the overwhelming whiteness of my life up until that point had not left its mark on me, but of course it did. Whiteness, like money, shows its privilege by hardly ever being discussed, and I considered myself "beyond racism" because my intentions were never to be racist. If only conscious intentions were enough. I was raised to believe that racism is easy to identify because it's so hateful. My own racism is the product of ignorance, but what does that matter to the people I've hurt with cluelessness, an "edgy" joke, a blithe comment? I started driving east because I don't want to be ignorant anymore. I decided I wanted to ask questions about the things I took for granted, especially about who I am and where I'm from. I want to interrogate the lessons my mom taught me about the world, about people, about men and women and how we relate to each other, what's polite and what's rude—a weltanschauung I believed was specifically southern.

I went to Beauvoir because I thought, naïvely, that it would place the Civil War in a historical context that acknowledged the role that enslavement of Black people for the economic benefit of whites played in the war. I was wrong. What I got instead was an eerie buffet of cognitive dissonance: a cheery and bloodless presentation of Jefferson Davis and the war as a high-minded, intellectual debate about "states' rights." Hadn't I started this trip because I wanted to confront the past, not just my own, not just my mother's, but the past of all the places we'd been together? Hadn't this whole thing started because I wondered who Moomat Ahiko was?

Palatka is coming, and as I turn Minnie back onto the 10, point myself east once more, I breathe deeply. Alabama has taught me that there is no looking at my mother without looking at myself, at this collection of heirlooms and accessories that were handed down to me, and that I took without questioning. I could say that this trip is like going to the attic, opening a big dusty box, and laying out all the delicate white things that my mother gave me, "Summertime" and "yes, ma'am" and watercolor paintings of Florida lighthouses, but that's not what this feels like. This feels like I am marching up to that pile of sleeping dogs; I'm prying open their jowls, cramming my arm down their throats, and bringing up their secret innards. I lay them out like the haruspex, scrying over a pile of steaming guts, trying to make sense of it all.

The National Memorial for Peace and Justice has documented over 4,400 lynchings but believes "thousands more lynchings occurred that will never be recorded." There is one lynching death not acknowledged here by the EJI, that of Michael Donald. Nineteen years old, Michael was randomly grabbed by two members of the KKK, beaten with a tree limb, his throat slit, and then strung up from a camphor tree. The reason the EJI does not include Michael Donald's death in their monument is because the monument only acknowledges racial terrorism deaths up until 1950. Michael Donald was lynched in 1981.[5]

HARRISON COUNTY, MISSISSIPPI

Edward Turner

02.12.1881

George Washington

07.23.1887

Charlies Maria

07.12.1894

Ed Russ

06.09.1900

Henry Askew

06.09.1900

Henry Lewis

12.20.1900

Samuel Adams

11.05.1903

Unknown

03.13.1904

Henry Leidy

11.10.1908

Alex Smith

03.21.1922

Chapter Twenty-Four

Her Death

The first real dead body I saw was my mother's.

I left college a bit earlier than when spring break officially began, to head home to Sacramento. Three friends were supposed to join me in Los Angeles, though one had read the tea leaves and graciously backed out. I was spending the day by my mom's bedside before flying south. I felt duty bound to meet my friends in LA. They'd never been, and the promise of two weeks in La La Land had gotten everyone giddy. I didn't feel like I could cancel on them.

By that time, Mom was so out of it, on painkillers and fading in and out of consciousness, that I could mime lighting a cigarette with my hand and put it to her lips, and she'd take deep pulls on the unlit thing. She asked for her blue American Spirits till the very end. I mashed up strawberries and fed them to her, wiping her chin. Sometimes I read to her. When I swapped places with Colin and retreated to the living room sofa, I'd sit down and immediately fall asleep. Soon enough it was time for Colin to take me to the airport. I went in to say good-bye.

"I'm going now, Momma. But I'll be back soon. I love you. I love you."

She held an unlit cigarette to her mouth and replied woozily, "I love Colin," her voice soft and dreamy.

"I know you do, Momma. And he loves you."

In Los Angeles I picked my friends up at the airport. I took them to see the Hollywood sign, and we went to the beach. Colin called. I needed to come back, as soon as possible. While I waited to hear how quickly I could get a flight to Sacramento, I sat with my friends and stared at a VHS tape of *Aladdin* playing. A couple hours later, I came down the escalator at the Sacramento airport. Colin was the only person standing there. He looked at me, and just nodded. I knew already that I'd missed it, but seeing him wordlessly confirm it, I sobbed helplessly.

By the time we got to the little house, she'd already turned green. Her body was starting to contort, and her head was cocked back. Her hardening tongue was visible as her mouth cranked open. She'd gotten very thin at the end. I shuddered in the doorway but made myself look. *This is death. This is real. Don't look away. Let the Tower crumble.*

It was because of this moment that I declined to see her body laid out in her coffin, dressed in a cream skirt suit she hadn't worn in years, her best wig. I didn't want to sully the horrible last view of her, to do myself the disservice of pretending any of this wasn't real and forcing my future self to confront it all again.

From the time she was diagnosed, December 2000, to her death in March 2002, time seemed to stretch on, as it does in Cancer Land. Waiting for test results, waiting to see if a procedure worked, and soon enough waiting for the orderly to come change the sheets, waiting for the pain meds to kick in. Waiting for her to die. Now that she had, I wanted to freeze this moment. Perhaps if someone you love has died, you know the feeling of not wanting to go to sleep on the last day they were in the world. To go to sleep and wake up without them is to be forced to acknowledge the new order of things. The same thing happened when Scott went missing. I stayed up all night, secretly knowing he'd already left the world, and aware of what I was doing: staging a protest, trying to stave off time and keep us both in the same world a little while longer.

My mother was buried on St. Patrick's Day. Communion was offered because one of my godmothers was sure that's what my mother would have wanted. None of her family attended.

In fact, they were all in Florida at a birthday celebration for my grandmother.

Chapter Twenty-Five

Jacksonville

> High crop yields and very low instances of disturbance support the evidence that just enough satisfaction, just enough stability, and just enough hope for the future could control a person as effectively as the whip.
>
> —KINGSLEY PLANTATION AUDIO TOUR GUIDE

Once more the 10 has swollen into a billion lanes of hot, pitted asphalt. From several miles out, I can see the interchange with the north-south Interstate 95 looming, a behemoth on the horizon. In fact, the eastern terminus of the 10, "the Big I," consists of seventeen bridges, twenty-one ramps, and twenty-five lane miles.[1] It seems the 10 doesn't exactly end the same way it doesn't totally begin; it merely goes on to become something else. This road has taken me across eight states and thousands of miles. So far, I've spent almost six months of my life on this road, which doesn't count the back and forth in 1996. Over sand and through rainstorms I thought would drown me, I have followed these long white lines. Back in Los Angeles at UCLA, Dr. Cuff had told me that getting on the 10 was akin to getting on an express underground subway, with all its utilitarianism—the only reason to pull off the exit ramp being to get gas, sleep a bit, and then get right back on. I'd be lucky to break down somewhere, she told me (to the horror of anyone who has driven through empty desert). Rather than a straight shot that spat me out on the far end, however, the 10 was more akin to an elevator I boarded and immediately pushed every button, each floor a different view, a microcosm of a larger whole. The 10 showed me that this country can break your heart over and over, while at the same time there can be beauty here so immense it makes you bigger somehow.

At this monstrosity of concrete, the 10 simply blurs away like any other common road; one highway becomes another, and it all carries on. I can't tell if that's demoralizing or thrilling; after all, where my mother's locket chain ends, mine begins. I was an egg inside her, just as she was an egg inside my grandmother. In high school, while my mom was dying of cancer, I was diagnosed with polycystic ovary syndrome and had to get an ultrasound of my uterus to check for endometrial cancer. I had dreams of being pregnant with my own dead mother, her shriveled body inside mine, rather than the other way around. Ouroboros.

Ever since I was tucked in my sleeping bag at White Sands, I have been emailing family members, cousins I remember from the few trips my mom and I took together to see family. Some of them can fill in the holes of her biography, and one thing seems to be clear: none of them remember her living in the South for very long. In fact, they all remember her as the consummate Northern California girl, going to concerts in the Bay Area, tagging along with her older brothers, smoking to look cool. The journalist in me is frustrated. I'm hungry for a breakthrough, something that makes all the chaos and hurt of her life, and mine, make sense.

I read through the white binder of my mother's poetry looking for her memories of our trip together in 1996, but come up empty-handed once more. The trip is there, but only in a handful of poems about the desert, the black flies, the casino boats parked muddy on the banks of the river in Baton Rouge:

those fabulous riverboats in the harbor
their white pain gleaming
smokestacks burning, engines churning

Instead, it's page after page of poems about the reign of Satan, the power of the Blood of the Lamb. As I made the drive from Mobile to Tallahassee, the entrance to Florida felt like the descent into a dream, a blend of the surreal and the hyperreal—truck nuts and "Salt Life" bumper stickers, billboards for Disney World and Universal Studios and Jesus, tent encampments beneath the overpasses out of the rain, and a green so lovely it hurts my feelings. If I pretend that nothing man-made is here, the landscape is fecund to the point of madness; if I look at these trees, these vines, this undergrowth for too long, leaves will erupt from my mouth, my eyes. If I don't keep moving, I will spring roots from my own toes.

After the whopping disappointment of the Big I, I pull off the road and over to the St. Johns River, the same river that runs through Palatka. You can't tell from here that we're close to the coast. Jacksonville is surrounded by delta marsh, fed by the waters of this slow-running river that has been the lifeline of "Timucua, early Spanish and English settlers, plantation owners, Civil War supply runners, and 1800s steamboat tourists."[2]

I get out of the van and realize it smells horrible. Truly rank. The muddy banks at low tide are exuding a cloying odor of still water and algae. Dead things. I get back in the van and drive to the coastal suburb of Jacksonville Beach, and there I have more of the moment I was hoping for: standing with my toes in the bathtub-warm waters of the Atlantic. It's windy, but the beach is hopping with families of all types, kids frolicking in what, to this West Coaster, look like brown waves.

I don't understand the Atlantic. My ocean is the Pacific: green-blue, and absolutely freezing. The irony of Southern California's beach and surfer culture is that the water stays frigid nearly the entire year, with temperatures in the upper sixties deep into August and September—something the Beach Boys never sang about. One of the smells of my childhood is the spongy warmth of a dry wetsuit, required for most summer swimming.

I saw the Atlantic coast in South Carolina in 1993, when my dad was filming *Forrest Gump*. I was eleven and I'd never seen a beach where people could ride their bikes on the hard-packed sand, or a beach so wide that with the tide out you could tire yourself out walking all the way out to the water's edge. I'd never been in an ocean so warm it felt like a pool. That was also where I saw my father afraid for the first time.

It was dark, and my father, Colin, and I were driving through the deep night along the coast. I was sitting in the front seat, and as we rounded a gentle curve in the road, our headlights quickly passed over something in the tall grass on the shoulder—a large, dark lump with a slash of shocking pink. In that split second it looked like someone's torso had been cleaved open. My dad pulled the car over. He got out and, while we held our breath, walked back along the road, still visible in the red glare of our brake lights. It was very quiet except for the bugs. Colin and I stared as Dad tentatively stepped into the deep grass.

"It's not a body," he said, climbing back into the car, wiping his forehead. It was a bag that had split and pink insulation was spilling out. It was the first time I ever saw my dad look anything resembling truly scared.

This was a far cry from the conversation we'd had at the beginning of that summer when he tried to explain southern hospitality to me. As a kid, I was wary of anyone being particularly friendly or kind right off the bat because it usually meant they wanted something from me. I was urged to hone those instincts and that cynicism, both by my family and by experience. Which made it all the more confusing when my dad explained that people in the South would probably be much more easygoing and friendly than I was used to. This wasn't them trying to get close to me to use me; this was simply How Things Were Down Here. That summer I learned how to crab, and had my first hint at the undertow, a current of southern violence that could shock but not surprise grown-ups. That's what I remember—that my dad hadn't seemed surprised that we could have found a body. A Black body.

"That spooked me," he kidded as we continued on the road. I had nightmares afterward.

I meander around the area near the beach. It's all strip malls and bars with music pumping, bistros with packed patios. With the beginnings of a sunburn already, I get back in the van and drive to the neighborhood where I'll be staying while I'm here. It's tree-lined with a cat lounging in the driveway, not inclined to move when I pull up.

After I settle at my rental, I go to the Kool Beanz Cafe on the recommendation of my host. I take the white binder. I flip through my mother's pages while eating an oddly salty version of coconut shrimp. (I asked if they were from the Gulf, and the waitress replied, "Honey, they're out of a bag.") My frustration with these poems makes it feel like my mother is sitting across from me and, just like when she was alive, she might as well be a million miles away. I want to ask her, "What do you remember about 1996, about our trip in the Winnebago? How did you feel about me then?" And all I get is a garbled mess of religiosity, warnings, and blessings. I get veiled references to bad things happening, and secrets we should never look at, we should never name. All I really want is my mom.

After Beauvoir, I thought to avoid going to any more Civil War historical sites, like plantations. However, on nearly every "What to Do in Jacksonville" list is the Kingsley Plantation. There isn't much else that catches my eye, outside of the Cummer Museum of Art, which I enjoy, though my favorite thing there is the absolutely incredible tree growing in its gardens.

The Cummer Oak, somewhere between 175 and 200 years old, festooned with Spanish moss, has branches as long and as wide as entire other trees. Some of these branches rise into the air, while others dip toward the ground, inviting you to perch for an afternoon read, if you were allowed to sit on it. There is no way to accurately photograph it, it's so epic, so I give up and try to remember the words to Walt Whitman's "I Saw in Louisiana a Live-Oak Growing." I saw plenty of gorgeous trees in Louisiana, but something about the Cummer Oak, so huge in the middle of the museum's dainty, formal gardens, stands out: "Without any companion it grew there uttering joyous leaves of dark green." It's 80 feet tall, with a span of around 150 feet, the moss swaying in the breeze off the river. Yet again the real thing makes me think of the ersatz version of my childhood: the big tree between Pirates of the Caribbean and the Haunted Mansion at Disneyland, where the fake Spanish moss waves in the hot, dry Santa Ana winds, across from the River of America, home to the paddleboat *Mark Twain*. (Little tip: if you ask, you might be allowed to "captain" the *Mark Twain*, and you get a certificate!) The Cummer Oak is stately and resplendent, and keeps my attention more than any of the very nice art inside.

Driving out to the Kingsley Plantation, you technically leave mainland Florida and cross over to Fort George Island, which is now a state park. From the highway, the way to the plantation road diminishes into a dirt road, long, unpaved, bumpy, and goes so deep into the Florida jungle, it is unsettling. Minnie groans as her weight shifts back and forth, and all my gear rattles around. The St. Christopher necklace swings wildly.

It is deafeningly hot, as if the heat itself drowns out any sound beyond the katydid symphony, and when I pull up, a family of three is limping with exhaustion to their car, one very annoyed, wrung-out child in tow. The ranger in the welcome center/gift shop tells me that the plantation is now a "Site of Sorrow"—state parks whose stated purpose is to mark the low points of American history. I ask her what other official Sites of Sorrow there are, and she tells me maybe some of the Japanese internment camps of California. Manzanar is in fact a national history site, but when I search later, I can find no mention about any national "Sites of Sorrow."

I sign up for the audio tour and start hoofing around the sixty-acre property. I love a good audio tour, and the one at the Kingsley is extremely well done—and it does not flinch away from telling the incredibly dark and complex story of the place.

Zephaniah Kingsley brought his family, three children and his wife, Anna, to Fort George Island in 1814. Anna was Anta Majigeen Ndiaye, a Senegalese woman whom Zephaniah had bought as a thirteen-year-old slave in Havana after she survived the transatlantic crossing. He married her, had children with her, and freed her. After Zephaniah's death, Anna would own land, businesses, and slaves herself. When Florida joined the Union in 1821 and life for free Blacks significantly worsened, Anna took her mixed-race family, and her slaves, to live and work in Haiti after its slave rebellion. They eventually returned to Florida, but during the Civil War the family sided with the Union and briefly fled north to New York, again returning to Florida once it was occupied by Union forces. It's as if they just could not stay away from Florida and its mesmeric pull, its current.

At the height of the Kingsley Plantation, Zephaniah and Anna owned around sixty enslaved persons, who worked the land to grow cotton, rice, oranges, and timber. Around the edges of the property, where the green gets so dense no light can penetrate it, is a semicircle of slave quarters, twenty-five of the original thirty-two still standing. In this area, enslaved peoples could grow their own foods, and sell them, adding to their savings to buy their own freedom.

I couldn't help but wonder at the perverse interconnectedness of the lives at the Kingsley Plantation, all so close to each other in tangled knots of dynamics. Like Anna, a woman who came to Spanish Florida as a slave and for a time lived in postrevolutionary Haiti, not to mention Union New York, but in her own will stipulated that the children of her slaves be sold and the profits go to her own mixed-race children. Or Zephaniah himself, who was a passionate proponent of slavery, but also pushed for the rights of free Blacks. Not only did he live alongside his family with Anna, but he also fathered five children with young Flora, the daughter of his freed general manager, Abraham Hanahan. In some ways it's as though they all lived on top of each other; but on the other hand, it's easy to imagine that the Big House and these small slave quarters on the edge of the impenetrable growth might as well have been different universes—transcended by only a handful. Much of the audio tour is dedicated to the tense relations between enslaved peoples and their Black managers, who most often doled out punishments rather than Zephaniah himself. The tour claimed that it was rare for there to be any real trouble at Kingsley; the faint possibility of being able to buy one's own freedom, or of Zephaniah gifting manumission papers, was usually enough to keep people from acting out. A mirage of hope is a very dangerous thing.

I'm standing in one of the slave quarters when I realize I'm not alone.

At some point in my sweaty ramblings around the property, I became aware that the only other person at the plantation (which, yes, still does weddings) was a young Black man. We circled each other for a while, and then I lost sight of him. That is, until we both end up in the same little slave cabin, made of a mix of crushed oyster shells and sand called tabby, a practice with Native American, West African, and Spanish roots.

I pull off my headphones, and he follows suit.

"This is fucking crazy, right?" I ask.

"Shit. You're not wrong," he says with a laugh.

His name is Isaiah; he is making up college credits during the summer semester, and his professor made him trek out to the island for a history course. He is tall, with a dark complexion, a polo shirt he's sweated completely through, and a flawlessly trimmed fade. We commiserate about the heat, and the eeriness of the drive out.

"I think my Uber driver thought I was gonna kill him," he jokes. When he asks what I'm doing here, I tell him I'm a writer. I ask him what he thinks of Jacksonville.

"Jacksonville's country as fuck," Isaiah says. We walk in and out of the slave quarters, talking about the lives of the people who lived and died here.

"It's just sad to think that, you know, I'm not too far removed from this. I could have been here. I could have grown up here, I could have died here. I'm twenty-two. It's a few generations away. Seeing this here, it's really fucking horrible. I wouldn't have had the strength to stay here. I would have been one of the ones to die," he says. Everything sort of spills out of him; it is as if we are both grateful to have someone there to compare notes with, to right-size our horror at it all.

"I just can't help walking about trying to think about what has changed and what hasn't," I say.

"What hasn't changed is the people. You don't see the error if it's always worked for you."

We start heading back toward the welcome center to drop off our finished audio tours.

"When people have this conversation, I've seen some white people get defensive: 'Well, I didn't do it,' or, 'It's not me.' But it's not about putting the blame on you. Obviously, none of us were here. But it's our job. It's our job to fix it."

"It's more my job than yours," I point out.

He eyes me to see if I'm serious, and then laughs. "It's hard to have that conversation with people sometimes. Because either they don't want to hear it, or they're not ready to understand. 'Cause that's what it's all about: just understanding. We're not pointing the finger at the new generation. We're pointing our finger at the establishment, and how you all aren't doing anything to fix the inequality of what we already have established. You'd rather keep it. And you want us to work twice as hard.

"I go to the University of North Florida. It's a quote-unquote 'white school.' It's a predominantly white institution. There's been several times I've literally been the only Black person in my classroom. As a white person going to UNF, you wouldn't know those kinds of feelings."

"Well, most white people have never been the only white person in the room," I say.

"That's the truth." While we enjoy the arctic blast of the welcome center air-conditioning, Isaiah and the park ranger both talk about how much they love living in Florida, even with the hurricanes. They sort of egg each other on, and it's nice to watch two people love where they live, even if Isaiah would pass on Jacksonville.

"I probably wouldn't want to live anywhere else in the South other than Florida," he says. "The laws and stuff make a little more sense to me. Like, I've been in Virginia, and they had a state tax, and local tax, and that freaked me out. Why are there two taxes? Like, why would I owe you guys more money? I don't want to do that."

Isaiah asks me for a ride back to the mainland, since his phone can't get enough reception to order an Uber. I warn him about just how much stuff I have in my van, and we trundle off down the road, arguing about saxophone players. He's a Bird man, while I prefer Coltrane. Isaiah says he wants to see New Orleans, but it seems too crazy for him; he's a Florida man, through and through. The conversation with this young man is one of my favorite things that's happened to me on this trip.

"You're really living in this van, aren't you?" He dubiously eyes the bed behind us, the camping gear I haven't touched since El Paso.

"I was, but the humidity put a stop to that. Now it's mostly Airbnbs."

I drop him off in a strip mall parking lot. We shake hands, wish each other luck.

That night I dream of the Cummer Oak—its colossal form against a dark sky. Its limbs grow out, searching, tangling with its own roots. Its trunk is slashed open and pink pulp blooms wetly. I stagger back, aghast.

"Dad"

no one was there who could help
and no one was saved
I watched him slowly die
as the waves of pain washed over him
wracked by a pain so severe he would
snap the iron bars
wreaking the bed
that held him hostage
when the pain became too intense
death was not silent
in the moisture and heat of that southern room
you could hear him whispering and pleading for a gun

—SJD

Things I Want to Know

Where did you grow up?

How did you grow up?

Did your father hurt you?

Did your mother hurt you?

Where did you go to high school?

What did you like to wear as a little girl?

What did you like to wear as a teenager?

Did you like being a sister?

What was your favorite book as a kid?

Did you pick at your skin?

Are you glad you had kids?

Why didn't we stop in New Orleans in 1996?

Were you afraid to die?

Where was your ropa vieja recipe from?

Do you miss me?

Are you still mad at me?

Chapter Twenty-Six

Palatka

> The idea that people do things for reasons, and that these reasons are worth trying to understand, can be a normative assumption. . . . That there is a conflict between the conscious and unconscious mind becomes broadly understood and casually recognized in this context, and is not a matter of stigma.
>
> —SARAH SCHULMAN

The shoes I bought in New Mexico are falling apart. On the way out of Jacksonville I stop at an absolutely enormous, mostly empty mall that randomly includes an occult store with two ornate witches' brooms in the window. I buy a new pair of sandals that I hope will last me until I get back to California, and in this thunderous humidity, they immediately rub my feet completely raw. The drive south to Palatka, along Highway 17, is just two lanes in either direction. It is lined with pine trees, Spanish moss, and an understory that looks like you could get ticks just by looking at it. That's what the first layer of green is called, the shrubs and vines that manage to survive with the light blocked out by dense canopy: the understory. As I get closer to town, driveways are dotted with rusty boats and RVs on cinder blocks.

Front yards filled with broken machinery are covered in green, as if the understory is trying to reclaim the land. A man in flip-flops rides a bike slowly on the side of the highway.

The first thing I do in Palatka is lie to my kind host. I've taken a room at the Grand Gables Inn, a tidy, poky bed-and-breakfast in the historic section of town. On the flats by the riverside are the grand houses of old Palatka, some in stages of repair, many in epic disrepair. I'm drawn to this strange neighborhood of what look like empty, sometimes crumbling mansions and river breezes. When I pull up to the inn, the owner greets me, fluttering around me and my bags like a nervous bird, and nearly immediately asks, "Are you Tom Hanks's daughter?"

I'm thrown and do something I haven't done in years: lie.

"Uh, no. No relation."

"Oh—I thought you might be." She sounds disappointed.

I'm suddenly worried that she's googled me and that maybe there's some sort of small-town phone tree that's been put into action, though I'm not sure that anyone in my grandmother's life was aware of her connection to my father, or that anyone she knew is still alive. More than the living, I suspect this town is full of ghosts for me, and I'm nervous about disturbing them.

The house is fully kitted out in typical bed-and-breakfast bric-a-brac, which clutters up its remarkable beauty. My room is high-ceilinged, with a imposing wooden bed that towers in the corner, and the hum of the air-conditioning is a comfort. My host recommends a spot for dinner: back out on the highway there's Corky Bell's Seafood at Gator Landing, a steak and seafood place. I eat at the bar, surrounded by cheery, hard-faced waitresses who don't let anyone's cup get close to half-empty and paunchy, funny men who flirt with all the women. I keep my nose mostly in a book, but a waitress with stop-sign-red hair dotes on me a bit.

Driving around brings up no memories, except for my grandmother Harriet's house, which I swing by and park across the street from. Whenever I visit Sacramento, I do the same thing with my mother's house, where I grew up. A family lives there now, with young children, and I try not to be obvious whenever I'm crying outside what is now their home. It's weird, and I don't want to be seen being weird. I have no tears for Harriet's house, though. Just vague memories of watching my mother drive my grandmother nuts trying to take care of things that were already handled, dusting already clean baseboards, moving furniture that was already well situated. Mostly I remember sleeping on a fold-out sofa in the living room and the way my grandmother pronounced it a "warshing machine." I don't stick around outside my grandmother's house long enough to discover if anyone is living there now. Instead, I drive around looking for something to be interested in.

The only thing that really draws my eye is what looks like an abandoned mansion, not in the historic area by the river but more directly in town. A large, weathered stone arch, which has clearly been around awhile and does not match the flimsy short metal fence that is being choked out by jungle vines, stands prominently along a main road. It looks like the sort of place I would have been obsessed with as a kid; that is, when I was here in 1996. It looks like it has a secret garden, or a magic fountain, or a hidden something, far more interesting than anything real, like where my grandmother lived for decades. I pull over and duck into an antique shop across the road to ask about the dilapidated splendor of the stone arch and the house beyond, but they send me a couple doors down with promises that the old-timer there would know more.

It turns out to be a notary shop, crammed full of stacks of papers and newspapers, and an old, fat dog, so old and so fat, I barely get a proper tail thump in greeting.

"Can I help you?" barks out the man behind the counter, entirely covered in papers, each pile precariously leaning on another.

"Yes, the ladies down the way at the antique store said you might know anything about that big mansion across the street—with the stone arch?"

"Yeah, yeah. It's old, but not before the war."

"Which war?"

I should have known better. "The Civil War," he says, looking at me over his glasses. "It's been sitting empty for forever, but I think some folks from up north just bought it up and are turning it into a hotel or something."

"Oh, that's nice."

"Well, we'll see if it happens. You just passing through?"

"I'm visiting."

"Most people visit St. Augustine, or Orlando."

"I had family here."

"Oh yeah, who's that, then?"

I hesitate before blurting, "Harriet Dillingham."

He thinks for a moment. "Don't know her. She must have been a newcomer."

I don't argue with him; I'm too busy realizing that I'm wildly relieved to hear he doesn't know her.

"Well, thanks for the info. Have a nice day."

"You take care now."

The next morning, after my breakfast of waffles and sausages, which the hostess brings out for me in the otherwise empty dining room, I set off for the Palatka public library. It is packed, delightfully busy with children, some speaking English, a couple speaking Spanish, all part of some summer programs run by adults who, even from across the room, project that steady, mildly amused energy of really good teachers. I'm distracted from the helpful librarian trying to show me how to use the microfiche machine, because I just want to listen to whatever these kids are talking about.

At some point I focus on what's in front of me; what is it that I am looking for? All I have to go by is my mother's accusation in the red journal that my grandfather raped and killed a little girl, and her subsequent allegation of cannibalism. I don't know where this supposedly happened, or when, or who the victim was. Maybe the story of my grandfather looks like a big mysterious mansion, but my story, and my mother's, and my grandmother's, is more like a little old house you'd drive right by without noticing.

Am I looking for headlines of some horrific crime? "Local Man Implicated in Rape and Cannibal Murder"? What the fuck am I doing here? What on earth did I think I would find? Did I really think I would drive all this way, over all these months, and discover something momentous in the Palatka public library?

Yes. I did. Because in the podcast version of my life, that's exactly what would happen. I've grown up with storytellers; I've been surrounded by narrative since my first breath. My only real faith has been that the story always had a beginning, a middle, and an end. This was supposed to be the end, just like the 10 was supposed to end, not just morph into something else. I'm furious and embarrassed with myself; I wasn't just trying to look at my trauma, or name it. I was trying to write it. Build it into an opera. Did I really think narrative was a solution for trauma?

Joan Didion wrote: "We interpret what we see, select the most workable of the multiple choices. We live entirely, especially if we are writers, by the imposition of a narrative line upon disparate images, by the 'ideas' with which we have learned to freeze the shifting phantasmagoria which is our actual experience."[1] Certainly, I've been picking the most workable choices, taking snapshots of the places and peoples I've met on this trip, trying to simultaneously understand their stories through these thin glimpses and grasp their place in the larger American story. Simultaneously I've been trying to discover my mother's story, to see if it overlaps with mine. Sitting in front of the microfiche machine, this all seems pathetic—a child's search: Can the story have a happy ending when its beginning is so bad? Meanwhile, the kids in the library are cracking up over something the designated class clown said.

Over the next couple of hours searching through the local newspaper—nothing has been digitized, so it's all microfiche—I find no mention of my grandfather John Raymond, but I do find one or two of Harriet, though mostly just society things: a list of high school graduates, a brief marriage announcement. Whatever it is I thought I would find, I haven't even seen its shadow.

What I do find is deeper roots in Palatka than I was expecting—my family are not at all newcomers here. Not only is Harriet buried here, so are my great-grandparents: Margaret McIlvaine Collins, who very nearly shares a birthday with me, and Percy Devereux Collins, who died at only thirty-one and whose obituary paints a portrait of a beloved local man.

> Percy Devereux Collins, one of Palatka's most popular and highly esteemed young men, died last Friday night in the government hospital in Gulfport, Miss., where he was carried several weeks ago for treatment. His condition instead of improving under hospital care continued to become more critical, and he gradually sank into his final earthly sleep. The

> news of the death of the estimable young man came Saturday morning, and though expected, the sad tidings cast a gloom over the community in which he was born and reared to useful manhood.

It's not stated clearly, but it seems he died of complications that began with injuries from serving in World War I.

> Of quiet, unassuming nature, Percy Collins was most highly esteemed by those who knew him best. With high ideals, his character was above reproach, and he always stood for the best moral interests of the community. He was a devoted son, husband and parent, loyal friend, and a Christian who exemplified his religion in his everyday life.[2]

The obituary mentions that his mother, Mrs. N. B. Collins, my great-great-grandmother, was also "of Palatka," so that's three generations of women I come from who have come from this place. Harriet is the first, though, to have her own proper obituary, which describes her as a devoted military wife who would raise her four children mostly on her own. She graduated from what was then Florida State College for Women, now Florida State University. There's the line "In 1989 she relocated to Palatka, where she lived the rest of her life."

Harriet had moved to Sacramento after her divorce from John Raymond to be near her brother, who had moved there because of his wife's family. My brother and I had ended up living in Sacramento because, during their divorce proceedings, my mother took Colin and me, without telling my father, to live with Harriet. My dad only realized we'd left Los Angeles when he went to pick us up from school on his allotted weekend, and a teacher told him that Colin and I had been missing. As a kid I had liked to imagine that I was descended from the settlers who came to Northern California as part of the gold rush, but my maternal roots in the west are only as deep as your average California blond's.

After David died, Harriet had had enough of living with my mother so close and returned to her childhood hometown. I guess everyone reached their limit with my mother, even her own mother. So Harriet moved back to Florida, "where she lived the rest of her life," which was until 2014.

I hadn't spoken to or heard from Harriet since I was in college, when I got a xeroxed letter that had gone out to all her grandchildren. In the wake of my mother's illness and death, when so many people not related to me by blood had stepped up and provided support, logistical and emotional, I didn't have much interest in being close to family just because they were family.

Driving around Palatka, I wonder if I regret not coming to some sort of peace with Harriet before she died. Not particularly. My feelings about her used to be anger, on behalf of my mother, especially my mother as a child. Before I read the red journal and had an idea of what had happened to her, there was still the fact that something wasn't right with her. In my young teens, a well-intended adult gave me a copy of E. Fuller Torrey's *Surviving Schizophrenia: A Family Manual.* While my therapist hypothesizes that my mother was more likely suffering from psychotic episodes of a bipolar disorder, both illnesses begin manifesting symptoms in women in their late teens, early twenties. There must have been signs. Whether at the time they were blatantly ignored, passively compartmentalized, or explained away, I don't know, but my anger at Harriet was that she had not protected my mother, had not gotten her the help everyone could see she needed.

My mother's best friend, who was alternately banished and invited back into her life over the years, was John, a gay man who survived the

AIDS epidemic and having a tumor the size of a fat lemon removed from his brain, and so consequently gave precisely zero fucks. They met in college, a couple of theater kids; he was witness to my parents' meeting. I asked him once, over tea in Sacramento, when he knew something was off about my mother.

"Oh, we all knew when something was up with Susan. It was always there."

He described a young woman who was sometimes thrilled to be the life of the party but midway through the same party would retreat to corners and stare daggers, swilling gin. She would report fights with friends that left everyone baffled because no such fights had happened, yet she spun stories of betrayal and sabotage. She stole, often blatantly obvious about it.

"So everyone knew?"

"Well, we didn't have the language of mental illness; we just didn't know about those things at the time. But, yes. Everyone knew something wasn't right. Or at least, everyone knew that your mother had good days and bad days. And even though I loved her so much, even I didn't want to be around on a bad day."

My anger at Harriet was the blame I placed on her for the life my mother never got to live. If Harriet, if anyone had ever talked to her in her youth and gotten her help, her life could have gone a very different way. John, and some of my mother's other college friends, told me that over the years if someone broached the subject of mental health with her, they were quickly excised from her life. Many of her poems talk about backstabbers who betray her when they suggest therapy or seeking out mental health assistance. While other teens hid porn or drugs, I hid my copy of *Surviving Schizophrenia*, and like all teen contraband, my mother found it and confronted me with it. I could only cry and say I hadn't bought it for myself, and she yelled that I was trying to destroy her.

But driving around Palatka, I don't feel that protective anger, a righteous sense of injustice. It's not that I forgive Harriet's abnegation of her only daughter, but I understand it better. Older now, all I feel is best described as mournful—all these lives, wrecked against each other like Spanish galleons in stormy waters. Harriet lived a quiet, difficult life that she brightened with the music she loved, her small church, her garden. She'd been married to a hard man, was shunted around the country, divorced before it was socially acceptable, and raised four children—probably the best she was able to. In many ways she abandoned my mother, who in turn abandoned me—but being angry at either of them feels like yelling into the wind. It would make for a tidier story if I had discovered some great, horrible secret, some original sin here in the dank swamps of Florida, but what I've done instead is just let go of the sand I've been gripping for so long.

Sitting with a plate of grits in a random diner, I was reading about the Library of Alexandria and I came across something that both shocked and saddened me. The truth is, it probably wasn't purposefully destroyed by fires set by uncivilized "barbarians," the way popular culture might depict it: "Rather than highlighting the cataclysmic nature of barbaric ignorance triumphing over civilized truth, Alexandria is a cautionary tale of the danger of creeping decline, through underfunding, low prioritization, and general disregard for the institutions that preserve and share knowledge."[3]

Boring budget cuts spread out over centuries are nowhere near as interesting as a horde of the ignorant burning your sacred place to the ground, are they?

I am the only person wandering around Palatka on foot, just like I'd been in Marfa and Montgomery. I try to remember anything from my time here in 1996, but it looks like every other southern town I've stopped over in. Six-lane-wide streets with few sidewalks in the busy spots, wide bumpy streets with sidewalks in the residential areas, though here I notice that some of the streets have patches of very old brick amid the cracked pavements. Spanish moss swings everywhere, and many blocks have abandoned homes midway through reclamation by the jungle. I'm chagrined, because I realize that I've been expecting someone to recognize me, not as my father's daughter, but my mother's. I've been cowering in restaurant booths and coffee shops, expecting someone to connect my face to a picture on a wall, and ask what it is I think I'm doing here. This is especially ironic because I have no idea if Harriet ever had a picture of me up on her wall. No one is looking for me; no one is expecting me; no secret has been waiting here all these years for me to stumble on it; no villain setting up a trap.

On the surface, the truth looks boring in comparison to the narrative. It's easier for us to understand the bad thing, the ill omen, when it's italicized, when it's sexy, when it's shocking; but the truth of it is, most of the time, wounds are "boring." Pain is so plentiful, if you go looking for it you'll almost always find it. More often than not, it's not from some grand, morbid event, but from a lifetime spent without much empathy, taking knocks from people who have been knocked around themselves. We don't need big, scary stories to be hurt; all it takes is a grandfather with a drinking problem, a grandmother happy to look the other way, and a lot of people content to let the trauma go unnamed. Nothing on fire, just a lifetime of hurt, an illness undiagnosed, and a pile of scrolls we all forgot about.

I don't want to be in Palatka anymore. I feel foolish and spooked. It's not ghosts of family who are haunting me, it's the emptiness of my experience. I don't feel closer to my mother here, or to my grandmother. Everything I've learned about my grandfather leads me to believe he spent as little time here as possible. I haven't discovered anything except for the knowledge that just because I want a tidy ending doesn't mean

I'm going to get one. Ending to what, anyway? It's been almost two decades since my mother died, and our relationship hasn't ended. I still wrestle with who she was, how she loved me, what I owe her. We are two paths that intertwine, we are inside each other always. Palatka can't change that. I don't even know if I came here to get closer to her, or if I came here to finally bury her, almost twenty years after we put her in the dirt.

The morning I leave, my hostess tells me I have to let her husband give the tour of the house and tell me some of its history. I begrudgingly say yes, fearful of being talked at when my head and heart already feel overfull and sloshing with unnamed thoughts and feelings, but my host is a good raconteur, and his house pride charms me.

Sherman Conant was a teenager from New Hampshire living in Massachusetts when he enlisted in the Union Army and eventually was made captain in command of H Company, the 3rd Colored Infantry, made up of Black soldiers with white officers. (Given that H Company occupied Jacksonville and large swaths of the east coast of Florida, I wonder if Conant ever crossed paths with Zephaniah and Anna Kingsley.) After the war Conant worked as a public servant in multiple capacities: secretary of state, judge, and state attorney general. His efforts on the voter registration board to sign up newly freed Black Floridians were not appreciated by whites, who quickly labeled him a carpetbagger, a term that often conjures war-profiteering Yankees making money off the limping South, but very often was applied to northerners who worked to make inroads with Black communities. Built in the mid-1880s, Conant's house fits the bill for the postwar Reconstructionist boom: ornate, monumental, a showcase for both wealth and power. It may also have been used to smuggle goods on the black market. Right on the banks of the St. Johns River, the house has a deep basement that features a hidden door to a tunnel opening onto the riverside, perfect for trafficking in untaxed goods. Perfect for keeping secrets. Perfect for burying things. Perfect for forgetting.

I get in the van. For the past six months I've been running toward something. Now I'm running away.

Chapter Twenty-Seven

Orlando

> I don't want the public to see the world while they're in the park. I want them to feel they're in another world.
>
> —WALT DISNEY

Palatka was supposed to be the end of the line, yet I'm still going. I'm going to Orlando, an entire city dedicated to happy endings of all sorts. In theory, it was a good idea. But this plan has backfired horribly.

Let me explain. I understand perfectly well that adults who love Disneyland are generally considered to be any number of bad things: Childish. Basic. Crass consumers of corporate-hack swill. There are aspects of Disneyland that I find as distasteful as anyone else: the rude crowds, the bad food in insane portions, the exorbitant price of nearly everything, of which they want you to buy as much as possible. Now I'm just complaining, but new additions like "Avengers Campus" (no one calls it that) and Star Wars Land (not the official name) are just excuses to sell you merch from bloated, crummy movies, and lack all the romance and possibility of Tomorrowland and Adventureland. Bah, humbug.

Speaking of, in my mind, Disneyland is a lot like Santa Christmas: there are many valid and important criticisms, the most damning of which might be that whatever its original purpose, whatever special magic was ever there, it has been completely drowned out by the tidal floods of commercialization. That it feels like you're being held up, forced to have fun with a porcelain-shattering grimace. The magic has been utterly smote. And yet . . .

All you need is one bleary morning watching a kid discover that the milk and cookies they left out for Santa are gone, and you get a little bit of that magic back. Anytime I've been to Disneyland, and that is more times than I can count, if there's ever a moment when I look around and am only disappointed, all I have to do is watch a kid meet the real Tinker Bell, and I remember something I'd temporarily forgotten. Disneyland teaches me time and again that creativity has no limit. Everywhere I look, I see art: in Cruella's smirking flourish as she flounces "offstage," performing to whoever just happens to notice her, or in the decorations atop the lights near the Dumbo ride (they're made of little piles of gold elephants), or in the guy selling churros who calls everyone of any gender wearing a princess dress "Your Majesty." There are theme park aficionados, Disney fans who wallow in the whole universe of Disney films, television, and merch. Most hard-core Disney fans tend to prefer Disney World in Orlando, simply because it's much larger. There are Disney subcultures of Pin Collectors, Cosplayers, the Dapper Day aesthetes, the Disney Bounders who use color schemes to signal their favorite characters. Of course, there are also my favorites: the Disney Goths, who mingle around the Haunted Mansion. I like them the most because they tend to be the most romantic, always holding hands with each other in their Jack and Sally *Nightmare Before Christmas* merch. It's sweet. All of that is fine and dandy, but for me, it's just Disneyland. I *love* Disneyland. So, so much. It's not the rides, or the food, or the merchandise—it's the gestalt of the place.

There are, of course, my family connections to Disney. My father played a particularly tidy version of Walt himself, and for many, many people, his most significant role is Woody, the high-strung toy cowboy of the *Toy Story* films. I cannot separate my emotional connection to Disneyland from my emotional connection to my father, because like many other California daughters, I have spent a lot of time at Disneyland with my dad, and because one day he'll die.

I was there one evening (nights are always better than days at Disneyland if you don't have children—less crowded, less heat, and the lighting is magic) with a friend whom I'd convinced to see the night show, *Fantasmic!*—a schlocky confection touting the power of the imagination while playing all the big hits. The exhilarating kicker is when a towering animatronic dragon rises above the River of the Americas and spits fire. A British friend once told me that this show embodied everything ridiculous and wonderful about America: "Only in America would someone say, 'Let's set the water on fire!' In England, we don't even set matches on fire."

At the end of *Fantasmic!* the paddleboat *Mark Twain* sails by the crowd, with all the characters you recognize waving colorful scarves in perfect synchronization to the soundtrack. There's Snow White! There's Goofy! On the very back of the boat that night was Woody, with his big, bulbous plastic head and scarf. I'm not sure what it was about this particular trip that put me in such a soft place, but watching *that* Woody wave a scarf around, I suddenly burst into tears. To anyone else it looked like a random white woman was sobbing because *Fantasmic!* had ended, but from my perspective, I was time-traveling. I know that one day, I hope many years from now, my father will die. But Woody will still be there, at Disneyland—and he'll speak with my father's voice. (Actually, sometimes it's my uncle's.)

I was thinking about that first time I will come back to Disneyland after my father dies—and how I will hear him when I hear Woody. In that moment, it was as if it had already happened, that I was somehow touching on what future me would feel, and I cracked open with emotion. I don't have any recordings of my mother's voice, that's gone and lost in the past; but Disneyland ensures that a part of my dad will live forever. Sure, he's been in a lot of movies, so why aren't I getting emotional thinking about the future day I watch *The 'Burbs*? Why isn't *Joe Versus the Volcano* causing a flood of tears? Well, I didn't spend countless birthdays watching *Turner & Hooch*. I haven't spent afternoons with my nieces giggling through *Road to Perdition*.

Disneyland has been more of a constant in my life than any house I have ever lived in. I have spent Thanksgiving there. I have spent Christmas there. I have spent more birthdays than I can count there, and on the day the forty-fifth president was inaugurated, I sat on a bench just inside the Sleeping Beauty Castle, watching the rain pour all day long while I wrote in a notebook. Someone also got engaged in front of me that day, and the newly affianced hugged everyone in the vicinity. I care about Disneyland because that specific place has become for me a monument for art, against death. Walt's vision survives, and some part of my father will too. Art survives.

So this is what I mean when I say I am a Disneyland girl.

And because of this, I don't remember the last time I've been to Universal Studios Hollywood, even though it does have a Harry Potter–themed area, which I was curious about. But the Harry Potter area in LA is very small and only has one ride, as opposed to Universal Studios Orlando, where Harry Potter attractions span two of the three parks and have an entire separate section, the Wizarding World of Harry Potter. Since I didn't plan on being in Orlando again anytime soon—I hadn't even planned on coming here in the first place—I thought this was my chance to get in the Harry Potter rides. So, while my heart said, "Disney World," my head said, "Universal Studios." This was the first time in months that I'd decided based on what I thought rather than what I felt, and it would not serve me well at all.

I book a room at one of the nicer, but not the nicest, of the Universal hotels; it is Polynesian-themed, which doesn't feel too far off base given that the humidity of central Florida in late August is epic. At this point, a daily thunderstorm and deluge is all but certain, and the heat has declared war on all the parts of my body that touch other parts of my body.

I sleep heavily, with no dreams, and wake surprisingly late the next day, excited for frivolity. Since the Harry Potter rides span two of the parks, you have to buy two different (pricey) tickets to ride all of them. To get to the main parks from the hotel, I decide to take a water taxi, but this doesn't save me from the Universal CityWalk, a row of stores and restaurants with names like the Cowfish Sushi Burger Bar or the Toothsome Chocolate Emporium & Savory Feast Kitchen. The slower you read these names, the more insane you feel. Each of them has a sound system blaring music out onto the streets.

It's not really fair. Like I said, I'm a Disneyland girl. I'm genuinely charmed by sugary music softly piped out of topiary hedges in the shape of beloved characters. So, it follows that I am not enjoying nineteen different types of Spring Break Rock at skull-fucking volumes playing at once. I briefly consider wandering into the Bubba Gump Shrimp Co., the *Forrest Gump*–themed restaurant chain, which I have never been in, and which my family doesn't actually have any business ties with, but my brain is already on the fritz, and that might just break it.

Once, in a Manhattan taxi, my dad and I were riding in peaceful silence that was broken when he mumbled, "Hrrm. Weird." I asked him what was up, and he explained that in the late seventies, he and my mother had lived in a wretched apartment in Hell's Kitchen. Colin was very young, and they couldn't afford a snowsuit that he would grow out of, so they bought him one much too big and used newspaper to stuff it. After wrapping Colin up, my dad would carry him to the bank to pick up his unemployment check, which he'd use for groceries, the rent, and bills, since he didn't trust my mother (deep into cocaine at the time) with the money.

"What made you think of that?" I asked.

"That bank is now the Times Square Bubba Gump Shrimp Company," which we'd just driven by.

I'm even underwhelmed by the entrance to the theme park. I'm so underwhelmed by it, in fact, I nearly walk past it, a surprisingly small collection of khaki umbrellas. This happens a couple of times: multiple attractions seem to have no signs or indications where their entrances are except for the scattered, melted tourists. Worse, several rides, including most of the Harry Potter attractions, require that you put all your belongings in a small locker beforehand because you can't carry anything on the ride. They recommend that you don't even carry your phone, which leaves the long lines interminable, and robs people of the great fun of playing dumb phone charade games together or with strangers, one of the things that makes the lines at Disneyland an occasionally great hang.

The lockers are their own (unmarked) area and, worse than a long line, there is no line. Rather, a miserable-looking employee halfheartedly reminds us all, "Only one person from a family enters the locker area," which no one pays attention to. Instead, whole parties cram into the dark, thronged area that is already so overheated, I worry for the grandparents and children who wilt against walls.

If I had been paying better attention, I would have known that this locker situation is spelling my doom. Nothing positive can come from a place that thinks this is good enough, as I will truly come to see. If you've got anything larger than a purse or fanny pack, which includes nearly all parents, you have to pay extra for a larger locker. The locker area is divided into dimly lit zones, about a hundred lockers per zone, maybe six zones total, all of which require a code, which you get from a small screen in the center of the one wall of lockers that does not have a line. Once you get assigned a code, a locker somewhere pops open. If it accidentally gets closed by one of the many people crowded into the area, whoops, it's now locked and your code to open it will only work once. If someone confused your locker for their locker, you have to try to find theirs to swap. If you lose the scrap of paper with your code on it, or it melts in your pocket, good luck finding an employee willing to jump into the horde of waiting people to help you override the system to get your locker open. I can't underscore enough how badly organized, ill-thought-out, and horribly executed I think this system is. It's insulting. Maybe I'd be less offended if I didn't know that ten miles away there's a perfectly executed version of optional lockers. Say what you will about the eerie perfectionism of a Disney experience, but surely that would be preferable to this Inferno moment I'm having on the edge of Hogsmeade. People are shoving, yelling, and moaning in discomfort at how hot and crowded it is. It feels like we are cattle jostling against each other in a truck with no air vents. And to add insult to very possible injury, we all paid a lot of money for this.

"Excuse me, it's way too hot for there to be that many people crammed in there. It's dangerous," I say to an employee limply waving their hands in no particular direction to aimless tourists all trying to figure out where to go. "There really needs to be a line, or a system, or a something."

Unsurprisingly (and who can blame them), the employee gives me an exhausted look, the subtitles for which would simply read, *Yeah, thanks, lady.*

By the time I make it to the newest ride, the wait time is already over five hours. I'm limp and haven't actually gotten on any attractions, so I decide to come back with a better game plan the next day. I have the same rule for theme parks as I do for strip clubs: the moment it starts to feel bad, you need to leave, because it'll only get worse. Everything about this place, the heat, the impatience, the rudeness of the people, the music, it feels bad. Gross, even. My skin starts to crawl, and I hightail it out of there. Clearly this is on me; this isn't my first rodeo, I should know better than to wander into a theme park in the midafternoon. It's either early morning, or early evening. Time to pivot: I'm just in time for lunch by the pool. What could go wrong there?

As I'm changing into my bathing suit and slathering on as much sunblock as possible, I wonder, is this what I should be doing? Does "should" even exist for me in this whole project? I consider merely climbing back in bed, then remember something Joan Didion wrote: "I spent what seemed to many people I knew an eccentric amount of time in Honolulu, the particular aspect of which lent me the illusion that I could any minute order from room service a revisionist theory of my own history, garnished with a vanda orchid."[1] Am I waiting for my personal history to be delivered unto me in this jejune tiki hotel room? No. For one thing, I planned on having my lunch by the pool. Secondly, I could have saved myself some serious gas mileage. Los Angeles has plenty of hotels, some of which have pools, ones that don't make me want to tear my hair out.

I pick a lounger fully in the shade and eventually manage to flag down a server who looks completely wrecked. I ask if he has any help during the lunch rush.

"We're a little understaffed today."

"Every day?"

He shrugs.

Something you cannot tell by looking down at the pool from your hotel room is that, just like at the Universal CityWalk, music here is constantly blared. The music is loud and bad. "YMCA" is a favorite, Chumbawumba's "Tubthumping" as well. It seems as if there's only twenty approved songs played on a loop. Every now and then a DJ interrupts to yell, "Who's ready for some Minions trivia!?!" I'm scarcely done scarfing down my turkey burger and frozen strawberry margarita in an attempt to get away as soon as possible, when the whole party is shut down; guests are not allowed to stay by the pool when thunder and lightning roll in. At night, I turn the air-conditioning as low as possible, curl up in a ball, and cry for a long time.

The next morning I've got my game plan in place: I get up early enough to enter the park with an early-entry pass and go straight to the one ride that ended up having any charm: the Hogwarts Express, which you can take from one park into another. The story among theme park enthusiasts is that Disney was going to host Harry Potter rides, but allegedly J. K. Rowling's requirement that the Hogwarts Express be included in the park busted up the deal. Walt Disney himself was a train aficionado, and no one at Disney was prepared to replace either the Disneyland Railroad or the Walt Disney World Railroad. Universal, on the other hand, was supposedly willing to build Rowling whatever she wanted for the rights to host the Wizarding World of Harry Potter. The train ride is delightful, though in my compartment I am seated with a family who do not once look up from their phones—it's the one Harry Potter ride where you're allowed to carry anything. Even with my time-tested theme park approach, every other line is already over three hours long. I tough it out for one attraction that I forget immediately, and call the whole thing a loss.

I spend the rest of my time in Orlando sequestered in my hotel room, regretting being here rather than at Disney World, where at least I know the exorbitant prices would bring me enjoyable experiences, and trying to wrap my head around driving westward. I came looking for a Happy Ending and have not found it. I feel like I've failed at something. Curled up in the air-conditioning, I read the obituaries of my Palatka family, research John Raymond Dillingham's military career, and try to piece together a timeline of my mother's life. My mother had three brothers, just like I have, and like my paternal aunt. All my families have one girl, three boys. I don't know these men, two of whom I've met only once, in 1996, on the 10—but I'm nervous to write them: I introduce myself, since they have not seen or heard from me in twenty-three years. I say I am on a long road trip. I am writing about Palatka and the American South. I say I would like to hear some stories about my mother, if they have any to share. I shoot off an email, then go wander around the hotel without my phone. I'm not sure why, but I'm afraid of their responses.

I fuss around the room, unpacking and repacking, picking at my skin while I await a response. It would make for a tidier story if I had discovered some great, horrible secret, some original sin here in the depths of Florida, but I'm reminded that a lot of trauma is boring. That is, unoriginal. A lot of people have mad, drunk parents who hit them, and there is some element of human nature in looking the other way so as not to rock the boat. Not to mention that all active addiction, in one way or another, meets the same fate.

Any acknowledgment of the abuse that marked my mother's early life, the mental illness that followed her the rest of her days, the wasting disease that killed her, and the legacy of dysfunction and madness that she left in her wake, well, that would have smacked of "making a fuss."

Whatever I thought or wished would happen here in Florida has not happened. I feel foolish, and unclear about what this whole thing was about anyway. Outside of El Paso, hiking along the ridge as the sun set, or in the Honey Island Swamp of Louisiana, it had seemed so clear to me that I was trying to understand something about America, about myself; but in Orlando, not only are the answers completely evading me, but I can't even remember what the questions were. I am packing up my bags when an email comes through. It's from my uncle Bruce. He says he has things to tell me. Things I should have known all along.

Chapter Twenty-Eight

The Bad Night III

It wasn't until I found the red journal and a collection of her writings that I understood her version of events:

Mumbling.
Praying and mumbling.
My attorney has called this sufficient reason
for my child to be taken away.
My crime an attempt at a slap
and the name of the Lord Christ.
These are held against me as a crime.
Not one of them
has not hit another, or their children.
Not one of them has forgiven,
while they expect me to forgive
to love, and never count their sins against them.
Not one of them wants me to tell the truth
they expect me to demonstrate the love
of Christ for them,

keep all their secrets
while ridiculing the source
and the name from which it comes.

I think it's perversely funny that this "poem" begins with the idea that this whole situation is blown out of proportion, that she could lose her child over some simple prayers (and an "attempt" at a slap), and dissolves into a martyrdom that would make the Christ blush.

I don't know how long it was before I got to Los Angeles, but I remember my dad coming to Sacramento, more meetings with lawyers because my mother could never keep one for very long, and many meetings with therapists and psychiatrists. One offered to pray with my mother and me, and urged me to pray for God to "guide my soul" in the right direction, i.e., staying in Sacramento. I refused to go back to that one. One therapist seemed pretty dubious of me and told me all teenagers think their parents are weird and difficult. She changed her tune when, later that session, my mother sat in her chair, talking to herself, and accused me of telling people she'd participated in the Holocaust.

The doctor asked to speak to me in private, and while my mother chain-smoked in the car, the therapist turned to me and with a refreshing lack of professionalism asked, "Where the hell did that come from?"

Eventually I packed a suitcase and flew to Los Angeles with my dad. He was in the middle of directing his first feature film, *That Thing You Do!*, and my stepmother, Rita, had two children under the age of five. It was not, in anyone's mind, good timing. I started classes at a small, conservative Episcopal school. One look at me in my unhemmed plaid uniform skirt, and the fourteen-year-olds of Los Angeles decided I was not up to par. Generally friendly with nearly all my classmates in

Sacramento, I was persona non grata at my new school. I'm ashamed to say that I reacted to this by trying to ingratiate myself with the cool kids and was cruel to the few kids I considered beneath me in the hierarchy. Once, early on, Mom came to Los Angeles, I think for a meeting with both teams of lawyers, and we ended up at Disneyland. Now every time I ride the carousel with my nieces, I remember her on the purple pony, white-knuckled.

For about two years, I was sleepless, awake from two till six in the morning. I struggled academically. I missed my friends and my life in Sacramento. While I was used to my Los Angeles family for a month or so during the summers, most of my time as a thirteen-year-old, and as far back as I could remember, had been spent alone. Suddenly I lived in a house where the phone never stopped ringing, and the doorbell was constant. I was transformed from the younger sister of a mysterious older brother into the older sister of two younger brothers. I resented school and dreaded the weekends when I would fly back to Sacramento. For a long while, my mother and I were never alone together. She'd gathered a cast of characters around herself as a shield. For years she had believed that my father was paying people to spy on her, following her and tapping her phone lines. It was made even worse when, during the legal proceedings around my move to Los Angeles, gossip magazines sent paparazzi to actually follow her, harassing her and possibly tapping her phones.

One weekend I arrived for my visit and in our living room discovered a random man with multiple guns and a German shepherd in tow, and was told he would be sleeping in our living room from then on. That was also when I started finding guns everywhere—in the old sewing box where we kept the remote controls for the television, for instance. We never spoke of my decision to move to Los Angeles, or what had happened. In fact, we often didn't speak. Until she bought a Winnebago and announced we were driving to Florida.

I walk into the small cedar house
There she stands with hair now silvered.
The house is a study in light and dark.
[. . .]
a room of robins egg blue, filled
with oriental china, as fragile as the woman
who stands before the fire place.
The room is filled with the books she loves so.
[. . .]
It is summer and the fans are spinning,
the summer breeze is blowing, and the curtains
soft voile are moving in the breeze.
Thru the open doors, the oaks
whose soft spanish moss tumbles gracefully
stand in silhouette, ageless.
Over the mantel the clock ticks slowly.
She pours me tea, with those funny little
english biscuits we loved so. Telling me
once again, as she has since I was a small
child, about my grammar . . . the correct uses
of the split participle,
the dangling of infinitives.
These rued correctives, once only to be endured,
I now cling to. Listening to every prized phrase
which she has chosen, carefully hoarding every
moment of our shared time.
My daughter impatient with heated youth
hearing only a school lecture
and yearning to be outside rebukes us.
She lectures us both on our attempts

to change one another. She with youth's
perspecuity has seen what other's could not.
We needed to just accept with each other with love.
My Mother and I who spent our lives trying to
change each other. We spent the time changing
each other's homes, rearranging pictures on
the walls, and trying to rearrange each other's lives.
[. . .]
That I would gladly exchange eternity
to be able to sit, frozen in time
here with her, listening to grammar.
Opera playing softly, issuing from the next room
and listening to her quiet voice,
it's southern music, slow southern tempos.

—SJD

Chapter Twenty-Nine

The Way Back

> Each mother can only react empathically to the extent that she has become free of her own childhood, and she is forced to react without empathy to the extent that, by denying the vicissitudes of her early life, she wears invisible chains.
>
> —ALICE MILLER

It feels surreal to be headed west. I'm so used to the clothes that I packed over half a year ago, I don't remember what the rest of my wardrobe back home is made up of. My espadrilles fell apart in Jacksonville. I bought them because of a *New York Times Style Magazine* story I read about how Simone de Beauvoir would go hiking all over the Alps eschewing real hiking gear for these summer sandals. My favorite pair of pink jeans has also died, as well as my preferred pair of butt pants, which were nice and light in the desert, and breathable in the land of humidity. I buy a replacement pair at a Target somewhere, but they're not as good.

Minnie, meanwhile, looks like a disaster but hasn't let me down once. Gas and a single oil change, that's it. She hasn't overheated, hasn't run out of gas or even window-washing fluid. There's sand in her cracks, spill stains everywhere, and I've given up on the packing cubes, so my clothes are all over, as are the books. If I left LA with twenty-five, I now have a library of seventy-five: books on lynching and delta erosion, on the Great American deserts, the Creole languages of Louisiana and the Gullah Geechee. I've got my father's collection of short stories, a guide to tarot, Keats's letters, and all of Didion's essays. Minnie smells like sunblock and dry tea bags. Amid receipts and photos, Post-its are plastered everywhere, as if she is one giant rolling notebook, reminding me to research more, read deeper, ask more questions. I love her.

The trip west begins with a baseball game in Pensacola, a breezy town that moves slowly, a wise approach this deep into summer. I'm staying on the Bayou Texar and would love to swim, but once more Google tells me that would be unwise. Instead, I spend a good hour in the morning simply watching the water. The quiet and calm here feel especially comforting after Orlando. At breakfast I make friends with a corgi puppy as distraught about the heat as anyone. He barely has the energy to roll over his limp noodle body for a belly rub.

My first attempt at seeing the Pensacola Blue Wahoos, a minor league team, is rained out, so I stick around another day to catch an evening game. I'm not a baseball fan in the way that I can list off statistics or the starting lineup for the Giants, but I know the difference between the American and National Leagues, I have feelings about the designated hitter, and I've been going to games with my dad since I was very young. I like the flow of the game, I like how it's the only sport outside of cricket where the defense has control of the ball. Even when I lived in Brooklyn, I would go to Mets games, sometimes by myself, reading and listening to the radio play-by-play in one ear. I can tell you that an evening in a baseball park is a lovely way to pass the time, almost meditative. You can pay attention to the game for as long as it holds your interest, and then feel free to let your mind wander to summer night thoughts until someone cracks a double and you're back in.

Getting situated with a beer and a program, I feel a pang for the games back home in Dodger Stadium, where if the Dodgers win, the loudspeakers blare Randy Newman's "I Love L.A.!" There are a lot of families in the stands around me, but the two on either side of me have given me a wide berth. One mother took her ten-ish-year-old child's hand and moved him two seats away from me when I sat down. At first I thought it was because she was concerned he might get too rambunctious, but he seems like a balanced enough kid, and besides, we're at a ball game. I have a suspicion it's because of my shirt, which I bought at the Los Angeles Book Fair. It reads FAMOUS WITCHES and features Cher, Marsha P. Johnson, Pamela Colman Smith, and others.

I try to ignore the vibe of this woman, who is staring daggers at me, and enjoy a hot dog. Speaking of dogs, the entertainment during the seventh inning stretch is a demonstration of the Pensacola Police Department's KP Unit. The crowd goes nuts when a German shepherd is sent to attack a man in a thick, padded suit. The Blue Wahoos win it, and I'm happy to have seen a game full of doubles, the upside of a minor league game.

Maybe because I am running from my expensive and joyless folly in Orlando, the drive west is harried and surreal. Was I really just in Palatka? Am I really going to meet my uncle? I always thought it was interesting that my mother had three brothers the way I ultimately came to have three brothers. I only knew a bit about her relationship with her youngest brother, who was closest to her in age and was sometimes confused as her twin. Her older brothers were as mysterious to me as they must have been to her. I can count on one hand how many times I got to see her as a sister, as a daughter; most of those instances were on the 10.

Then and now, it makes me sad. Being a sister to three brothers can mean a lot of things, but for me it means trying. Trying to listen, to help, trying not to get in the way, trying to understand, trying to ignore, trying to learn from them. I don't know what my uncle Bruce's relationship with his sister was like, but I'm hoping he'll tell me. Did my mother try? Did they try with her?

The drive west through Texas is the only time I ever pull over and sleep at a random hotel. I've been bending my rule not to drive at night and can't find a truck stop that allows overnight parking. Exhausted, I pull off the highway somewhere north of San Antonio, maybe around Junction. I book a room, run across the road to the only restaurant nearby (a Subway), and then park Minnie directly in front of my door. I've been spooked by stories of U-Hauls and vans being stolen from motel parking lots, but I'm too tired to drag everything out of Minnie and bring it inside. I'm back on the road early enough that it's before the heat hits.

When I roll into El Paso, signs everywhere read "El Chuco Strong." The city has been brought low by a mass shooting in a Walmart on the east side of town. It happened right by the 10, all stroads and box stores. Twenty-three people have been shot dead. It's the third mass shooting in Texas in less than two years. A 2017 shooting in a church left twenty-six people dead and twenty wounded, and in May 2018 a shooter killed ten people and wounded thirteen others at a high school. In 2022, nineteen students and two teachers will be murdered at Robb Elementary School in Uvalde.

I go to pay my respects and lay some flowers at the large *ofrenda*-like altar that has been growing around the gates of the Walmart. The area is in a huge strip mall, so I park near the Hooters and walk over. I leave my flowers by some little stones that a child has painted with the words *peace* and *faith*. There is a therapy dog named Daisy on hand, her pink vest embroidered with her name. Her handler brings her over to two little girls with chocolate on their faces.

"Do you want to say hello?" the handler asks in Spanish.

The girls are thrilled to say hi to Daisy, but their parents stand to the side, looking shell-shocked. When I choke up and start crying, I realize it's time for me to go.

Viva El Chuco.

Of my mother's three brothers, Bruce is the one I know the least, in large part because my mother was convinced that he was, in her words, a "spook." A former marine, he and his wife, Pat, went on to live in West Germany, which was enough to convince my mom that he was a hitman for the CIA. When I emailed my uncles, he was the first to respond, quickly and kindly, and noted that on the original trip on the 10, the only time we've ever met, I apparently said to him as a means of good-bye, "You're not as bad as everyone says." The things I said to grown men as a child. Apparently, I once looked a theater colleague of my mother dead in the eye and announced, "You're a fluff cat. You were born in a tree, and you're gonna die in a tree." I have no idea what I meant, but I think it's great.

When I was driving east, I purposefully bypassed Bruce's house in Arizona, not too far off the 10. I had an innate sense that I didn't have the right questions to ask yet, and also I was scared. Of making an ass of myself, of finding out something that I didn't want to know, of not finding out anything. Talking to my uncle before I made the trek felt like putting the cart before the horse. Now, who the fuck cares about carts and horses, what am I doing here?

The morning of my meeting with Bruce, I'm parked in a motorhome/tiny home park where I've rented a spot not much bigger than Minnie, but it has a kitchen. As I get ready to go, I simultaneously feel I've been on the road for years, not months, and also that I could drive around this country interminably and never feel ready for this conversation.

Like all desert houses, Bruce's blends into the surroundings, brown and sandy, but with flashes of color popping in pinwheels stuck into the gravel front yard. Without the peculiarities of the desert necessities, the things that keep this entire neighborhood from shriveling up and blowing away, this could be an Anywhere USA home. As I walk up the pathway, the sun already stinging the back of my neck, I try to remember walking up this same path with my mother, but nothing comes. I'm alone.

When my uncle opens the door, my reaction is physical, my weight shifting back to my heels. My mother only lived to be forty-nine, but there it is: what she would have looked like had she gotten more time.

"You look exactly like your mother," he says, welcoming me in out of the sun.

"I was going to say that you look exactly like your sister," I reply.

Bruce is tall, auburn-haired, freckled, and frank, and seems unfazed that this stranger with his sister's face has wandered into his house. His wife, Pat, is kind, and gives me a big hug, telling me she's so glad I've come. Inside, I remember more from 1996. Not much has changed, though there are more souvenirs from trips around the world: steins from Germany, ceramic plates from Italy and Latin America. There are silk Japanese cloths, which it turns out my grandfather brought back from the tour that ended his marriage, and which my mother had framed for my grandmother at some point. Bruce has a slew of old photo albums out, mostly from Harriet herself, as well as some more recent photos on the iPhoto stream on the television.

I don't ask to record the conversation for fear of scaring anyone off, and we fall into conversation easily, aided by our mutual frustration that the iPhoto stream won't work at first. It's nice to have a familiar crossover to my other family: I am slow to anger, unless technology is involved. If a Bluetooth won't pair, or I'm prompted for a password there's no way I'll remember, I erupt with a blue streak, Shakespearean in length and volume, just like every other Hanks. We do not do well with malfunctioning technology.

Eventually Bruce gets it working, and there's a bunch of photos from the nineties: my mom and I outside the O.K. Corral, my cousins and me looking put-out over parents and their cameras. Then there's a photo of my grandmother smiling at a buffet, a large corsage pinned to her blouse, her sons Michael and Bruce in the background.

"That must be the birthday party," I say.

"Yes," Bruce responds.

I never heard from any member of the family in the wake of my mother's death. Later, my brother and I learned that her family had all been in Palatka for Harriet's eightieth birthday. My grandmother had not come out while my mother was dying because, as Bruce tells me over the Pepsi and Ritz crackers that Pat set out for us, "She didn't feel like she'd be able to do anything."

While Bruce sits across from me on the other side of the glass coffee table, Pat perches beside me on the comfortable sofa and pats my hand once or twice to comfort me. It is nice, and a little foreign, to have comforting maternal energy by my side.

"It was Michael who told me she'd died," Bruce says, toggling through photos on the TV. Michael is the eldest, then Bruce. Eric is the youngest of the four siblings. "Michael and I were in the car. Eric called him and Michael just said, 'Susan's dead.'"

They decided not to tell Harriet until later. My family had known she was sick, of course, but it had not been made clear how close to death she was. But this did not explain why I did not hear from anyone after her death.

"I'm sorry that's how you heard that your sister died," I say to

Bruce, and I mean it. I'm angry on his behalf. "I wish everyone had spoken to each other."

Pat takes my hand. "That's what I keep thinking, what you must have thought."

What I had thought was that no one had wanted to talk to the Hollywood kids. I thought no one wanted to deal with my crazy mom. My experience of silence was that it always meant, *Don't make me deal with this, don't make me responsible for you. Don't make me care more than my heart can handle.*

Sitting on that sofa, I am hit with a wave of relief, as if the people I had worried for so long were bad people were suddenly absolved of that badness, and I did not have to worry anymore about them being my people.

It will only be hours later, trying to fall asleep, that I wonder: But why did no one come when she was sick? Wasn't having cancer reason enough to visit? Didn't she deserve that, even if she was sick before the cancer? Why did no one call us when she died, even if Harriet wasn't to know anything? Why had no one said anything? Why had no one helped her? Why had no one helped us, her children?

She was a quiet kid, Bruce says, and a little strange. Sensitive. She burst into tears as a teenager when her brothers struck too sarcastic of a joke. She picked at her skin and plucked at her eyebrows until she didn't have any. As Bruce talks, and Pat offers more snacks and occasionally chimes in, it's clear to me that these are the remembrances of an older brother to whom his little and only sister was a bit of an oddity. On the different bases where the Dillinghams lived, my mom would open the front door to find a herd of little girls waiting. They would play horses, running around the lawns pretending to canter and jump things. For some reason it never occurs to us to pretend to ride horses; no, we *become* the horse and jump and kick and snort and run together, because it is more fun in a group. It is safer.

After an hour or so of talk, I begin to work my way toward the question I have come all this way to ask. At first, I ask Bruce when he knew my mother was functioning in a different reality than other people. His response is that years later, paranoid and scared, she asked him if he could use his telecommunication spy skills to find out who was hacking her computer, tapping her phone lines, and following her. He also adds that he didn't work for the CIA (but that even if he had, he wouldn't tell me).

"You can have a conversation with someone and hear their version of events, and it's not at all like yours. I mean, not at all. Totally different." He shrugs.

Pat asks if my mother ever had a clinical diagnosis. I tell her that to the best of my knowledge, no one was ever able to get her into continuous treatment, but that conversations I've had with various doctors, and my own therapist, have led me to believe she was possibly bipolar with bouts of paranoia and delusions. I think I am running my ship up against the harsh rocks of generational differences.

Saying that my mother was mentally ill, that she was possibly "bipolar with episodes of extreme paranoia and delusion," makes sense of the nights sitting with her on a blanket in the driveway, my mother sobbing and convinced there were men inside the house, bugging the walls, waiting for us in our bedrooms. Waiting for me in the dark. But these words seem to only make my aunt and uncle uncomfortable. They say a lot of the things my godmothers would say: "Susan was odd, Susan had a different perspective, Susan had funny ideas sometimes, like there were men listening in on her phone calls."

"Was it fun growing up on the bases, having all those other kids to play with?" I ask.

"Yeah, of course. There were a couple things, well, things that happened that weren't—it wasn't good," he says. I file his hesitation away but move on. I ask about his older brother, Michael.

When I wrote Michael to ask if he'd be willing to talk with me, he wished me luck, but as he was nearly a decade older than my mother and moved out early to join the military, he had little memory of her as a child and missed the majority of her childhood. Bruce tells me that since Michael left the house as soon as possible, he didn't know him particularly well, but perhaps he was the most like Jerry Dillingham of all the siblings. (Not long after I sat with Bruce and Pat I heard that Michael had died.)

"Did your dad ever hit you?" I ask Bruce. I don't know if he was expecting this line of questioning, but I certainly haven't surprised him. He responds without hesitation:

"Well, he never laid a hand on me. My dad was intimidating enough that he only had to look at me, and I would stop whatever it was that I was doing."

I take his tone as an opening to go on. I describe how, toward the end of her life, before she was diagnosed with cancer, my mother seemed to be getting worse. She went out less and less, losing her already tenuous connections with the outside world. I talk about the canceled plans: to go to seminary, to become a Latin professor, to move to Ireland, to move back to New York, to write fantasy novels. I mention the strangers who would people her life before she banished them, the religious fervor that had crossed over into obsession years before.

"When I look at her life, at this inability to function, I wonder if something happened that stunted her, that set her off on this broken path."

When Bruce doesn't immediately disagree, I continue. I tell him about how my mother never, ever spoke of Jerry Dillingham. I tell him about the red journal.

"Were you ever aware of any sort of abuse or sexual violence that your father inflicted on my mother, or anyone else?"

Bruce does not immediately say no, or yes, or kick me out of his house. He thinks for a moment.

"Like I said, my father never put a hand on me, and I never saw him put a hand on any of the other kids. But that doesn't mean it didn't happen. I mean, you hear about these things, when people say, 'I never thought he'd be the sort of guy to do that sort of thing,' or 'He seemed so nice,'" Bruce continues. "And of course, it turns out that they all did it. So, I don't know. I don't think so, but that doesn't mean he didn't do it, or that something didn't happen."

He pauses again, and it takes everything I have to just sit and wait. After months of listening to people, I've learned that I have a horrible habit of jumping in on a subject's response, as if I'm trying to help them finish their thoughts, sometimes just cutting people off. I'm working hard to let silence do more of the work.

"When I was talking about growing up on the bases, there were some things that happened. There was a boy. He was molesting his sister, and he brought other kids to watch. So maybe . . . I don't know. And I heard things about stuff on other bases."

I imagine living on a military base with four kids. I imagine a husband who was hardly ever around, a woman desiring just her books and classical music. I imagine that my grandmother didn't pay much attention to where her kids ran off to during the day.

I can see the back door opening in the morning, maybe one of the base kids would barge in, looking for one of the Dillingham kids to play with, and off they would go. In some regards a military base must have been the best place for a bunch of kids; how much trouble could they get into? They were out the door in the morning, and if they didn't show up for dinner, well, chances were they were with a family three doors down because they had a better television. It was a village, and everyone looked out for everyone's kids. Except.

What about quiet, strange Susan Jane, who still carried her pink blanket, and liked to canter around with the other little girls, jumping fences and braiding her thin hair like it was a pony's mane?

I hoped that Bruce would offer some piece of information that would crack through all the mist with the clarity of lightning and light up the gray that surrounds my mother's life. Was she, as Bruce seemed to think, merely a would-be actress who never recovered from her ex-husband's catastrophic fame?

When I ask Bruce what my grandmother thought of her daughter, he sighs. "Harriet could not, would not, ever speak ill of a family member," Bruce says, the ice in his glass of Pepsi clinking slightly. Behind him, a small desert rabbit hops by, while a hummingbird flits about an empty feeder. Eventually Pat gets up to refill it. A quail, with many little chicks following her closely, scurries by.

"She was the only true southerner in the family, and I think that was part of it. She could not speak badly about a family member." I think of being in Harriet's house in Palatka and seeing, for the first time, that fuzzy picture of my grandfather on the floral wallpaper. When I asked about him, she'd merely waved her hand and said, "That was all a long time ago."

For Bruce, their military upbringing surpassed any major influence the South had on the Dillinghams. They were not a southern family; they were a military family. Are those very different, when it comes to talking about the past?

* * *

We look at more photo albums that Bruce has from when he cleared out Harriet's small Palatka house. They all reflect the eras they've come from: florid green from the seventies, shiny veneer from the eighties, and one that is a sort of shellacked piece from Japan during the war. Bruce has thoughtfully laid them all out for me to inspect and promises to make me copies of any photos I'd like. I wonder if he and Pat were as nervous about this as I was. I think about spontaneously hugging him, but instead focus on all the pictures.

My mother, with her freckled nose, her tiny white socks on Easter Sunday, showing off her little white purse with pride. It looks like she's wearing a proper crinoline underneath her Sunday dress.

Looking annoyed while posing next to a stagecoach, giving me Tombstone flashbacks, waiting for her mother to take the picture already. Like me, she has downy blond hair as a child, which eventually turned a dark auburn. (Brown, really.)

As a baby, with elfin eyes and dimples (here I see my middle niece), and when she is a young girl, with a filly's long legs, I see my eldest niece.

As a teenager sprawled across the back of a seventies-era Yamaha motorcycle, wanting to look cool, wanting to be anything other than soft, quiet, a little odd. Sensitive. "That was my motorcycle," Bruce says.

But there are also pictures of my great-grandmother, Margaret McIlvaine Collins, who served in the Women's Army Corps, and in 1931 made inroads as a woman lawyer—not very common in Jacksonville at the time. She was born the day before me, albeit in 1895. There is her mother, also a woman of Palatka. I can't get enough of the pictures of these women—I've never seen pictures of my mother as a child, my grandmother as a mother, my ancestors. Who were these women with chins like mine and skin like mine and cheeks like mine? How did I not know I was so hungry for this until I had my first taste?

I have returned to the south
With my daughter who is curious
About her heritage.
To visit with my Mother in her home
[. . .]
The three of us, generations of women together,
Are funny. My daughter and I relish the South
Where older women are respected
Counted as sources of wisdom.
It's wonderful to see the care and tender love on
Her face as she has realized her Grandmother is
Older now. She assists in her Grandmother's
Smallest effort.
All the women in our family were strong
Rugged, pioneers, lawyers, even hunters
For their families during the depression.
The men left for world wars, or looking for jobs
During the depression. The photos of the solemn
Faced women
In the black and white photos of the past which
Hang in her house have fascinated me all my life,
Have haunted me. How did I let myself become so
Shallow and passive in the face of these women?
How did I let myself make so many foolish mistakes?
[. . .] I am here
To examine where our family found its strength, in
Old southern life, where females were expected to
Be well educated in Shakespeare, Ovid, and Proust.
Where women were required to be strong
Individualists. The deceptively easy way of

Life, the courtesy which is required and where
Culture and family are ways of life still. [. . .]
[My daughter] is
Fascinated by the southern women of this land which
Is so foreign to her. The tropical rains and
Hurricanes, sugar canes and strange foliage, large
Red blooming hibiscus and blue plumbagos, the
Strange exotic birds such as pink flamingos and
White egrets. We are here to [. . .]
retrieve those good
Portions of the southern traditions
for a place
In our lives.

—SJD

Chapter Thirty

Pacifica

> Experience has taught us that we have only one enduring weapon in our struggle against mental illness: the emotional discovery and emotional acceptance of the truth in the individual and unique history of our childhood.
>
> —ALICE MILLER

The truth exists with or without our help, but narrative requires an author, and authors are prejudiced. I thought I could craft a cogent narrative from what I learned of my mother's life. I was unable to prove that my mother was assaulted by her father, but I know violence was definitely part of her childhood, quite possibly sexual violence. Both in and out of her family. I know that my grandfather was a successful army man, a drunkard, a charmer, and a dark presence who was expelled from his own family.

I leave the trailer park somewhere between Tombstone and Tucson early the next morning. It'd never occurred to me that I could have stayed with my aunt and uncle, and returning to Minnie felt like returning to solid ground after jumping from ice float to ice float. I scarf protein bars and black tea for breakfast and hit the road.

I'd meant to stop back in Phoenix to see if Dana Armstrong had opened up the resurrected Dirty Drummer bar. I'd meant to stop in Palm Desert and research tribal laws regarding the Morongo Casino Resort, but nearly unconsciously, I just kept driving. I didn't even listen to music, I just thought about the pictures Bruce had shown me of my great-great-grandmother McIlvaine, standing in her dour Victorian garb, all petticoats and corsets, on the dirt streets of old Palatka, looking serious and strong. I thought about Harriet, Grandma Haha, how she would play *Peter and the Wolf* for me, and how much of her life she must have spent just trying to find a little peace. I thought about the pictures of my mother as a little girl, something I'd never seen before, her crooked bangs, her big dark eyes. The pride in her smile at her little white purse on Easter Sunday. I thought about these women for miles and miles, and only now, months later, do I realize that not once in those last hours in the van did I ever think of John Raymond Dillingham. Let him remain in shadow.

Right over the border into California I stop for gas and find myself in the longest line at a gas station I've ever been in. It's almost September now, but the sun is still beating down on us as we all wait. I watch a group of motorcycles pull up to the minimart. When the riders and their passengers take off their helmets, I see that most of them are my age, a collection of men and women. I wonder what it would have been like if I had done the same trip, but on a motorcycle. Certainly less room to bring a miniature library with me everywhere I went. I dated a man once who had no form of transportation other than a motorcycle, and he took me out on it at night around Elysian Park, the land that cradles Dodger Stadium. At some point he pulled over and asked how I was doing, and my immediate, breathless response was,

"The only thing better than that would be if I got my own."

Watching the pack of friends get back on their bikes and pull out of the gas station, I pull out my phone and research places to get my motorcycle license back in LA.

I don't even drive all the way to the Pacific, back through the McClure Tunnel I passed through half a year ago. When downtown Los Angeles appears on the horizon, I am already in the thick of rush-hour, bumper-to-bumper traffic, and I might have been gone awhile, but I immediately click back into Angeleno thinking and calculate how long the traffic will take me. I don't have the patience to spend another three hours in Minnie to go fifteen miles. The Pacific will keep.

When I merge off the 10, there's relief. Every night for months now, I have gone to sleep feeling I haven't done enough. I haven't found out enough, talked to enough people, understood enough. I haven't read enough—why haven't I tracked down a truck driver to interview? Why didn't I stop in Bagdad, Florida? There is a city named Bagdad in Florida, for Christ's sake. Getting off the 10 feels like stepping down from a long watch through a dark, if starlit night. Remarkable things can happen when you walk into a room of strangers with an open mind—now I want to know what happens when you come home with that same curiosity.

The I-5 north is the highway I have driven to Sacramento more times than I can count. The tangerine light of dusk hits Dodger Stadium on the hills above me. Dodger Stadium, a beautiful place to watch a long game and fireworks, has its own history. Before the Dodgers left Brooklyn, the area where the stadium now stands was known as Chavez Ravine, named after Julián Chávez, who held several civil servant jobs, including assistant mayor and city councilman. The Ravine was home to a longtime community of Mexican American families who fought the eminent domain evictions in 1959—pictures show police dragging women out of their homes. But the families were no match for the city; the stadium opened in 1962. The only older Major League Baseball stadiums are Boston's Fenway (1912) and Chicago's Wrigley Field (1914).[1]

I roll down my window and get a whiff of car exhaust and eucalyptus; I can't get enough of the Dr. Seuss profiles of the palm trees and succulents along the highway.

When I walk into my house, it's cleaner than when I left. While I was gone, a friend who has been trying to get her business off the ground had been staying there. I was expecting to have to tidy and grocery shop, but she's kindly done both. I do a lot of laundry, shelve all my new books, and sleep in until noon for a few days, getting used to being back in my home. I meet up with my friend at Bob's Doughnuts in the old farmers market at the Grove on Fairfax. We park at the table favored by the writer and director Paul Mazursky, who would sit at the same spot every Sunday and hold court. When I return her St. Christopher necklace, I feel a welling up of emotion, something deeper than gratitude. It's odd to be done with the trip, and all these little goodbyes keep throwing me for emotional loops. It's strange not to have the necklace dangling from the rearview mirror.

About a week after I get back, I climb into Minnie, now cacophonous like an empty apartment, get back on the 10 when the traffic won't be so bad, and go to visit the Pacific.

I go through the McClure and ease up the Pacific Coast Highway to the mouth of Topanga Canyon, my favorite place to park at the beach, since parking lots are usually both a nightmare and expensive. There's a gravel patch just beyond the Malibu Feed Bin, a livestock and pet supply store in a red barn that has been there for fifty years. There's also a crosswalk so you don't risk your life rushing across the highway, infamous for drunk drivers even now that ride-sharing services exist.

I stand for a while in the absolutely frigid water, keeping an eye out for dolphins, which are common in this spot. Some birds are dive-bombing a kelp forest—must be a school of fish feeding somewhere nearby. I am having a moment with my own personal deity, Pacifica.

Maybe I was so keen and able to make up my own goddess because it's not the first time I've done it. For years my family has had a running joke about the goddess of show business, Pelicula. Have a big audition? Pray to Pelicula. Submitting a packet? Make an offering to Pelicula. There is no more fickle goddess; the best way to book a gig is to tempt Pelicula by buying a nonrefundable trip somewhere. Beware Pelicula!

Pacifica could be Pelicula's cooler, older sister. To me, she is a goddess of constant change and yet steady presence. She's cold and yet she harbors abundant life. She takes and she gives in somewhat predictable cycles. She may take out your Subaru, but she will bless you with a Ford Transit. Her blue-green colors flash with beauty, but she's not afraid to toss some garbage up on the shore as well. Pacifica taught me that the point of dancing is not to master the steps before you go on the dance floor.

Sometime in the year my mother was sick, she went to the Northern California coast with one of her dearest friends, my godmother Marnie. There's a picture of her—her hair is chemo short and starting to go gray. She's smiling while holding a towel around Marnie's tall, lanky son Alex, who is severely developmentally disabled. She was always very gentle with him. It must have been the last time she saw the ocean. This is my favorite of her poems:

I will loosen and unbind these wrappings,
unbraid and let down my hair
and with long hair flowing
stride into the face of ocean surf
letting the sea waves warm waters wash
clean these limbs, these arms, this breast.

Standing with my feet in the cold water, so far from Jacksonville and the foreign Atlantic, I say a prayer to Pacifica. To her, and my mother, and Scott, and Grandma Haha, and anyone else who helped keep me safe in White Sands and Juárez, in the Bywater and on the Houston interstate. I ask Pacifica to curse the poolside speaker system of any hotel affiliated with Universal Studios Orlando. I say thank you.

And then I leave.

I think there must be something between the truth and narrative. As much as narrative can give us meaning, it can just as easily deceive. I took to the road in an attempt to find out what really happened, to try to divide truth and narrative. Back home, in my own big bed with music on my own radio, I look over the white binder one last time before setting it on the shelf, next to Yeats and Whitman and Plath. Reading my mother's words was a conversation with her on her own terms, and she told me that she lived honestly, in accordance with the story she needed to survive.

My brother Chester recently said to me, "The truth has no temperature." He told me that he got this from Cormac McCarthy, which is true, but it means nothing to me coming from McCarthy and everything coming from my brother. Maybe there are people who run too hot, too cold, to live in the truth. My mother was such a person. So, what can I offer her, here at the end of a trip that will go on to become something else? The same thing that she told me, again and again, is the only thing that really matters: grace.

Joan Didion felt that being from Sacramento set her life on a course that was fated—landscape was destiny. Georgia O'Keeffe preached a gospel that it didn't matter at all where you were from; it was where you decided to go and what you decided to do when you got there that counted. Narrative versus truth. I am not sure we can survive with just one and not the other. Balance is needed. El Paso needs Juárez, and vice versa. The tide must come in and the tide must go out. Ken Burns, talking about Billie Holiday, said that the greatest thing America has offered the world is the idea that "every individual matters, and that every individual can make art out of themselves, if they are honest, and true, and willing to take the incredibly courageous stand of not just being the one thing or the other, but they have mitigating wisdom to see both. Then we're running on all cylinders."[2]

Perhaps there is something that is both, something like divination. Not quite creating story, but neither cold, hard fact. Maybe divination is the meaning we discover not by digging down to bedrock, but when we are struck by lightning; all we can control is where we happen to be standing when it happens.

I was struck by lightning when I found the red journal, but I was also struck by lightning watching Mexicans and Americans and those in between dance to polka music in the waters of the Rio Grande. I was struck by lightning when the Grand Chief of the Yellow Pocahontas tribe danced with me in the name of Dr. John. The best moments on this trip happened when I just said yes and found myself in a moment—meeting Isaiah in the midst of the Kingsley Plantation, talking with Julie in a bar in Marfa, hiking over the ridge in El Paso.

One particular moment makes me well up as I'm flipping through my memories. It's nothing big, nothing important. I was just sitting inside Minnie in New Orleans when it started to pour while the sun was still out. I didn't want to get out, not for fear of getting doused, but because WWOZ started playing a song that was so beautiful, I didn't want to move. "The Beauty of Dissolving Portraits" by Ambrose Akinmusire. From the first notes of the strings to when Akinmusire's tentative trumpet comes in, it sounds like the first steps you take toward love when you've been so hurt before. It's tender and awkward and there's so much hope in it. I wasn't able to move. The beauty of it all: the light coming through the rain, the sound on Minnie's roof, the wet greenness and the broken concrete all around me, and the sounds a trumpet can make. I almost couldn't breathe for fear of breaking up a moment of perfect, sublime mystery.

I didn't solve my mother, or either of her parents, or discover who she really was. I already knew, but in the twenty years since her death, I was starting to forget. I spent dedicated time over nearly half a year just to think about her and remember the way she taught me to use lipstick as blush because it stays longer, or the time she let maggots infest our entire pantry. I took time to think about my grandmother, and learn about her life, and the women who raised her in a small southern town. I wandered around the labyrinth inside of me, shook hands with all the ghosts and monsters I found there, and slithered back out, the rose on my tongue just beginning to blossom.

I think that we are all looking for some point of origin, or perhaps an original sin, that makes us who we are. Am I my mother's daughter? Yes. Because of her, I love Bach and Beethoven, my skin freckles, and I have to work hard to open my heart to the person standing right beside me. But I am equally my father's daughter because he taught me to tell the truth and move forward.

At home, in my own bed, I look through the pictures on my phone with soft eyes, trying to see the whole trip at the same time: eating out of a bag of dehydrated food on top of a sand dune in New Mexico; the Indians masking for Leah Chase and Malcolm John Rebennack; Ding the cat, patron saint of the Bywater; Brandon with a plate of enchiladas; flowers outside a police barrier in El Paso; a Pensacola home run. It feels like I haven't really come home yet.

A funny thing is happening at night: I'm not sleeping. When I first got back, I was so exhausted that if I sat down I passed out; but I've been back for a while now, and suddenly the nights are sleepless. While LA often has fireworks, they're a summertime thing, and deep into September, the only sound I'm hearing is the occasional police helicopter. Something is missing.

It's the katydids. For months I'd been sleeping to the symphony of katydids, crickets, and frogs, the sounds of summer where lightning bugs flash and humidity still floats in the dark over damp concrete. I was used to daily thunderstorms and wearing deodorant on my thighs to keep them from chafing in the heat, and the soundscapes of a southern night. When I start playing looped sounds of katydids on my phone, I am finally able to sleep. This goes on for a month or so, until I wake up in the night hearing something else—the Griffith Park coyotes.

I happen to live on the border of the 4,210 acres of wilderness that make up Griffith Park, which lies within the Santa Monica Mountains. Its elevation reaches 1,625 feet above sea level, and it is filled with a plethora of flora: oak and walnut trees, sage, eucalyptus, toyon, and sumac. It's home to the Hollywood sign, a zoo, and the Griffith Observatory made famous by *Rebel Without a Cause* and *La La Land*. There's wildlife as well: hawks, deer, skunks, possums, at least one mountain lion, and coyotes. It's not uncommon to see a pack of them trotting down my street at night, their thin legs illuminated by some of the four hundred different types of streetlights in Los Angeles.[3] There was a period of time when I first moved back to Los Angeles from Brooklyn, when I would get up in the dead of night, pack a backpack with pepper spray, work gloves, and garbage bags, and go clean up trash in an abandoned lot where street artists would put up their work. One night, while I was wrangling broken Styrofoam and beer bottles into a bag, three coyotes dashed across the high brush of the lot. I don't know who was more surprised to see the other. Two of them scattered off quickly, but the third lingered, eyeing me up. Maybe it was an invitation to run with them for a bit.

Home, in bed, in the dark, I hear a brief, sharp yowl. I sit up. There they are: I can hear the coyotes yipping and howling. It's hard to tell how close or far they are, the sound carries so strangely in the canyons. I lie down and dissolve into sleep. The coyotes are home and so am I.

Acknowledgments

First thank-you must go to everyone in this book who took the time to have a conversation with me. Thank you also to Letter Perfect Transcription for wrangling all said interviews. To everyone at Gallery and Simon & Schuster for making this happen, and deepest of gratitude to Isabel of Creative Authors for sticking it out.

Immense thanks and love to Madeleine Eve Ignon for her wonderful drawings and for being a part of it all from the beginning. You are Cher. To Nat Moonhill for their perfect iconography. To Veronica Moonhill, the pinkest of ponies, for sewing me curtains and always inspiring me to fuck the moves.

Thank you and all the love, so much and every day, to my family everywhere, including the East Sac round table.

Special thanks to Brandon Presser, Book Husband, who held my hand and more. There is no one I'd rather get lost with.

And to Mark, of course.

To Mister, who carries my heart in his pocket everywhere we go. This story may not have begun with you, but I could not have finished it without you.

And more than anyone, to Brother Bear, without whom I wouldn't be here.

Notes

Introduction

1. Bertolt Brecht, "Journals," in *Writing Los Angeles: A Literary Anthology*, ed. David L. Ulin (New York: Library of America, 2002), 290.
2. Reyner Banham, *Los Angeles: The Architecture of Four Ecologies* (Berkeley: University of California Press, 2009), 143.

Chapter Two

1. Dan Flores, *Horizontal Yellow: Nature and History in the Near Southwest* (Albuquerque: University of New Mexico Press, 1999), 154.

Chapter Four

1. Dan Flores, *Horizontal Yellow: Nature and History in the Near Southwest* (Albuquerque: University of New Mexico Press, 1999), 127.
2. Flores, *Horizontal Yellow*, 25.

Chapter Six

1. Tom Clavin, *Tombstone: The Earp Brothers, Doc Holliday, and the Vendetta Ride from Hell* (New York: St. Martin's Press, 2022), 22.

Chapter Seven

1. Alice Miller, *The Drama of the Gifted Child: The Search for the True Self*, trans. Ruth Ward (New York: Basic Books, 1981), 12.

Chapter Eight

1. Georgia O'Keeffe, *Georgia O'Keeffe* (New York: Viking, 1976), 24.
2. O'Keeffe, *Georgia O'Keeffe*, 82.

Chapter Nine

1. "U.S. States Comparison: Arizona vs New Mexico," countryeconomy.com, https://countryeconomy.com/countries/usa-states/compare/arizona/new-mexico?sc=XE34.
2. Clarissa Pinkola Estés, *Women Who Run with the Wolves: Myths and Stories of the Wild Woman Archetype* (New York: Random House, 1992), 36.
3. Georgia O'Keeffe, *Georgia O'Keeffe* (New York: Viking, 1976), 71.

Chapter Eleven

1. Nicole Maxwell, "Officials: 70-Year-Old German Man Died while Hiking White Sands," *Alamogordo Daily News*, June 10, 2019, https://www.alamogordonews.com/story/news/local/community/2019/06/10/white-sands-national-monument-german-man-died-while-hiking-peter-rudy-cramer/1411421001/.
2. "Hiker Found Dead on Same White Sands Trail Where French Couple Died in 2015," *El Paso Times*, September, 14, 2014, https://www.elpasotimes.com/story/news/2018/09/14/hiker-found-dead-white-sands-trail-where-french-couple-died-2015/1303495002/.

Chapter Twelve

1. James R. Murphy, *Images of America: El Paso 1850–1950* (Charleston, SC: Arcadia, 2009), 20
2. Sara Sanchez and Aaron Montes, "Months after Jakelin Caal's Death, Medical Examiner Releases Autopsy Report," *El Paso Times*, March 29, 2019, https://www.elpasotimes.com/story/news/2019/03/29/jakelin-caal-autopsy-report-released-el-paso-medical-examiner-migrant-girl/3313850002/.
3. Mary Hudetz, "New Mexico Medical Examiner Confirms Guatemalan Migrant Boy Died of Flu," *El Paso Times*, April 4, 2019, https://www.elpasotimes.com/story/news/2019/04/04/migrant-boy-guatemala-died-flu-new-mexico-medical-examiner-confirms/3364783002/.
4. "Chinese Exclusion Act (1882)," National Archives website, https://www.archives.gov/milestone-documents/chinese-exclusion-act.
5. Dan Olson, "This Is Financial Advice," Folding Ideas YouTube channel, https://youtu.be/5pYeoZaoWrA?si=eJI40N0fa-wXRxz-; F.D Signifier, "Why Everyone Is Wrong about Interracial Dating," https://youtu.be/O-KoABq6ygA?si=7ioLTbN_78EWIkxl; Natalie Wynn, "Tangent: Liminal Spaces," June 16, 2023, ContraPoints Patreon page, https://www.patreon.com /contrapoints/.

Chapter Thirteen

1. James R. Murphy, *Images of America: El Paso 1850–1950* (Charleston, SC: Arcadia, 2009), 20
2. "The Twelve Traditions (The Long Form)," Alcoholics Anonymous website, https://www.aa.org/the-twelve-steps.
3. "Dream of the Rood," lines 60b–62, trans. Ophelia Eryn Hostetter, Old English Poetry Project, https://oldenglishpoetry.camden.rutgers.edu/dream-of-the-rood/.

4. Dámaris Arellanes Cruz, "Narcoviolencia dejó 26 ejecutados en 'Días Santos' en Juárez," *Tiempo: La Noticia Digital,* April 21, 2019, http://www.tiempo.com.mx/noticia/narcoviolencia_ejecutadosfin_de_semana_dias_santos_ciudad_juarez/.

Chapter Fourteen

1. Joseph Campbell, *The Power of Myth* (New York: Anchor Books, 1991), 53.
2. Gabe Schwartz, "Prada Marfa," Atlas Obscura, April 10, 2010, https://www.atlasobscura.com/places/prada-marfa.
3. Bryon Schroeder, Tre Blohm, and Meradeth H. Snow, "Spirit Eye Cave: Reestablishing Provenience of Trafficked Prehistoric Human Remains Using a Composite Collection-Based Ancient DNA Approach," *Journal of Archaeological Science: Reports* 36 (April 2021), https://www.sciencedirect.com/science/article/abs/pii/S2352409X21000109; Rachel Monroe, "The Bodies in the Cave," *New Yorker,* October 3, 2022, https://www.newyorker.com/magazine/2022/10/10/the-bodies-in-the-cave.
4. Natalie Wynn, "Tangent: Liminal Spaces," June 16, 2023, ContraPoints Patreon page, https://www.patreon.com /contrapoints/.

Chapter Eighteen

1. Lawrence Wright, *God Save Texas: A Journey into the Soul of the Lone Star State* (New York: Aldred A. Knopf, 2018), 90.
2. No disrespect, Rhode Island! Pour me another cabinet!

Chapter Nineteen

1. Dean MacCannell, *The Tourist: A New Theory of the Leisure Class* (Berkeley: University of California Press, 2013), 5.
2. Clarissa Pinkola Estés, *Women Who Run with the Wolves: Myths and*

Stories of the Wild Woman Archetype (New York: Random House, 1992), 445.

3. James B. Twitchell, *Romantic Horizons: Aspects of the Sublime in English Poetry and Painting, 1770–1850* (Columbia: University of Missouri Press, 1983), 21.
4. Aaron Schrank, "Santa Monica Tries to Repay Historically Displaced Families," *Greater LA*, KCRW, January 31, 2022, https://www.kcrw.com/news/shows/greater-la/toxins-santa-ana-edu/santa-monica-displaced-black-families-housing.
5. Peter O'Dowd and Chris Bentley, "How a Black Neighborhood in New Orleans Fits into Biden's Plan to Fix Urban Design Inequities," *Here & Now*, WBUR, April 2, 2021, https://www.wbur.org/hereandnow/2021/04/02/highway-new-orleans-treme.

Chapter Twenty

1. Pamela Eakins, *Tarot of the Spirit* (Boston: Weiser Books, 1992), 344.
2. Dean MacCannell, *The Tourist: A New Theory of the Leisure Class* (Berkeley: University of California Press, 2013), 98.
3. Lawrence N. Powell, *The Accidental City: Improvising New Orleans* (Cambridge, MA: Harvard University Press, 2013), 163.
4. Cole Kinchen, "The Legend of the Honey Island Swamp Monster," Pelican State of Mind, https://pelicanstateofmind.com/louisiana-love/legend-honey-island-swamp-monster/.
5. Willie McNabb (@WillieMcNabb), "Legit question for rural Americans - How do I kill the 30-50 feral hogs that run into my yard within 3-5 mins while my small kids play?" Twitter (now X), August 4, 2019, https://x.com/WillieMcNabb/status/1158045307562856448?lang=en.
6. Jeff Daniels, "Feral Hogs Cause up to $2.5 Billion in Damage

a Year, so the Government Is Boosting Efforts to Fight Them," CNBC website, August 3, 2018, https://www.cnbc.com/2018/08/03/hogs-run-wild-but-usda-doubling-efforts-to-fight-problem.html.

Chapter Twenty-One

1. *Jazz*, episode 1, "Gumbo," directed by Ken Burns, written by Geoffrey Ward, aired January 2001 on PBS.
2. Jack E. Davis, *The Gulf: The Making of an American Sea* (New York: Liveright, 2017), 234.
3. Brian Palmer and Seth Freed Wessler, "The Costs of the Confederacy," *Smithsonian*, December 2018.
4. Davis, *The Gulf*, 234.
5. Palmer and Wessler, "The Costs of the Confederacy."
6. "The Civil War in California," California State Parks website, https://www.parks.ca.gov/?page_id=26775#:~:text=Like%20other%20Northern%20states%2C%20California,with%20state%20regiments%20back%20east.
7. *My Next Guest Needs No Introduction with David Letterman*, Netflix, April 29, 2024.
8. "Bring all of those Confederate statues to Biloxi, Beauvoir says," *Biloxi Sun Herald*, August 17, 2017, https://www.sunherald.com/news/local/counties/harrison-county/article167854697.html.

Chapter Twenty-Two

1. Aja Romano, "Why Satanic Panic Never Really Ended," Vox, March 31, 2021, https://www.vox.com/culture/22358153/satanic-panic-ritual-abuse-history-conspiracy-theories-explained.
2. "David Mitchell: The Art of Fiction No. 204," *Paris Review*, Summer 2010.

Chapter Twenty-Three

1. Wayne Flynt, *Alabama in the Twentieth Century* (Tuscaloosa: University of Alabama Press, 2004), 154.
2. Ersula J. Ore, *Lynching: Violence, Rhetoric, and American Identity* (Jackson: University Press of Mississippi, 2019), 11.
3. Equal Justice Initiative website, https://shop.eji.org/products/monumentparkprint.
4. Janice Simpson, "Pivotal Moments in Broadway's Black History," *Playbill*, February 12, 2022, https://playbill.com/article/pivotal-moments-in-broadways-black-history-com-342101.
5. "Donald v. United Klans of America," Southern Povery Law Center website, https://www.splcenter.org/seeking-justice/case-docket/donald-v-united-klans-america.

Chapter Twenty-Five

1. "FL: I-10/I-95 Interchange 'The Big I,'" America's Transportation Awards, https://americastransportationawards.org/past-projects/2011-2/fl-i-10i-95-interchange-the-big-i/.
2. "River of Lakes Heritage Corridor," Florida's Scenic Highways, https://floridascenichighways.com/our-byways/central-region/river-lakes-heritage-corridor/.

Chapter Twenty-Six

1. Joan Didion, *The White Album* (New York: Farrar, Straus & Giroux, 1979), 11.
2. Percy Devereux Collins obituary, *Palatka Times-Herald*, July 4, 1924.
3. Richard Ovenden, *Burning the Books: A History of the Deliberate Destruction of Knowledge* (Cambridge, MA: Belknap/Harvard University Press, 2020), 35.

Chapater Twenty-Seven

1. Joan Didion, *The White Album* (New York: Farrar, Straus & Giroux, 1979), 14.

Chapter Thirty

1. Elina Shatkin, "The Ugly, Violent Clearing of Chavez Ravine before It Was Home to the Dodgers," LAist, May 1, 2023, https://laist.com/news/la-history/dodger-stadium-chavez-ravine-battle.
2. Ken Burns on *Charlie Rose*, PBS, January 8, 2001.
3. India Mandelkern, "Chasing Streetlights," Curbed Los Angeles, August 1, 2018, https://la.curbed.com/2018/8/1/17635608/streetlamps-urban-light-history-design.

Bibliography

Abbey, Edward. *Desert Solitaire: A Season in the Wilderness*. New York: Ballantine Books, 1968.

Babitz, Eve. *I Used to Be Charming: The Rest of Eve Babitz*. New York: New York Review of Books, 2019.

Banham, Reyner. *Los Angeles: The Architecture of Four Ecologies*. Berkeley: University of California Press, 2009.

Bruder, Jessica. *Nomadland: Surviving America in the Twenty-First Century*. New York: W. W. Norton, 2017.

Campanella, Richard. *Cityscapes of New Orleans*. Baton Rouge: Louisiana State University Press, 2017.

Campbell, Joseph. *The Power of Myth*. New York: Anchor Books, 1991.

Cantú, Francisco. *The Line Becomes a River: Dispatches from the Border*. New York: Riverhead Books, 2018.

Clavin, Tom. *Tombstone: The Earp Brothers, Doc Holliday, and the Vendetta Ride from Hell*. New York: St. Martin's Press, 2020.

Davis, Jack E. *The Gulf: The Making of an American Sea*. New York: Liveright, 2017.

Didion, Joan. *The White Album*. New York: Farrar, Straus & Giroux, 1979.

Eakins, Pamela. *Tarot of the Spirit*. Boston: Weiser Books, 1992.

Estés, Clarissa Pinkola. *Women Who Run with the Wolves: Myths and Stories of the Wild Woman Archetype.* New York: Random House, 1992.

Flores, Dan. *Horizontal Yellow: Nature and History in the Near Southwest.* Albuquerque: University of New Mexico Press, 1999.

Flynt, Wayne. *Alabama in the Twentieth Century*. Tuscaloosa: University of Alabama Press, 2004.

Gabriel, Louise B. *Images of America: Early Santa Monica.* Charleston, SC: Arcadia, 2006.

Gratz, Roberta Brandes. *We're Still Here Ya Bastards: How the People of New Orleans Rebuilt Their City.* New York: Nation Books, 2015.

Guzmán, Alicia Inez. *Georgia O'Keeffe at Home.* London: Frances Lincoln, 2017.

Kipen, David, editor. *Dear Los Angeles: The City and Diaries and Letters, 1542–2018.* New York: Modern Library, 2018.

Lavender, David. *The Southwest.* Alburquerque: University of New Mexico Press, 2002.

Loomis, Jan. *Westside Chronicles: Historic Stories of West Los Angeles.* Charleston, SC: History Press, 2012.

MacCannell, Dean. *The Tourist: A New Theory of the Leisure Class.* Berkeley: University of California Press, 2013.

Miller, Alice. *The Drama of the Gifted Child: The Search for the True Self.* Translated by Ruth Ward. New York: Basic Books, 1981.

Murphy, James R. *Images of America: El Paso 1850–1950.* Charleston, SC: Arcadia, 2009.

O'Keeffe, Georgia. *Georgia O'Keeffe.* New York: Viking Press, 1976.

O'Neal, Bill. *Images of America: Texas Gunslingers.* Charleston, SC: Arcadia, 2014.

Ore, Ersula J. *Lynching: Violence, Rhetoric, and American Identity.* Jackson: University Press of Mississippi, 2019.

Ovenden, Richard. *Burning the Books: A History of the Deliberate Destruction of Knowledge.* Cambridge, MA: Belknap/Harvard University Press, 2020.

Pfaelzer, Jean. *California: A Slave State.* New Haven, CT: Yale University Press, 2023.

Poling-Kempes, Lesley. *Ladies of the Canyons: A League of Extraordinary Women and Their Adventures in the American Southwest.* Tucson: University of Arizona Press, 2015.

Powell, Lawrence N. *The Accidental City: Improvising New Orleans.* Cambridge, MA: Harvard University Press, 2012.

Solnit, Rebecca and Rebecca Snedeker. *Unfathomable City: A New Orleans Atlas.* Berkeley: University California Press, 2013.

Theroux, Paul. *Deep South: Four Seasons on Back Roads.* Boston: Houghton Mifflin Harcourt, 2015.

Tidwell, Mike, *Bayou Farewell: The Rich Life and Tragic Death of Louisiana's Cajun Coast.* New York: Vintage Books, 2010.

Treuer, David. *The Heartbeat of Wounded Knee: Native America from 1890 to the Present.* New York: Riverhead Books, 2019.

Twitchell, James B. *Romantic Horizons: Aspects of the Sublime in English Poetry and Painting, 1770–1850.* Columbia: University of Missouri Press, 1983.

Twain, Mark. *Life on the Mississippi.* New York: Modern Library, 2007.

Ulin, David L., editor. *Writing Los Angeles: A Literary Anthology.* New York: Library of America, 2002.

Wells-Barnett, Ida B. *On Lynchings.* Mineola, NY: Dover Publications, 2014.

Woodward, C. Vann. *The Burden of Southern History.* 3rd ed. Baton Rouge: Louisiana State University Press, 1993.

Wright, Lawrence. *God Save Texas: A Journey into the Soul of the Lone Star State.* New York: Aldred A. Knopf, 2018.

About the Author

E. A. Hanks lives in Los Angeles, California. Formerly a staffer at *Vanity Fair* and the *Huffington Post*, she has contributed to *Time*, the *Guardian*, the *New York Times*, and others. Follow her on Instagram @EAHanks.

Moonat Ahiko
Santa Monica, CA
Palm Springs, CA
Phoenix, AZ
Tucson, AZ
Tombstone, AZ
Ding
I've been absolutel terrified
moment of my li
I've never let it
me from doing
single thing tha
I wanted to do
- Georgia O'Keeffe